Reagan, Thatcher, and the Politics of Decline

£7 95

Europe and the International Order
SERIES EDITOR: JOEL KRIEGER

Published:

Peter Hall, *Governing the Economy: The Politics of State Intervention in Britain and France*

Forthcoming:

Judy Hellman, *Journeys Among Women*

Stanley Hoffmann and George Ross (eds), *The Mitterrand Experiment: Continuity and Change in Modern France*

Reagan, Thatcher, and the Politics of Decline

Joel Krieger

Polity Press

© Joel Krieger, 1986

First published 1986 by Polity Press, Cambridge, in association
with Basil Blackwell, Oxford.

Editorial Office:
Polity Press, Dales Brewery, Gwydir Street, Cambridge CB1 2LJ, UK.

Basil Blackwell Ltd, 108 Cowley Road, Oxford OX4 1JF, UK.

British Library Cataloguing in Publication Data

Krieger, Joel
  Reagan, Thatcher, and the politics of decline. —
  (Europe and the international order)
  1. Great Britain—Politics and government—1979—
  2. United States—Politics and government—1981—
  I. Title   II. Series
  354.4107'2'09   JN231

ISBN 0-7456-0272-X
ISBN 0-7456-0273-8 Pbk

Typeset by Pioneer Associates, Perthshire
Printed in Great Britain by Billing and Sons, Worcester

13/1/87

294458

Contents

Acknowledgements

A vast number of people aided me in the writing of this book, some perhaps unknowingly in conversations, comments, and rejoinders the value of which they may not have realized. Their contributions can be only partially noted here.

I wish first to thank Kris Glen who challenged and encouraged me in many ways, who kept reminding me what the book was (or should be) about, and as a consequence improved the result enormously. She has truly been a partner to me throughout. I thank Alicia for her summertime research assistance; and, Sam, for his many "low fives" of encouragement. I am grateful also to my brother Alan and my parents, Lucille and Phil, for the quiet support they always provide. I also wish to thank my "Wellesley family," Bill Joseph, Sigrid Bergenstein, and Abigail for their friendship and encouragement.

Parts of this study were presented to many audiences, including: Harvard University, Center for European Studies, British Study Group; New York University, Institute for the Humanities, "New Right" Seminar; University of New Mexico, Department of Political Science Lecture Series; Columbia University, Seminar on the State; Columbia University, Institute on Western Europe; American Political Science Association; and Council for European Studies conferences. I am grateful for these opportunities to work through my arguments and for the stimulation and useful commentaries they provided.

I am indebted to many friends and colleagues for critical comments and important suggestions, among them: Teresa Amott, Samuel H. Beer, David Douglass, Anthony Giddens, David Held, John Keeler, Mark Kesselman, Martín Sanchez-Jankowski, Paul

Thomas, and Allan Silver. Special thanks are due to Peter Hall for his painstaking review of an earlier draft of this book.

I am grateful to Wellesley college for providing generous leave support which enabled me to come to grips with the project, and to the Whitehead Chair for assistance in the final stages. I would like to thank Margaret Helck for research assistance, Ron Roel for editorial work and his encouragement in the early going, and Hope Hodson for her help in the preparation of the manuscript.

Finally, I thank Anthony Giddens and David Held at Polity Press for their crucial support and assistance, and Susan Rabiner and Rachel Toor at Oxford University Press for their insights and encouragement.

Introduction

There is a moment in every failing government, it seems, when the full quality of disarray is revealed. Before, central policies were slipping and political support may have been strained, but supporters still had reason to hope that a recovery was possible. But now, all at once, some magnificent weakness becomes obvious (and in time it comes to represent the fatal incapacity of the regime). From then on there may be victories — support momentarily recouped, advantages taken — but there is little likelihood that political defeat and harsh historical judgement can be avoided.

For president Jimmy Carter this unfortunate moment came coincidentally, just as the new British prime minister, Margaret Thatcher, was putting her stamp on British politics. By the early summer of 1979 the signal political achievement of the Administration — the signing of the Camp David agreement by Carter, Anwar Sadat, and Menachim Begin — seemed an anomalous high point in an ineffectual and fast-declining presidency.[1]

The government's index of leading economic indicators showed a 3.3 percent drop, the most precipitous decline since the 1974 recession, and OPEC-triggered gasoline (petrol) shortages were mounting. Carter's popularity was falling rapidly and his political troubles were legion. The Congress rejected one presidential initiative after another: on hospital cost containment, tax reform, Rhodesian sanctions; and most dramatically on energy, specifically gasoline rationing and decontrol of oil prices. Carter was also unlucky, taking considerable flack for the accident at the Three Mile Island nuclear power plant.

In July a *New York Times*/CBS News Poll indicated a 4 percent 1 month decline in the presidential approval rating to 26 percent — the same as Richard Nixon's lowest rating (in an ABC/Harris Poll) 2 months before he resigned.[2] Equally troubling to an administration having to face down a growing "Dump Carter—Draft Kennedy" movement in the House, the poll also indicated that despite repeated assurances by the Massachusetts senator that he was not a presidential candidate, Democrats preferred Kennedy to Carter as the 1980 nominee by a sizeable 53 percent to 16 percent margin. Add to this New York senator Daniel Patrick Moynihan's caustic remark that unless Carter acted decisively to take control, the President would be governing soon only "by the sufferance" of Edward Kennedy.

At the same time, Washington talk of cabinet dismissals — at Energy; Health, Education and Welfare; Transportation; and Treasury — contributed to a sense of inner division and mismanagement. Criticism of the White House staff and signs of inner conflict completed the picture of an administration in disarray. With a growing sense of crisis in the Carter camp, some summer intervention to put the administration back in shape seemed certain. The specific form of the White House gamble to recapture initiative soon took shape.

At the start of an economic summit of Western powers in Japan at the end of June, OPEC announced a 15 percent increase in oil prices. Then, with angry drivers suffering through longer and longer lines while waiting to get gas, and temperatures (literally and figuratively) heating up with the start of summer, a very damaging memo about the energy crisis leaked out of the Carter White House. Written to the President by his domestic affairs advisor, Stuart E. Eizenstat, the sharply worded document — gleefully reported in the press — shocked Carter into a series of highly public gestures which would crucially influence the course of his administration:

> I do not need to detail for you the political damage we are suffering from all this . . . . nothing which has occurred in the administration to date — not the Soviet Agreement on the Middle East, nor the Lance matter, not the Panama Canal Treaties, nor the defeat of several major domestic legislative proposals, not the sparring with

Kennedy, or even double-digit inflation — have added so much water to our ship . . . . Nothing else has so frustrated, confused, angered the American people or so targeted their distress at you personally.[3]

Carter would have to risk it all on energy. Eizenstat recommended a major policy address — not a very new idea in the Carter administration. Four times before, the President had delivered speeches about energy with decreasing attention paid to his pronouncements. Carter had consistently expressed distrust in big oil companies and espoused increased reliance on coal and solar energy, removal of price controls on natural gas, and the introduction of aggressive conservation strategies. In his one notable reversal of energy policy, Carter had recently succumbed to pressure from Secretary of Energy James R. Schlesinger and agreed to phase out price controls on crude oil as an inducement to private investors. So his record was well known and his focus on energy as a high administration priority made his inability to get comprehensive energy legislation through Congress a serious political embarrassment. OPEC's pressure on American consumers, and Carter's uneven responses, were not only the substance, but also the symbol, of Carter's incapacity. "What is it that troubles people?" asked a *New York Times* editorial about Jimmy Carter, "He appears weak, many say, vacillating. On July 29, for example, he angrily condemned OPEC for increasing oil prices; by July 9, he was heaping America's gratitude on the Saudis, the leaders of OPEC, for increasing oil production."[4]

With this record staring him in the face, the challenge to Carter was formidable. The President had gone to the well often on energy, most memorably in an April 1977 speech proposing new taxes on gasoline and investment credits, but notable mainly for his characterization of the coming effort to rationalize energy policy as "the moral equivalent of war." The MEOW speech, as Washington insiders quickly dubbed it, could not easily be outdone for fervor. Nevertheless, on Monday, July 2, upon his return from the economic summit in Japan, Carter accepted Eizenstat's suggestion, and announced that he would offer a major address on energy 3 days later. As high-level staff and Cabinet officials drafted a set of proposals, on July 3, Carter removed himself to the presidential retreat at Camp David in the Maryland mountains. Abruptly, at mid-afternoon on July 4 — hardly an auspicious day to sound the call for retreat from the United States' moral equivalent of war — Carter ordered his aides to cancel the planned speech.

For the next 10 days except for two quick helicopter journeys to confer with "ordinary citizens" — once in Carnegie, Pennsylvania and once in Martinsburg, West Virginia — Carter remained sequestered at Camp David. The press dutifully reported that some ten dozen people — elected officials, church and labor leaders, industrialists, academics, economists — made the pilgrimage to the Maryland mountain retreat. Carter asked questions, sought their advice and evaluations, took longhand notes on yellow legal-size pads, and reflected not simply on energy policy, but on the United States' "moral tone" and the need for new directions.

Finally, on July 15, Carter came down from Camp David to Washington for a feverishly touted television address (which, ironically, on one national network replaced a special broadcast of "Moses the Lawgiver.") An estimated 100 million viewers watched a solemn, introspective Carter — at his very best and worst.

Looking firmly ahead, hands folded, speaking assuredly, Carter addressed the nation first about a subject which he considered "even more serious than energy or inflation." Carter spoke about "a fundamental threat to American democracy." This was neither a military threat nor a threat to political liberties. "The threat is nearly invisible in ordinary ways," intoned the President. "It is a crisis of confidence. It is a crisis that strikes at the very heart and soul and spirit of our national wills."

Quoting the often critical advice he had received during his 10-day retreat — from a Southern Governor, from the black mayor of a small town in Mississippi, from a Pennsylvania woman — the president acknowledged the widespread mistrust in his own leadership, the alienation people felt from big government in Washington, the lack of confidence in the future, the fear that no longer would "the days of our children . . . be better than our own." Carter admitted sharing the fears of so many that the future held, "paralysis and stagnation and drift," and concluded: "You don't like it and neither do I."[5]

The 10 day delay heightened attention to the speech, and the openly self-critical homily promised leadership but offered very little that was new programmatically. Carter's risk was enormous. Even Moses was spurned the first time he came down from the mountain. "I watched in amazement," recalled Joseph Califano, outgoing Secretary of Health, Education, and Welfare, fearing for the worst in the 1980 campaign, "How could we run against Washington and government when the President was both?"[6]

For Prime Minister James Callaghan and Britain's last Labour government, the moment of truth had come precisely two years earlier, in the second week of July 1977. Carter's problem was how to rekindle national confidence after what was for Americans a new, and therefore extremely demoralizing, experience: being on the receiving end of economic pressure by others. Given a history of declining comparative advantage in economic performance which reached back nearly a century, and a decade of growing internecine struggles between the trade union and the party wings of the UK's labor movement, Callaghan's problem was perhaps more prosaic. How should the prime minister respond to growing trade union restiveness and their increasingly public threats to bring down an incomes policy which was the cornerstone of the government's economic strategy? Such a challenge from below was definitely not the moral equivalent of war, but a beating could quickly become the political equivalent of surrender.

Perhaps no area of public policy has shown the fragility of political rule in postwar Britain more than the government efforts to introduce political regulation of labor markets. Throughout the 1960s, first the Conservatives and then Labour tried to gain trade union approval for voluntary wage restraints by encouraging their participation in consultative bodies which were inspired by the French example of indicative planning. Despite the limited influence of these efforts and the often speedy criticism from trade union quarters when the upward movement of wages slackened, the 1974—1979 Labour government expanded the design.

In fact, Labour's new plan — the most comprehensive ever in the UK — was hatched during a period of trade union struggle with the Conservative government of Edward Heath, which was in office between 1970 and 1974. The timing was probably not coincidental, since a program to tap trade union support for a labour government offered considerable partisan advantages during a period of bitter confrontation over Heath's 1972 Industrial Relations Act, which mandated the "registration" of unions and assigned them financial liability for the non-sanctioned actions of members in breach of contract.

The contrast could not be more clear: Tories brought industrial strife while Labour engendered cooperation and harmony. The new Labour strategy, it was hoped, would stabilize the economy by involving the Trades Union Congress (TUC) in an expanded agenda of shared responsibility for economic and social policy. The "Social Contract" agreed by the TUC—Labour Party Liaison Committee in February 1973 called for wage and price controls "within the context of coherent economic and social strategy — one designed both to overcome the nation's grave economic problems, and to provide the basis for cooperation between the trade unions and the Government."[7]

Unfortunately the pressure of economic exigencies — mounting inflation, a substantial run on the pound — quickly removed the more expensive (and for the TUC, the most attractive) elements of the Social Contract. The promises of expanded social provision were jettisoned, and discussion of industrial and economic democracy (however vague those concepts had been) was shelved indefinitely.[8] After the electoral victory in February 1974, the new Labour government and the TUC agreed to a formal but voluntary incomes policy. New terms would be bargained for each of four annual "phases," with decreasing TUC, trade union, and rank-and-file support. If a Labour government couldn't manage its trade union allies — whom could it govern?

Both economic and political solvency required success in the promulgation of these income policies. As the term "Social Contract" implies, the agreement took on enormous normative significance in domestic political debates. Equally important, restraints on incomes and promises of reduced social expenditure had been the government's collateral to the International Monetary Fund (IMF) in return for a $3.9 billion credit to slow a feverish run on the pound in late 1976.

With trade unionists feeling the pinch of 2 years of wage restraint, and the government unable to offer the promised non-wage supplements, by the time of Phase Three the Social Contract had been reduced to an increasingly strained anti-inflationary alliance. An open rupture between the government and the trade union movement would considerably damage Callaghan's domestic credibility, and would risk further national embarrassment before the IMF.

Now, in the summer of 1977, it was obvious to even the most dogged supporter of Callaghan's austerity program that the TUC could not much longer police the incomes agreements. The most the government could expect from the unions this time was an agreement to honor Phase Two contracts for 1 full year (the "12-month rule") and the vague promise that the return to "normal collective bargaining" — by now a radical demand — would be "orderly." Yet, on this second Monday in July, Callaghan was still taking a hard line. Chancellor of the Exchequer Denis Healey, who served Callaghan both as worldly counsel for IMF-endorsed macroeconomic strategies and as the government enforcer with the unions, took a strong message to TUC leaders: no wage restraint, no Labour government come the next general election. While Healey perhaps had the temperament, he lacked the timing of a skilled blackmailer. Coming too far in advance of the general election, the ultimatum only sparked increasing union opposition to the government.

By mid-week, mounting pressure from the union and bitter arguments in Cabinet convinced Callaghan to abandon the Phase Three policy paper. The government would go it alone and attempt to hold the line at 10 percent without formal TUC endorsement. On Friday July 15, Parliament heard a subdued James Callaghan withdraw the Phase Three incomes policy while at the same time claiming that the Social Contract — now reduced to bromide assurances of "cooperation" from the unions — was "healthy and alive." The next day Callaghan ventured forth to the annual Miners' Gala in Durham, just south of Newcastle, a traditional rock-hard base of Labour support. The gala is always a remarkable event, but this year it would hold special meaning for Callaghan and the fate of his government.

On the second Saturday in July each colliery marches from the village into the town behind a silk banner that may bear the image of anyone from Lenin to Harold Wilson, a scene from the general strike following one from the Bible. Speakers for the event are chosen in a local union election, and the invitation to speak is a great honor. (No-one is quite sure whether Prince Kropotkin, who once addressed the gala, was invited because he was a prince or because he was an anarchist. It is said that he received votes from more than one quarter).

The gala is also a good forum for a major policy statement. The audience included ambassadors from the United States and the Soviet Union, Israel, and several East and West European countries. Traditionally the Labour Prime Minister or a senior Labour Cabinet member has a prominent place on the program. The ranking party member is introduced as "my friend Tony" or "my friend Michael" — the trappings of power are left elsewhere. Quite the opposite, the homespun message of commonality between trade unionist and party leader — workers together in a great movement — is a central theme of the celebration. Facing 10,000 miners and their families, it is clear to the ministers — and to the television cameras — that the movement is deeply divided. Where the balance of power resides is also clear. The party leaders try to tap this power and market it via the cameras to the nation.

In 1977, however, the featured speaker was not Prime Minister James Callaghan. It was NUM's Yorkshire area leader (later national president) Arthur Scargill, Callaghan's sharpest critic among the union leadership. In June the NUM had sent the government's pay policy skidding when it approved a wage demand of 91 percent. Nor was Callaghan likely to forget that it was the miners who eased Heath's exit from No. 10 Downing Street in 1974, defying the Tories' last attempt to impose wage controls by calling their second national strike in 2 years.

Of course the miners would remove a Labour government less willingly. But the invitations to the gala made it clear that rank-and-file miners felt that Callaghan had not held up his side of the bargain as a Labour Prime Minister. They were tired of the Social Contract which obliged them to accept wages lower than what they could have gotten through collective bargaining with recourse to strike action. They blamed Callaghan for the decline in their industrial power and, whatever the merits of their objections, they felt cheated financially.

Although not invited to speak, Callaghan was on the podium.

He looked increasingly owlish as Scargill, turning to him several times in the course of his speech, heaped abuse on him for the government's "betrayal" of the trade union movement. "No wonder the CBI [Confederation of British Industry, the business counterpart of the TUC] have welcomed with open arms Mr Healey's statement on limiting wage increases to 10 percent at a time when profits are running at a record 47 percent in increase over last year." Scargill assured both Callaghan and the Durham miners that the NUM pay claim was no mere public relations ploy or a sop to militants. Then, in closing, the Yorkshire leader spoke beyond the local miners to a wider audience. "I want to urge the whole trade union movement," intoned Scargill, "To ignore the advice and pleas of the government for further wage restraint policy."

After more harsh speeches, followed by a couple that took a more conciliatory tone, Callaghan asked to address the crowd. Reluctantly, the master of ceremonies introduced him in a clipped regional accent that rendered the name "Kaligan," skipping the part about "my good friend." Despite a jeering audience, the Prime Minister hit his message hard. "For the sake of the country — and miners are part of the whole national family — the government's first priority is to get down the rate of inflation which was destroying us three years ago. That is the objective we have set ourselves, and the tide is beginning to turn." Warming to the offensive, he accused the miners of demanding "the lion's share" and trampling on the needs of "the weak and the sick and those whose bargaining power is not so strong."

Unlike his Labour predecessor Harold Wilson, Callaghan rarely took on hecklers. But today he engaged in sharp repartee. "He who laughs last laughs best," he told the crowd, to which one miner responded, "You can afford to laugh." "Jeers are what we hear from the Tory benches every day," Callaghan replied, "from people who argue that the government cannot succeed in bringing down inflation." He concluded on a more ministerial note, buttoning his waistcoat, looking straight into the television cameras and choosing carefully the message that — he guessed rightly — would appear on the news that evening:

Next year the miners' claim will be £200 a week, and the next year £300 a week. Is the miner worth it? Certainly he is, provided he is paid in real money, and that is what we have got to do. Therefore, let no one think I can be carried away on this particular issue. What I am looking for is the real standard of improvement and advancement for our people, not easy slogans.[9]

Callaghan was, after all, a Labour Prime Minister, and he had waited his turn and boldly faced down his detractors. Callaghan struck the right chord by appealing to the miners' natural sympathy for the less powerful and drawing them in to a broader movement perspective. Equally important, he appealed cleverly to the national audience. The miners have their sectional interests, Callaghan was saying, but we have the interests of all working people and diverse constituencies at heart. For his efforts Callaghan won the crowd's grudging support; but in the end Callaghan could *not* afford to laugh, as disgruntled trade unionists pushed the government into an increasingly defeated posture, and widespread strikes in the winter of 1978 contributed significantly to the Callaghan government's defeat.

In the end, Califano was right, of course, Carter could not run successfully as an anti-Washington incumbent who admitted that the nation was directionless, lacking confidence in its leadership and expecting the future to be worse than the present. In the first few days after the speech the White House staff was euphoric, however, as Carter's approval rating shot up 11 points and 77 percent of his core constituencies — those with the least education, Democrats, southerners, blacks — agreed that there was a "crisis of confidence."[10] But by mid-week, five Cabinet members had been dismissed, the White House staff had been shaken up and the Georgia guard — the object of most staff criticisms — was actually strengthened with Hamilton Jordan's elevation to Chief of Staff.

The gains of the speech were largely squandered, and hope was replaced by the old miasma, by a continued sense of things being stirred up at the top but not improved. Unfortunately for the President, not Carter's resolution, but the dramatic reassertion of a "crisis of confidence" would be confirmed in the coming months. Carter's indecisive handling of the economy and the dual Iranian crisis — the fall of the Shah and the taking of the hostages —

meant that the confidence theme would tail him right to the end of his political career in the presidential election 15 months later.

Likewise for Callaghan, the comeback at the Durham fairgrounds represented only a short-lived victory amidst a very clear statement of mounting problems that would in the end defeat his government. For a year the Callaghan government scraped by on the remnants of Social Contract agreements: inflation was down, the IMF was mollified, and wage increases averaged 6.4 percent above inflation so the trade union sector was surprisingly inactive.[11]

But with Phase Four everything came undone. The government insisted on a 5 percent pay norm and, affronted, the TUC overwhelmingly rejected *any* "arbitrary pay limit" at its September, 1978 conference, despite the belief cultivated by Callaghan that an announcement of an early general election was only days away. A host of rank-and-file and official strikes, fueled by a seemingly endless series of leapfrogging pay demands, erupted into a "winter of discontent" which battered the government in its last pre-election season. Both dismay with Callaghan by traditional union voters and dismay with the unions by a great many others were to make Thatcher, surprisingly, a consensus politician and the UK's Prime Minister before the spring had passed.

There is a poignancy to the fates of Callaghan and Carter, for as the scenes above suggest their points of no return were also among their finest hours. They stood their ground and faced their most intractable problems wisely but, in the end, not well. What could they have done?

Criticism can be directed at them as leaders and as personalities: Callaghan for ill grace and poor timing; Carter for an obsessive attention to detail which left the direction of government unattended and for his proclivity to temporize in crises. In the end, however, these personal qualities had little to do with the failures either of the Callaghan government or the Carter administration.

Ultimately, Carter and Callaghan succumbed to fatal weaknesses, not so much in their own leadership as in the visions of society, respectively, which came with their Democratic and Labour inheritances. They lost the initiative for a deceptively simple reason: for each, the *economic* and *geopolitical* preconditions for their brand of politics (as for that of their centrist Republican and Conservative counterparts) had largely disappeared.

For the United States a policy package of international liberalism inaugurated as Bretton Woods and mild Keynesian-welfarism at home was jeopardized by the budgetary excesses of the Vietnam War — and effectively killed by declining US competitiveness since the oil shock of 1973–1974. In the subsequent decade the United States' average annual rate of change in productivity was roughly one-seventh that of most of its trading competitors; real wages stagnated; the real rates of return earned by manufacturing investment fell substantially below the yield of passively held bonds (an indication of the inability of US firms to produce goods profitably in the context of international competition); and the merchandise trade balance which had been positive from 1893 to 1970, has (except for positive blips in 1973 and 1975) been in decline ever since (as has been the US share of high-technology exports).[12] A recent report of the President's Commission on Industrial Competitiveness aptly noted, "[a]s the result of unprecedented changes in the international economy, the United States, which once dominated most major aspects of the world economy, is now a nation that must compete."[13] The same might be said about the American position in the geopolitical sphere. A series of epochal defeats and withdrawals — of the policy of "containment" with the Vietnam War; of the use of regional surrogates with the fall of the Shah of Iran; of "Detente" with the Soviet invasion of Afghanistan — have signaled a significant decline in the United States' global pre-eminence.

For the United Kingdom the indications of increasing economic distress are well known and diverse. At an average of 2.3 percent, the UK's annual growth rate in gross domestic product (GDP) was 70 percent of the Organization for Economic Cooperation and Development (OECD) average from 1957 to 1967; from 1973 through 1978 the UK slipped further and GDP growth declined to an annual average of 1.1 percent — only 45 percent of the OECD average. Similarly, the UK's inflation rate was well above the average throughout the 1970s, and about twice the OECD rate from 1975 through 1977; manufacturing output has yet to match its 1973 peak; and by 1975 the UK's real GDP per capita exceeded only Italy in a comparison of the six major OECD nations.[14] In geopolitical terms the UK also suffered decline during the 1960s and 1970s. Suez, de Gaulle's rejection of UK entry into the European Community, Wilson's futile efforts to influence the United States' war policy in Vietnam, the Callaghan government's forced capitulation to IMF loan terms in 1976 — all these suggest the UK's retreat to the bottom of the middle rank of nations.

These rather sombre descriptions of declining economic competitiveness and reduced geopolitical influences suggest the context in which the defeats of Carter and Callaghan can best be understood. The Fall of the Shah and the Soviet invasion of Afghanistan left Carter's foreign policy exposed, much as declining US competitiveness and stagflation defeated the residue of New Deal liberalism at home. Likewise, by playing the IMF card while he orchestrated an historic collapse of Labour's traditional trade unionist base of support, Callaghan confirmed at once how far Britain had fallen from its imperial past, and how weak his claim to successful governance had become.

Callaghan's predecessor, Prime Minister Harold Wilson, once observed about the UK, "We are a world power and world influence or we are nothing." With this remark Wilson unwittingly anticipated the valediction for a whole age of politics based on combined geopolitical and economic strength. In the United States and the United Kingdom, it will be argued, the political success of mainstream postwar governments presupposed first the benefits and future expectations of economic growth and successful international competitiveness, and second a national geopolitical identity and position in the international hierarchy of nations which was consistent with the politics of the "growth coalition" at home. By the close of the 1970s economic and geopolitical realities had changed, but the domestic politics of Carter and Callaghan remained strangely out of phase with the altered circumstances.

Callaghan and Carter could not adjust to a political world in which a large proportion of voters were liable to reject the premises of traditional European social democracy and American New Deal liberalism: that governments should foster the redistribution of resources in society, promote egalitarianism, harmonize interests and guarantee basic provisions (housing, jobs, education, health care) as part of the universal rights of citizenship. They could no longer consolidate a political base when an economic downturn exacerbated the differences of interest among their own constituencies and turned many of the nonaligned against trade unions — and when new industrial patterns reduced the size and fragmented the influence of their working-class support. Finally, schooled in welfare state traditions of public finance they had no economic nostrums with which to replace an increasingly discredited Keynesianism, and no national vision to buoy spirits and galvanize support as the United Kingdom slipped toward the bottom of the second-rate powers and the United States lost some of its huge comparative advantage, *vis-à-vis* Europe, the Soviet Union, and especially Japan.

These were fundamental tensions which the tired politics of Carter and Callaghan were unable to resolve, and their failures raise important questions about democracy, participation, and the formation of a national political community. What would replace the universalist ethos of the welfare state, the social visions of New Deal liberalism and European social democracy, the economic approaches of Keynesianism? How would durable electoral support be constituted in the absence of traditional coalitional politics? Could a national community be unified amidst racial, ethnic, gender, and class divisions — and how would these nation-states behave in a post-hegemonic order?

The arrival of Thatcher and Reagan signaled new strategies to resolve the tensions which followed the eclipse of Keynesianism and the welfare state: the decomposition of the working class, and the upsurge of internecine warfare within Labour and Democratic constituencies; the precipitous decline of UK fortunes and the notable reduction of US prerogatives in the international order. Indeed, the Reagan and Thatcher governments have provided often surprising answers to these questions, and this is what makes them significant far beyond the particularities of contemporary UK or US politics.

Of course, their answers are not the only source of interest in the political successes and policy innovations of Margaret Thatcher and Ronald Reagan. It is also true that these redoubtable leaders have overcome the most fundamental liabilities of their predecessors. Reagan has rekindled widespread confidence in government, and Thatcher has, through legislation and strategies of direct confrontation in the state sector, considerably reduced the power of trade unions. There are few enough success stories in contemporary politics, and it is interesting to ponder political success (on whatever terms).

Thatcher and Reagan are fascinating, also, because they break the mold. They are not normal Tories or Republicans; they reject the verities of the welfare state and Keynesian economics. In their free-market maxims and in some actual economic programs — deregulation and privatization, "cash limit" financing and tax reform — they offer an export package of resurgent pro-capitalist economic policies. So part of the significance of Thatcher and Reagan lies in their conscious and widely heralded departure from the norm of mainstream non-ideological governments and centrist politics.

Their true significance, however, lies much deeper, in the ways these governments try to resolve the fundamental tensions of a post-welfarist, post-hegemonic order — and in the grave questions their "solutions" raise about democracy and about the nature of political community. If the visions of cross-generational solidarity, cohesion, and equality which motivated the welfare state are gone — are the appeals to sectional interest, individualism, and competition which replace them too costly for the political community? Can a society adjust to changes in international standing and reduced economic performance without further fragmenting the international economic order or engaging in dangerously aggressive foreign policy adventures? Does the breakdown of the normal coalitional politics of the period of the welfare state change the way the state conducts its affairs — and has power become so concentrated in the executive that political participation loses meaning and democratic control becomes more difficult to achieve?

These are the issues which will focus this book, but a few qualifications may be in order. This study has been inspired by a fascination with how Thatcher and Reagan did it — gained their seats of power against all odds and traditions — and with what makes them tick — how do they hold on to support, use their powers, put their visions into force. But I am equally concerned with some elusive deeper understandings, which are still partly buried. Hence, intertwined with the narrative there are a set of more theoretical discussions: about democracy, state formation in a post-hegemonic world, and the autonomy of the executive within the state.

This arrangement means that the book can be read on two levels: as an account of the evolution of the Thatcher and Reagan governments, and as a theoretical discussion which applies the substance of the Thatcher and Reagan governments illustratively. This also means that the book must be defined also by what it is not; namely, a full theoretical account of a new regime-type or, alternatively, a comprehensive record of both governments. In fact the book is a highly selective interpretive essay, and it is my hope that narrative and theory develop symbiotically, to mutual advantage.

In keeping with this approach, Chapter 1 considers the effects of geopolitical decline on domestic images of political community and discusses what the eclipse of the welfare state may have meant for the evolution of British and American politics — and for growing tensions between capitalism and democracy.

Chapters 2 and 3 examine the rise and fall of British Labourism and "one-nation" Toryism, in turn, and discuss the transformation of British political expectations which resulted in the victory of Thatcher in May 1979. Chapter 4 discusses the political and programmatic basis of Thatcherism.

In chapter 5 I review the evolution and ultimate demise of Keynesianism in America, and draw connections between the international and the domestic ramifications of American decline management. Chapter 6 exposes the complex bases of Reagan's electoral triumphs; chapter 7 demonstrates the full measure of Reagan's mastery, as represented by his capacity to secure a quite unusual degree of independence both for the executive within the state, and for the state above the typical interplay of forces.

In chapter 8 I evaluate the Reagan and Thatcher governments, challenging the validity — and the certainty — of economic performance criteria, and close by considering the implications of these governments not only for politics in the UK and US but also more generally for the issues they raise about the state, democracy, and political community in contemporary capitalist societies.

1

The Context of Decline

During the two decades or more of expansion at the close of World War Two, before a growing set of economic troubles (high interest and inflation rates, reduced growth, crippling sectoral and severe general unemployment) challenged the complacency of the capitalist democracies, an often unreflected optimism pervaded discussions about the prospects of Western society. Growth meant that distributional decisions would be relatively consensual, since diverse constituencies could often be appeased. Class struggle seemed almost anachronistic as trade union elites routinely participated in the formation of economic policy. Political conflict often seemed reduced to the problem of rational administration, and nowhere more so than in the US and UK.

In a famous interview with André Malraux, John Kennedy, the United States' first dyed-in-the-wool Keynesian President, captured the sentiment. Malraux remarked that in the nineteenth century, ostensibly the fundamental issue was monarchy versus republic, but the real issue was proletariat versus capitalist. In the twentieth century, continued Malraux, the ostensible issue was proletariat versus capitalist. What did Kennedy consider the real issue? "The real issue today," replied the President, "[is] the management of industrial society — a problem . . . not of ideology but of administration."[1]

Whatever else may be said about the contributions of Reagan and Thatcher to the course of contemporary history, there is no question that they have returned ideology to center stage and re-politicized public administration. In so doing they have helped reverse a powerful tendency among observers from diverse traditions to view political choice and ideological conviction as almost incidental to governmental decision-making. In this vein, Claus Offe wrote in 1972:

> The margin of decision . . . becomes barely visible. The conservatives then are partly correct in their assessment of the welfare state as creeping socialism, not because it is socialism but because it creeps. The welfare state is developing step-by-step, reluctantly and involuntarily.[2]

The range of decision, of course, seems far less marginal today: welfare expenditure follows a less certain evolutionary course and is subject to intense ideological conflict. This change is both a cause and a consequence of the consolidation of power by the Reagan and Thatcher governments. So pervasive is the joint influence of economic uncertainty and the resurgence of sharp-edged ideological politics, that it is hard now to recall that there was a time not too long ago when European politics was a study in the stability of fairly quiet and predictable democracies. High and relatively steady rates of growth, a very rapid increase in worker productivity accompanied by a mounting demand for more labor, the positive contribution of wage-earners and their representatives to the processes of state-sponsored economic management, a high domestic rate of investment and hence the prospect of continued "full" employment — all this signaled a period of economic prosperity and political moderation which most observers expected would endure indefinitely.[3] It was taken as axiomatic by many, certainly by the vast majority of American policy-makers, that US military and technological pre-eminence set the terms for a new world order in which growth assured global equilibrium and domestic Keynesianism suitably complemented the international liberalism of Bretton Woods, free trade, and multilateralism.

Pax Americana granted the United States a capacity to control the institutional terms which would govern international co-operation and the wherewithal to coordinate a world economy consistent with American policy aims. In the early years of the postwar world, "[a]ltruism and self-interest worked hand in hand"[4] to secure American hegemony in the world political economy. At the same time, the US applied the advantage of its economic pre-eminence to secure geopolitical goals, as it exploited the fear of unknown Soviet intentions to impose its own foreign policy "consensus" on sometimes reluctant allies.

Although the period of American pre-eminence in some ways mirrored that of earlier periods of national dominance — notably *Pax Britannica* of the nineteenth century — *Pax Americana* was also in certain important respects *sui generis*. Like the United Kingdom in the period of their predominant influence, the United States after 1945 had preponderant control over sources of capital, raw materials, and markets; retained significant competitive advantage in the production of advanced, highly valued (and value-added) goods; and had the power and political will to determine basic rules and institutional arrangements among states, and particularly among trading partners.

The comparison between the characteristics and the extent of US hegemony in the twentieth and UK hegemony in the nineteenth century, however, is both apposite and instructive. The US threatened reciprocity to secure "free trade" while the UK retreated into markets within its Empire. The US dependence on foreign investment was consistently lower than that of the UK, and its comparative advantage in productivity was greater. Finally, the UK relied on military and political rivals as major trading partners (thus forcing a division between economic influence and geo-political control), whereas the US created a more unified international hegemonic bloc of trading partners which were also political and military allies (and subordinates). "American hegemony, rather than being one more instance of a general phenomenon," observes Robert O. Keohane, "was essentially unique in the scope and efficacy of the instruments at the disposal of a hegemonic state and in the degree of success attained."[5]

This idyll, however, could not and did not last. By the end of the 1970s each of the conditions which had defined American hegemony had eroded considerably. The increased significance of Eurocurrency markets and international banks substantially privatized international monetary policy[6] and reduced US government control over capital. The growth of powerful cartels (notably OPEC) and the increased influence of regional trading blocs (such as the European Community) lessened American control over raw materials and markets. Growing trade deficits in automobiles, steel, and electronics reflected reduced international competitiveness. Perhaps most troubling to American interests, between 1960 and 1980, according to a Department of Commerce study, US export shares declined in eight out of ten crucial high-technology sectors[7] — despite the depreciation of the dollar in the 1970s which generally enhanced price competitiveness. However, by the 1970s it had also become clear that the United States could no longer impose rules which would govern the terms of international political-economic interaction among states: the regime of stable international exchange rates, with the dollar pegged to gold at a set price (the Bretton Woods system) was gone; protectionist pressures on trade policy led to increasing disregard for General Agreement of Tariffs and Trade (GATT) provisions to secure liberal (i.e. open) trade policies, and, in geopolitical terms, Vietnam (and later Iran) encouraged fragmentation within the Western alliance alongside the open defiance of American interests by an expanding "neutralist" and third-world bloc of nation-states.

Thus a post-hegemonic order was born. The United States entered the 1980s with diminished geopolitical influence and suffering from what some have called a "scissors effect." The United States had "simultaneously become more dependent on the world economy and much less able to dictate the course of international economic events.[8] In this sense at least, Jimmy Carter was right to link American crisis of confidence and loss of national purpose to fear that the future would not compare favorably with the past. It may have been the born-again preacher in Carter who warned that "the erosion of our confidence in the future is threatening to destroy the social and the political fabric of America"[9] — and it is easy to remain aloof from Carter's calculating pathos. But if the exaggeration and the tone are ignored, an important truth remains: the end of the United States' glory years of unquestioned economic pre-eminence and geopolitical mastery would have significant consequences for the nation's self-appraisal, its social visions, the bases of cohesion among diverse groups and interests. *Pax Americana* and the welfare state were animated and politically sustained by a "growth coalition"[10] of New Deal Democrats and Republican and business internationalists. Even a modest decline — measured against what the US had been at the start of the postwar order and what Japan, ironically, might become — could have serious political repercussions. The UK, of course, has suffered an incomparably greater fall in international influence and comparative economic performance, but the political implications are surprisingly similar.

The United Kingdom's decline has lasted much longer, dating from the 1880s when *Pax Britannica*, based on free trade and unrivaled naval power, lost viability as its supremacy was increasingly challenged by the economic competition and the expanding military capacities of the United States, Germany and Japan. More to the point, the UK's decline is of a wholly different magnitude. There is no denying, in fact, that the UK is in profound economic straits. Ajit Singh has argued persuasively that the UK economy has suffered from a "structural disequilibrium, whereby the trading position of the manufacturing sector in the world economy continues to deteriorate, in spite of increasing cost and price competitiveness." De-industrialization, measured by the loss of one million jobs in manufacturing between 1968 and 1976, is only one of the more heralded symptoms of this disequilibrium.[11]

A recent study by the OECD extends Singh's measured pessimism. The 1983 economic survey noted a severe fall in production in the UK economy and observed that despite a declining rate of inflation, "the downturn in output and employment has been greater [in the UK] than in most other member countries." The report emphasized a sharp fall in manufacturing production to a level roughly 16 percent below the UK's 1979 peak, and stated that UK international competitiveness measured in relative unit labor costs deteriorated by some 55 percent in the course of the 1970s. The OECD study concluded bleakly: "Under these circumstances it is not surprising that the industrial base has contracted and unemployment risen strongly."[12] As the narrative which follows will seek to demonstrate, the UK equivalent of the US growth coalition — Tory modernizers and Labour/trade union optimists who touted the "white hot technological revolution" — would see their political fortunes decline alongside the UK's economic performance and geopolitical standing.

Times changed, and although the changes did not foreordain the advent of Reagan and Thatcher's new age of politics — they did encourage the development of a post-hegemonic, post-welfarist orientation. There is a simple premise, which I shall ask to bear considerable weight: that the experiences of decline meant that when the generalized economic crisis of the 1970s beset Western Europe and the US, in the UK and the US in particular, neo-conservative and new right forces would be better positioned to take advantage of the political-electoral openings. The eclipse of Keynesianism and the welfare state left the center-left — and even mainstream Conservative and Republican — alternatives out-positioned and in considerable disarray. Indeed, it is in the rise and fall of the Keynesian welfare state that one can best trace the origins of Reagan and Thatcher.

THE ECLIPSE OF THE KEYNESIAN WELFARE STATE

As is well known, a world recession began with the sharp rise in petroleum prices in 1973—1974. Compared to the previous 10-year period the period from 1973 to 1981 saw a significant reduction in the average increase in world trade (from 8.7 percent to 3.1 percent). Not surprisingly, the most notable development in world trade after 1973 was the large increase in exports by oil-producing developing countries — an increase of 7.7 percent to 15 percent of the world share. During the same period the industrialized nations' share of world exports slipped 7 percent (from 71 percent to 64 percent).[13] Throughout Western Europe and the US this recesssion signaled an epochal shift in the patchwork of growth-based economic and social policies that political elites pursued. Suddenly, economic management problems had become intractable and efforts to secure the requisite quotient of popular acceptance to ensure electoral success had become far more complex.

While there never had been a true "end of ideology," mainstream sociologists and political scientists were right until then to note tendencies toward class de-alignment in electoral behavior, and to identify a broad consensus in party political (and to a lesser but significant degree in trade union strategies) in favor of what might be called "Keynesian society" or the "Keynesian welfare state" (KWS). This was true, in particular, if "Keynesian" refers *not* to an economic doctrine, but to a vision of society which involved state efforts to harmonize interests through diverse economic and social policies, to politically regulate the market economy, and to take a tutelary role in securing business and trade union approval for central economic policies. Keynesianism refers here to the political regulation of the capitalist economy, and includes the institutionalized arrangements for interest intermediation (sometimes labeled "corporatism") which emerged during the postwar period of economic growth and political stabilization of the capitalist democracies.

Of course, a range of factors would determine the precise fix of the deals struck between capital and labor which influenced in turn the extent and character of the political regulation of the economy: the balance of class forces in a particular state; pre-existing institutions for mediating conflict and managing the economy; the strength of socialist and communist parties; the power and strategic capacities of trade union movements; the resolve and level of cohesion of capitalist elites. But everywhere these "postwar settlements" included at their core a central premise: "full" employment through governmental demand management and increased social welfare expenditure in return for relative social harmony and labor peace.[14] There would be a better-managed capitalism, with considerable limits placed on private prerogative: a capitalism tilting toward a non-ideological social democracy.

The marketplace, as location of industrial conflict and mechanism for calibrating the allocation of resources in society, was augmented by non-market political institutions. Governments, the leading actors in a tripartite matrix of power shared with capital (more so) and labor (less so, but for exceptional cases such as Sweden), took on a wide range of management, ownership, and control functions which were previously the center of capitalist prerogative and the source of private labor-management disputes. Many capitalist-democratic states increased their ownership of basic industries, paid the wages of a sizeable percentage of a nation's workforce, and they often set prices and incomes. Keynesianism meant, above all, that whenever possible conflict would be mediated through non-market political institutions, such as the National Board for Prices and Incomes (NBPI) set up by the Labour government in 1965 to determine whether prospective increases were in the national interest, and which was empowered to freeze prices and incomes as it deemed necessary.

During the heyday of Keynesian society, a period of some 25

years from the end of World War Two to the oil shock of 1973–1974, there were shifts, of course, in political sentiment and in the balance of class and coalitional forces. One could expect the alternation of center-right and center-left governments; but nearly all governments were committed to the institutionalized compromises of the welfare state. As a result many observers and government officials alike were lulled into thinking that growth, welfarism, artful demand management, and political moderation might go on for ever. Eventually, however, the global capitalist recession of the 1970s eroded the terms of the postwar settlements and reduced the prospects for a victimless mixed-economy capitalism.

Growth had done wonders to reduce political conflicts and ease the problems of governance, since expansion meant that the needs of diverse — and even antagonistic — constituencies could often be met. Wages could rise without a decline in profitability; improvements in the provision of health care or education did not require a reduction in unemployment benefits or pensions.

With recession the Keynesian consensus was lost and political life became very much more complicated for actors on all sides. Trade union and allied social-democratic interests must respond to rising new economic orthodoxies — monetarism, supply-side economics, the "new economic pragmatism" — before they have developed an adequate post-Keynesian strategy of their own. They must construct programs which can reclaim majority support in an era when economic reversals mean a retreat from redistributive and universalistic welfare measures, except when they serve a particular group's self-interest. Rightist and pro-capitalist elites must re-invent strategies which lead the economy toward a growth equilibrium through "free market" forces, in a period when oligopolistic powers on a global scale have long since obscured the world of Adam Smith, and trade unions bent on protecting jobs may obstruct strategies for improved productivity.

Governing parties, whether of the right or left, must maintain support from millions of voter-consumers stretched among diverse constituencies, precisely at a time — as we shall see — when declining economic growth exacerbates class tensions, and receding opportunities deepen racial, ethnic, and gender divisions within the nation-state. The economic boom gone bust, all bets for smooth political mediation are off. Throughout the capitalist West governments are scrambling to adopt new strategies with which to overcome the constraints of the international economic order and break the pattern of national policy failures.

All is not Reaganomics and Thatcherism, however. In Sweden, just before the Social Democratic Party was turned out of office in 1976, a path-breaking strategy was conceived to arrest the unusually high concentration of capital, provide new sources of accumulation and investment, and redistribute both wealth and economic control in society — in short, to "transcend the compromise between labor and capital" which marked the period of the Keynesian postwar settlement. The idea of the "Meidner Plan" — named after the head of the trade union commission which developed the strategy — was extremely simple in principle. Part of the profits from every enterprise would be transferred to the employees collectively, as newly issued stock to be held in a wage-earners fund. After 30 years or so the majority of enterprises would in this way come under employee control.

Despite political difficulties, as John Stephens writes:

> the Swedish labor movement will continue to push for the passage of wage-earner funds, because from the labor movement's point of view, they are the *only* workable solution to the key problem facing Sweden today: the search for a policy that will both insure sufficient rates of investment *and* result in a distribution of income and wealth that is acceptable to the labor movement.[15]

However, since the return of the social-democratic government in September, 1982 it has become increasingly clear that the pressures of international competitiveness faced by Swedish firms have eroded the principles of traditional Swedish solidaristic wage bargaining. "Just as growth tends to strengthen *both* labour *and* capital," observes Jonas Pontusson, "so do crises entail tendencies that weaken capital *and* labour."[16] As a result the political difficulties of implementing the wage-earner funds proposal are heightened and the transformative impulse blunted. As a consequence, "ultra-Keynesian" employment policies are shelved.[17]

The Swedish case, like the French — in which continued

international recession has pushed the Mitterrand government from a left-Keynesian debut toward a "Colbertist austerity" since March, 1983[18] — suggest that enduring economic troubles have had widespread and profound consequences throughout the capitalist democracies. They have eroded confidence in the assumptions of the Keynes-inspired class compromises and necessitated new strategies to meet economic and political problems which are highly resistant to solution. While the crisis limits governmental options and reduces the likelihood that any economic management strategy will be successful, it does not mandate one kind of solution. Why only in the Anglo-American world did the eclipse of Keynesianism result in such unabashedly pro-capitalist, anti-welfarist, and powerfully statist governments?

THE SIGNIFICANCE OF EMPIRE

At the height of their influence, imperial states often secured a national interest which is consistent with an unusually broad range of elite and non-elite interests. Indeed, a powerful coalition may emerge historically from the connection between the growth of empire and the development of the welfare state. Quite consciously, political elites increase state-sponsored social provision as part of a governmental strategy to secure widespread support for imperialist expansion. Indeed, this is one of the reasons why the early growth of the welfare state, ironically, remains the gift of Conservative governments. Thus, as German historian Hans-Ulrich Wehler observed, "Bismarck's social policy was the internal aspect of a stabilization programme, whose external aspect was imperialism."[19]

The Conservatism of Disraeli brings the themes of empire and social reform — which forged the nineteenth-century "growth coalition" — a good deal closer to home. In fact the speeches of the British Prime Minister in 1872 in many ways represent the first expression of the modern Tory Party. As Paul Smith notes:

> Imperialism, offering the kind of romantic image whose influence on men's minds, Disraeli so well understood, appealed forcefully to a bourgeoisie beginning to tire of change at home but ready to assert the nation's greatness overseas and to large elements of the

working class whose essential chauvinism it gratified. Social reform reinforced the appeal of the working man's patriotism with the promise of care for his well being.[20]

The Conservative Party was able to consolidate a cross-class base of support precisely because, at this stage in the Empire, Disraeli could unify the themes of international pre-eminence and social reform (the symbol of inner greatness). The Conservatives emerged as a national party, and remained so for three-quarters of a century until the postwar era, because their appeal to national greatness fulfilled patriotic yearnings and encouraged belief, at the same time that material needs might be satisfied.[21] In a similar way the grand designs of the Kennedy administration, expressed through the upbeat messages of the "New Frontier" and the "New Economics," linked new leadership abroad to economic growth and social improvement at home. The economic and geopolitical advantages of empire were the source also of hard political currency, and the basis for powerful domestic appeals.[22]

The growth of empire, it seems, encourages a compatibility between social reform—welfarism and grand patriotic designs for geopolitical pre-eminence. Hegemony, therefore, occasions unusual programmatic consensus among otherwise divided interests. If growth reduces social tensions and distributional conflict, then growth enhanced by the patriotic messages of international grandeur becomes an even more powerful resource for sustained governmental support.

It is a premise of my argument that the contrapositive holds equal force. The prism of decline tends to refract national interest into divided particularistic and sectional interests and to reduce the political/electoral utility to which a governing party can put promises of welfare provision. There is more at work here, however, than a logical premise. It will be my intention to show how in the UK and the US the eclipse of Keynesianism combined with eroding geopolitical position and reduced economic capacities — in very different ways — to hasten the dissolution of symbiotic attachments among the modernizing, welfarist, internationalist elites.

The first truly post-Keynesian governments in their construction of political meanings, Thatcher and Reagan have been extremely skillful in creating a new political community and in forging a potentially durable electoral base. In this sense they have earned their stay, for they have instinctively recognized the tensions immanent within the KWS package, and have acted decisively to reorganize society accordingly. By challenging basic beliefs about political participation and democracy which were nurtured during the era of the welfare state, however, and by altering the modus operandi of the state, Reagan and Thatcher have also generated a host of new problems. Here it is only possible to introduce two such themes that will be developed more fully in the narrative which follows: the repudiation of integrative strategies and the expanded independence of the executive.

ANTI-WELFARIST LEGITIMATION

National political life changed considerably once mass political parties that were linked more or less directly to the working class began to compete with parties of order and business for success in the political realm. Parties such as the German Social Democratic Party, the British Labour Party and, to stretch a point, the American Democratic Party, began to serve as "transmission belts between the population at large and the governmental structure."[23] In this task the "class-mass" parties were remarkably successful, integrating out-groups into the mainstream of politics, thereby harmonizing the prevailing order.

This very process of integration, however, is oddly self-negating, since constituencies which are brought in typically are depoliticized by the process of social and political integration, resulting in transformed party structures and expectations. The success of class—mass parties as electoral parties has led to a decline of class-oriented, issue-based parties, and their replacement by "catch-all" parties, which appeal to diverse intra-class constituencies on leadership and performance criteria. The rise of parties less concerned with the needs of a specific social class or religious/ethnic clientele involves a weakening of the integrative role of the party system as a whole and encourages a class de-alignment of electoral behavior. Moreover, these integrative functions of the parties decline as interest group activities and direct encounters with state bureaucracies come to connect the citizen with the state in ways that are more sustained and significant.

The locus of integrative strategies tends to shift from the party to the state apparatus. Efforts at integration become focused on social policies, such as Johnson's "War on Poverty," which are designed to incorporate a particular social group into the mainstream of political and social culture, however marginally or negatively. At the same time, governments in tune with a Keynesian motif introduce new institutional arrangements which are intended to mobilize consent among potentially combative groups, characteristically by setting labor and capital to bargain with state managers over nationally fixed wage increases. During the era of the welfare state, nothing taxed the imagination of government officials more than efforts at harmonizing interests in society, and integrating potentially disruptive groups into the much safer realm of consensus politics. It was easy to see that governing elites would have an abiding self-interest in maintaining social harmony by buying people into the good life of democratic capitalism. To many observers, social welfare expenditures were the essential integrative, demobilizing tool of state managers. Aren't increasing welfare expenditures, amidst the continuous provocations of immiseration and asymmetries of power, the necessary minimum for maintaining social harmony? It seems not, by the look of things in Whitehall and Washington.

Clearly, the governments of Thatcher and Reagan repudiate traditional KWS integrative politics. Instead, the legitimacy of these governments comes to rest on an ideology which combines the doctrine of the social market economy ("monetarism") with a neo-laissez-faire rejection of public intervention in the economy and the universalist and redistributive ethos of the welfare state. This doctrine belies practices of economic policy intervention that continue, such as Thatcher's tight-fisted control of state sector industrial relations or Reagan's shifting industrial policy disguised as tax policy. More significant, here, are the divisive appeals which replace the integrative, welfarist norms: Thatcher's explicit characterization of striking miners as "the enemy within" and the increased marginalization of the black community in the British Nationality Act 1981; Reagan's assault on the reproductive rights of women, and a systematic refusal of the Justice Department to pursue discrimination cases, even as it argues before the Supreme Court that statutory approval of affirmative action quotas to advance racial equality be revoked. There are, of course, positive appeals, but these are directed to particular sectoral constituencies — potential council-dwellers cum homeowners in the UK or investors in oil reserves in the US. Except for often bellicose assertions of national pride, the lingering universalist appeals of the KWS ethos are offered narrowly — protection of the "truly needy" and legally constructed issues of "equal opportunity" and civil rights.

As politically potent as these de-integrative strategies are, they nevertheless raise some troubling issues. Thatcher and Reagan have arrested — and partly reversed — the historic tendency for citizenship rights to expand from *civil rights* (securing individual freedoms) to *political rights* (participation in the governmental exercise of power) to *social rights* (provisions for need which reduce the natural pattern of social inequality in a capitalist society). T. H. Marshall observed that "class-abatement" was the aim of social rights, which invariably involved "the subordination of market price to social justice."[24] If this is true then the current Anglo-American resolution to the problems of the KWS has, in turn, brought a new set of problems to the fore. Confidence in government has been restored and the power of trade unions reduced, but not without cost in terms of the rights of citizenship: not simply social-welfarist rights, but also the more modest nineteenth-century goals of political participation. For an effective de-integrative strategy also effectively disenfranchises groups which are outside the mainstream — people of color, for example — who were the most recently integrated into national politics. It also makes meaningful participation by women, ethnic minorities, gay people, and the unemployed or even the non-unionized employed workers far more difficult — and it deepens a central tension in society.

There is, after all, no natural compatibility between capitalism and democracy. If market principles divide groups by economic situation and foster competition — how can political arrangements reconcile these abiding conflicts of interest? If the capitalist economy creates inequalities of wealth and labor market situation — how can governments both enforce these market principles and at the same time maintain popular support in accordance with principles of fairness and the universal rights and entitlements of citizenship? In the nineteenth century a wide range of thinkers — from Karl Marx to John Stuart Mill — thought that capitalism and democracy based on equal and extensive suffrage were incompatible. For part of the twentieth century the KWS, the artful use of politics to secure social rights, and the economics of growth made a practical if not theoretical reconciliation possible. Compromise obscured for a time the tension between capitalism and democracy.

Today, ideologically determined governments in the US and the UK raise once again the old concerns that vigorous capitalism and full democracy may not mix. Have Thatcher and Reagan altered the formula, by reducing the participation of non-mainstream groups and narrowing the terms of citizenship? How costly is their program to the character of political community, to democratic values, and to the meaning of citizenship? These questions are closely linked to a second theme associated with politics in the age of Reagan and Thatcher: the unusual statism of these governments.

THE EXPANDED INDEPENDENCE OF THE EXECUTIVE

The demise of the KWS represents more than the eclipse of an economic theory or the reduction in some categories of social expenditure: it signifies also the decline in support for a kind of society. Keynesianism meant that state managers would seek compromises among competing social groups and that, whenever possible, industrial conflicts would be mediated through political institutions. State efforts to regulate the market economy enmeshed government in a set of political exchanges with major social actors and, as a consequence, positioned the state as the arbiter of competing interests and the object of explicit class pressures. The state's tutelary role in the formation of policies which previously lay within the prerogative of the private sphere — the setting of incomes, the allocation of resources in industrial contexts — implicated the state directly in class and market relations. But what motivates state involvement? Does the state act as a power broker for a capitalist class? Or does it act from a more independent

posture to keep the society and economy operating smoothly —
contravening the political aims of business elites and challenging
their prerogatives as it sees fit?

The more active and transparent the performance of the state in
the processes of economic management, the greater the urgency
of questions such as these which address both the class context of
state power and the character and extent of its institutional
constraints. The era of the KWS made obvious that the political
regulation of market forces — through planning initiatives,
industrial policy, incomes policy — actively structured economic
outcomes. Robust performance obscured the political—ideological
determination of policy, since growth encouraged class compromise and ensured an unusual degree of satisfaction with state
programs. The recession of the post-1973 period, however, made it
clear that when economic constraints exacerbated distributional
conflicts, then governments (and diverse state actors) were forced
to advantage some constituencies and disadvantage others.

Class politics re-emerged vigorously in many West European
countries, and new constituencies — discontented youth, ethnic-
nationalists, women, racial minorities — made demands which
states were little inclined (and not always able) to meet. It became
clear, once again, that states were sites of struggle and that state
institutions and practices — from the statutory enactment of wage-
earners' funds to the legalization and funding of abortions, to the
expansion of centralized police powers or the reduction of trade
union rights — reflected the dynamic balance of class and other
political forces in society. By institutionalizing the power of certain
interests in society (e.g. through corporatist arrangements with
trade union associations) or, alternatively, by fragmenting political
opposition (e.g. through economic policies that divide the
employed and the unemployed), states radically condition the
future evolution of political forces. These practices in some
important ways identify the character of the class—state nexus.

During the KWS, therefore, it seemed sensible to reject a view
of the state as the instrumental reserve of any one class (the
capitalist class) and to see the institutional arrangements and the
policy outcomes of the postwar settlement as expressions of the
"relative autonomy" of the state from the control of capitalist
elites. It was possible to define the state as a determinate agency

which would ensure capitalist business as usual, but one which articulated class compromises in a range of institutions and common practices.

But how are class—state relations explained when state practices depart from the KWS norm, and when governments withdraw from the institutional connections which expressed their "relative autonomy" and articulated the hard-won compromises of the postwar settlements? The modus operandi of the Reagan and Thatcher governments point to a theoretical blind spot — and raise crucial issues about the political consequences of an unusual introjection of state power.

There are serious indications that, through very different institutional means, both the Thatcher and the Reagan governments have secured for themselves — and notably for their chief executive officers — an unusual sphere of decisional independence. In the UK, as a consequence of economic crisis and the declining international competitiveness of some domestic segments of capital, the intra-class divisions endemic to capitalism have deepened. Thus, after an early campaign against Thatcher and in defense of manufacturing interests, the Confederation of British Industry (CBI), the central corporatist representative of capital, became too internally divided to pursue policy interventions.[25] At the same time the government has, for ideological reasons, associated with its broader de-integrative strategy, pulled back from institutional ties to the TUC. However, as Leo Panitch notes, in the UK the National Economic Development Council (NEDC), the central "planning" agency, "has withstood not only Heath's 'Selsdon Man', but also the more extreme ideological and policy shifts of the Thatcher regime."[26] While some institutions may be enduring, more ad-hoc arrangements within a KWS motif (such as incomes policies) require that all negotiating parties have some expectation that they can "deliver the goods" to their constituencies. Both economic decline and ideological antipathy between the government and trade unions make this condition quite unachievable.

In the United States, where even the shallow planning capacities of the NEDC have not been structured into the institutional arrangements of the political economy, the Reagan government has achieved its unusual independence through rather different institutional means. The very irresolution of the American process of economic policy formation — which involves routine combat among the Treasury, the Congress, and the ostensibly independent Federal Reserve Board — gives the American President a structured opening to "divide and conquer" these competitive interests. I will suggest in the narrative which follows that Reagan's manipulation of the "politics of the deficit," which was *permitted* by the existence of a political base outside his party and Congress and an institutional restructuring of the budgetary process, and *encouraged* by an unusually determined leadership at the Fed, helped secure for the President an atypical moment of autonomy.

Have Thatcher and Reagan expanded the independence of the executive? In some sense their distinct missions in coming to office required that they do so — that Reagan remove the White House from the influence of "special interests" as part of the process of reviving confidence in government; that Thatcher disentangle the state from institutional binds to trade unions and return management prerogative to the capitalists. Both have used free market ideology as a potent mechanism for taking politics above the traditional interplay of interests, and both are the chief executives of powerfully *dirigiste* states — states which are not readily subject to the arrangements of the postwar settlements nor the traditional interplay of Keynesian coalitions. But they have gotten to this comparable place through different paths and for distinct institutional reasons.

For Thatcher, the increased *concentration* of state power — the reduced influence of local councils as an oppositional force, the state's withdrawal from "voluntary" corporatist arrangements — has provided the opening for expanded independence. For Reagan, on the contrary, the state's very institutional *fragmentation* and irresolution — the separation of powers in economic policy formation, the "independence" of the Federal Reserve, the shallowness of party discipline, the weakness of the budgetary process — have provided him with the leverage to secure an unusual insulation from the pressure of interests.

If, as I hope to show, the current UK and US executives are unusually assertive and strongly independent, then there may be important, although by no means unambiguous, consequences. For a start, state theory which would anticipate that ideologically pro-capitalist governments would act invariably on behalf of, or directly at the behest of, capitalist class forces would seem strangely out of tune with the contemporary political moment. Perhaps far more important, such developments would raise a cautionary note about the consequences for democracy. Is a state which is above the interplay of coalitions and the normal constraints imposed by interest intermediation — that much further removed from effective democratic control?

The chapters which follow will consider both the paths these governments have taken to power and in power — and assess some of the implications of their policies and programs for the contemporary meaning of capitalism and democracy. It should be noted that their political approaches are similar in important ways, as I suggest by referring to a common age of politics associated with Reagan and Thatcher. Nevertheless, very different locations in a trajectory of decline, and fundamentally dissimilar institutional realities within each state and society, mean that contemporary UK and US politics involves the telling of two rather different stories: the one, more a story of parties and the dissolution of a social-democratic vision of the society; the other, more about the demise of a hegemonic international order and the politics of economic policy. It is to these two stories which I now turn, beginning with the UK and the decline of the KWS.

2
The Break-up of Labourist Britain

Far from representing the failures of leadership or the mischance of one administration, the dissolution of the last Labour government — and the demise of the tradition of politics and vision of society it expressed — are firmly grounded historically. The first industrial nation, the United Kingdom can also lay claim to a less estimable title as the European state longest in decline. Already by the time of the "second industrial revolution" in the last decades of the nineteenth century, the UK had begun to fall behind her continental competitors (and the US) in crucial areas: technological innovation, the securing of mass markets, the scale of organization of production.[1]

By the 1890s a 30-year decline in profitability, investment in home manufacturing, and economic growth introduced a period of rapid political change. Although wages continued to rise until the turn of the twentieth century, increasing unemployment focused the dissatisfaction of working people and a rash of studies on the "condition of England" question — housing, the aged poor, the provision of the Poor Law and others — challenged the complacency of middle-class society. At the same time the political influence of the "aristocracy of labor" — skilled, comparatively well-paid workers who were unionized along traditional craft divisions — rose steadily after their enfranchisement in the 1867 Reform Act. Finally, by the 1880s a set of new unions representing the "unskilled" workers of the second industrial phase — notably dockers and mineworkers — heightened class tensions through a bold use of the strike weapon and an explicitly political (often socialist) approach to trade unionism. In response the 1890s saw both an increase in efforts by capitalists to reduce the power of unions by threats of dismissal and the use of lock-outs, and a state-sponsored counterattack on the rights of trade unions.

THE EMERGENCE OF THE LABOUR PARTY

In 1870 the Liberal Party of Gladstone had dominated the landscape, containing within it a significant sector of aristocratic opinion and, remarkably, a majority both of the politically active working class and of manufacturing and commercial interests. By the 1890s, however, the Liberals were split, with City and manufacturing interests relocating in the Conservative Party. In 1900 the Labour Representation Committee was formed and from it there emerged a new and very different kind of party. The Labour Party was founded in 1906 to achieve direct working-class representation in the Commons and secure the political demands of a restive trade union movement with sufficient confidence to break away from political vehicles, like the Liberal party, which were not of its own making or class affiliation.[2]

Thus the period from 1860 until World War One, which marked the beginning of the end of UK hegemony, was also the end of an era in another sense. As Dangerfield wrote in his study of political crisis in the 1910—1914 period:

I realize, of course, that the word "Liberal" will always have meaning so long as there is one democracy left in the world or any remnant of a middle class, but the true pre-war Liberalism — supported, as it still was in 1910, by Free Trade, a majority in Parliament, the ten commandments and the illusion of Progress — can never return. It was killed or it killed itself, in 1913. And a very good thing, too.[3]

As both the material and ideological advantages of empire declined, liberal England — the England of free trade, limited franchise, and stable leadership by the Liberal Party — died because the terms of the compromise it represented between capitalism and democracy could no longer be sustained. The UK's economic decline, its loss of geopolitical pre-eminence, pressure from the newly enfranchised and unionized laboring classes, and increasing middle-class distress with the social costs of industrial capitalism — all these factors transformed state—society relations in the period from the 1880s to the 1920s.

By the end of World War One it was increasingly apparent that the old compromise between capitalism and democracy — a robust imperial economy and a limited (although expanding) franchise exercised through support for parties which shared a narrow laissez-faire view of the role of the state — could not hold indefinitely. Thus World War One ended the classic phase of English liberalism, a fact confirmed as much by the dramatic expansion of state involvement in the economy during the course of the war as by the extension of the franchise to all adults in its aftermath in 1918.

Liberal England died as the "interventionist state" and a mass representative democracy were born.[4] The death of Liberal England signified a fundamental reappraisal of the meaning of capitalist democracy, for the terms of reference had been dramatically recast. The creation of the Labour Party, and its full arrival with the formation of minority Labour governments in 1924 and 1929, indicated the extensive political integration of the working classes into the affairs of state. At the same time, the deepening participation of the state in the running of the wartime economy suggested its gradual transformation in accordance with a new interventionist mandate.

TWO POSTWAR SETTLEMENTS

Generally when political scientists refer to the "postwar settlement" (PWS) they are referring to a set of implicit and explicit arrangements made by representatives of labor and capital under the tutelage of the state which changed the balance between public and private power in the period after World War Two. The UK is no exception to this theorem. After World War Two the British state deepened and diversified its responsibilities for the conduct of the economy and the provision of social benefits like other Western European states.

It is noteworthy, however, that the "interventionist state" emerged in the UK to a significant degree during the conduct of World War *One*, although that earlier postwar era cannot be identified as one of political harmony and a negotiated settlement among state, capital, and labor. The state took increasing control of a number of industries, including railways, mining, and shipping; it set prices and restricted the flow of capital abroad; and it applied fiscal policy to the task of channeling private resources into production geared to the war effort. As Eric Hobsbawm notes:

> In fact between 1916 and 1918 Britain was forced to evolve a first incomplete and reluctant sketch of the powerful state-economy of the Second World War. It was dismantled with unseemly haste after 1918 . . . Nevertheless, nothing could be quite the same again.[5]

Thus, in one crucial way, the wartime experience transformed the structure of British political economy. State intervention would no longer proceed only *negatively*, by the use of legislative enactments and administrative measures to reduce constraints in the operation of a free market — augmented only by homeopathic treatment ("the infinitesimal dose") to produce healthy responses in the economy by the tapping of its own natural reserves. Rather, to a new degree, the British state would conform more closely to the continental practices of *positive* intervention which involved, among other things, the rationalization of industry through amalgamation of production into larger units and the regulation of prices, the creation of government cartels, and the application of protectionist duties.

THE POLITICALLY REGULATED MARKET ECONOMY IN THE UK

In this sense, with the growing political regulation of the market economy in the interwar years, an underlying motif of the PWS began to take shape in the United Kingdom well before World War Two. The picture is complicated, however, by consideration of the political repercussions of state involvement in the conduct of World War One. As unemployment skyrocketed at the end of the postwar boom — from 2 percent in 1919—1920 to 12.9 percent in 1921[6] — industrial tension erupted in a set of epochal showdowns. A Triple Alliance of powerful unions (railway workers, miners, and transport workers) challenged the government's decision to ignore the recommendation of a royal commission that the coal industry be nationalized. The coalition government of Lloyd George invoked emergency powers amidst threats of a general strike and won capitulation from the miners. Five years later the general strike of 1926 confirmed both the intensity of class antipathy and the capacity of the state — now deeply enmeshed in industrial management — to wield its power to fragment the trade union movement and resist a transformative agenda.

In retrospect, the PWS after World War Two, therefore, represents both *continuity* and *discontinuity* with the experiences of the earlier postwar era. The evolutionary trend toward expanded economic governance by the state gathered momentum, but in the second postwar era the political crisis and class bitterness of the interwar years was averted.

The more sustained economic growth of the 1950s and 1960s accounts, in large measure, for the relative political calm which surrounded the significant changes in the UK political and economic order during the latter period. The UK shared with other capitalist democracies an extremely propitious set of economic conditions during the first two decades of the postwar order which — at least in combination — are not likely to be seen again. Increasing worker productivity encouraged a solid rate of domestic investment. At the same time the UK enjoyed low inflation, virtually full employment, and a steady rate of growth.

By comparison with the interwar period, the UK's postwar growth rate of 2.8 percent represents a record of solid achievement and provides — if just barely — sufficient expansion to encourage widespread support for increased government expenditure on social welfare provision. Nevertheless, a comparison with other European postwar experiences suggests also the narrow limits within which the UK's PWS was cast. Lacking the much-vaunted "miracles" of economic growth which occurred elsewhere during the same 20-year period — 6.7 percent in Germany, 6.0 percent in Italy, 4.5 percent in France — the UK's room for maneuver was far more cirumscribed than elsewhere. Equally significant, the structure of growth reduced trade union influence in the conduct of macroeconomic and social policy, since economic performance followed a now-traditional British pattern: the financial sector bailed out a consistently declining manufacturing sector.[7] With a short period of Labour government (1945—1951) and a far longer stretch of Conservative power (1951—1964) accompanying a rather shallow record of growth, the political regulation of the market economy in the UK assumed strictly limited proportions.

For example, state involvement in economic affairs, apart from the role of public enterprises, has been notable mainly in its efforts to "fine-tune" the economic aggregates by adjusting state revenues and expenditures. Thus, when the economy heated up — production rose, inflation increased, credit expanded, labor markets tightened and the balance of payments was jeopardized — government would act to cool off the economy by running up a deficit and raising taxation or triggering a rise in interest rates to tighten credit and attract capital inflows to the country.[8] In this way UK economic management involved predominantly state regulation of the market economy through the manipulation of monetary and fiscal policy centered in the Treasury and the Bank of England.

Welfare provision, like economic management, illustrates the limits of the postwar settlement in the United Kingdom. The increased cost of social services in the UK, as elsewhere in capitalist Europe, is one of the most dramatic facts of state policy in the twentieth century. From about 4 percent of the GNP in 1910, social expenditures — for income security (which includes pensions, unemployment, family allowances, and national assistance or "welfare" in American terms); medical care; education; and housing — increased by 1970 to some 24 percent of the GNP. In fact, during the rise of the postwar settlement welfare provision expanded to a point where it accounted for one-half of all state expenditures.[9] Nevertheless, this growth was modest in comparative OECD terms where in 1960, for example, UK social expenditure approximated the OECD average for the major economies — and the annual growth in "real expenditure" was the lowest for the major economies.[10] Nevertheless, with growth during the period of the PWS substantially below the OECD average, there is reason to believe that welfare costs were difficult for the UK economy to bear.

CALLAGHAN'S INHERITANCE

At the start, therefore, with Labour victory and a post-war social consensus, the PWS involved a fine-tuned compromise among class interests and corresponding political elites; in its denouement the PWS has involved increasing concessions to a growing universe of economic constraints. Two decades of stop—go shallow interventionism sapped the ardor and reduced the influence of Labour and labor activists who had hoped for more. A moment of broad consensus and unusual social harmony viewed in terms of potential programmatic innovation, was largely squandered. The continual downward spiral of the UK's economic performance would, by the mid-1970s, reduce the options available to any government.

In the case of a Labour government, reduced performance and geopolitical standing would mandate choices that significantly damaged the party's electoral future. Thus, when we encountered James Callaghan at the Durham fairgrounds in July, 1976, his options were few. He carried the message of an exhausted social democracy turning in on itself, and Callaghan as leader is only a small part of the drama and defeat which followed.

Callaghan had become Prime Minister upon selection as party leader by Labour MPs in April, 1976, following Harold Wilson's sudden resignation, and Callaghan departed immediately from the style of his predecessor. Where Wilson was an intriguer and back room politician, Callaghan was more in the style of a union official (which he had been): pragmatic and apparently guileless. Where Wilson would appease, Callaghan challenged opponents head on. Under attack for his incomes policies, Callaghan took on all comers, both the embittered trade unionists and leftwingers in his own party and the capitalists who were hurting his economic recovery program by refusing to invest. It took a Callaghan to intone at an openly hostile Labour Party Conference: "I say to both sides of industry, do not support us with kind words and then undermine us through unjustified wage increases or price increases. *Either back us or sack us.*"

The fact that Thatcher got to No. 10 is proof that Callaghan's audience got the message. More important, it is a sign of the historic turn in Labour Party fortunes — and of the rancor instilled by Callaghan's resistance to trade union demands — that the electoral blackmail failed, shifting working-class votes from Labour to Tory and winning Thatcher the election in May, 1979. Whatever his personal responsibility, it is undeniable that Callaghan (and Wilson before him) steered the party from a moment of rare optimism in 1974 into an historic crisis 5 years later, when the British Labour Party would display fully the multiple contradictions embodied in party structure and vision.

John Saville recently pondered Labour's riddle: How it comes about that

> those who win election with socialist phrases on their lips — and most are not conscious hypocrites — ... then proceed to administer a capitalist society, which they have previously denounced in as efficient a way as possible, is one of the central ironies of modern British history.[11]

It is an irony for Party leader and Prime Minister best hidden, but one artlessly paraded by Callaghan to the incalculable harm of the UK's social democratic project.

The triangle of contradictions between Labour Party and Labour government, Labour government and trade union movement, trade union movement and Labour Party — cannot be undone. The contradictions are especially telling now, when diminished national prerogatives press cruel choices on any administration. These conditions raise the ante, particularly, for a Labour government which must either appease economic elites at the expense of working-class and allied interests or go for broke with a tranformative strategy.

So too much, perhaps, should not be laid at the door of the leader. Callaghan, temperamentally and ideologically cautious, had the natural middle course taken from him by the disarray of the international economy: there is no pragmatism in caution when political stasis invites disaster. By mid-term in the last Labour government, global economic forces severely reduced the option of a declining middle-ranked nation-state, reinforcing the familiar contradictions of UK political life. The erosion of economic prerogatives and labor movement fragmentation pressed in on

Callaghan. Caught, as we shall see, between the IMF and the TUC, Callaghan and the tired Labourism he represented were not to survive unchanged.

CORPORATISM AND THE SOCIAL CONTRACT

Earlier, in 1974, an architect of the Social Contract, then leader of the Transport and General Workers Union (TGWU), Jack Jones, had reportedly said to the Trades Union Congress that a vote for Labour would "help to build the new Jerusalem." Five years later trade unionists helped lead the country to less hallowed ground. As David Coates observed,

> Under this Government, trade union leaders gained not so much power as a new role: that of increasingly hard-pressed guarantors of pay restraint and overseers of falling real wages in the face of sustained inflation and intolerably high levels of unemployment that both they, and seemingly the Government, could only regret but not prevent.[12]

In the end they regretted the deal they had struck as much as the result. What went wrong?

The Social Contract — a series of policy statements formulated by the National Executive Committee (NEC) of the Labour Party and the General Council of the TUC — was a characteristic artifact of the UK's hesitant social democratic vision and relatively weak capacities for corporatist institutional arrangements. In the UK significant corporatist arrangements have never endured because at least one crucial ingredient — the sustained integration of organized labor — is not present. Whatever the perspective of government or business, the most typical corporatist agreement — an incomes policy — could not hold because of three related structural features of the labor movement: the division of interests and lack of strategic coordination between trade union and party within the working-class movement; the incapacity of the Trades Union Congress to bind individual unions to negotiated agreements; and the inability of trade union elites to force rank-and-file compliance with policies.

While the arrangements of the KWS were maintained, however

tenuously, the effective negotiation of class compromises could for a time conceal these contradictions within the form of corporatist interest intermediation. Today the transitory character of these forms, their historically contingent and frail quality, seem more clear. But this is partly a matter of hindsight. The contradictions of corporatist arrangements were played out in full force during the UK's last Labour government. Perhaps to no-one's real surprise in labor movement or party, but to nearly everyone's dismay, the forces which Callaghan and Jones unleashed could not easily be controlled.

Peter Gay wrote about the German Social Democratic Party in the period before World War One: "a democratic Socialist movement that attempts to transform a capitalist into a socialist order is necessarily faced with a choice between two incompatibles — principles and power."[13] The corporatist strategy could not, of course, reconcile the two. In this sense the Social Contract bore the unmistakable signs of its authorship and design — with an attractive outer padding of somewhat unlikely out-of-office promises stuck in place to cushion the shock of a power play to be executed against the unions once the returns from the general election were in. There was thus in the design of the Social Contract something for every taste, and its demise seriously damaged a whole range of associated interests which would even extend into the Conservative Party.

THE TERMS OF THE CONTRACT

Callaghan, from the start, saw in the Social Contract the basis for a voluntary incomes policy which would draw the TUC into sharing "bad news" responsibilities with the government. Jack Jones, mastermind of the agreement but also TGWU leader with classical trade unionist concerns, saw the Social Contract as guaranteeing basic minimal standards for workers and pensioners, and granting the unions new authority to bargain directly with government over an ever-widening range of social and economic issues. For him, the Social Contract "above all . . . place[d] Industrial Democracy . . . into the centre of Party thinking and policy." Harold Wilson placed the Social Contract at the heart of his promises to govern on "the basis of social justice" and considered it "the central mechanism to ensure national economic recovery." Coates notes that:

> [F]rom the beginning it was given different emphases by different labour leaders. But though the emphasis differed, the content of the Government's part of any future "social contract" was clear — radical and innovatory policy in the field of industrial relations, housing prices, social benefits, investment and industrial democracy.[14]

What was not clear to either trade unionists or parliamentary labor leaders in 1972, in the heat of growing opposition to Heath's labor policy, was that an economic crisis of new dimensions in the mid-1970s would make implementation of the broader vision of the Social Contract very difficult. Worse, the annual effort to coerce the trade union wing of the movement to accept the stick of incomes policy — with no carrot proffered in return — would hasten the labor movement's fragmentation, quicken constitutional and organizational chaos in the party, and push Margaret Thatcher to center stage.

The syndicalist power of the labor movement brought Heath to a celebrated U-turn in 1972, when the trade unions refused to swallow an Industrial Relations Act which could bring bankruptcy by making them legally responsible for the costs of broken contracts during strikes.[15] While the union movement could be (nominally) politically integrated by corporatist arrangements at the top, the industrial-syndicalist pressures below could not be so easily defused, as the Labour government was soon to be reminded.

As government policy was inaugurated, Callaghan probably underestimated the difficulties. His was a government which never fully recognized the futility of its actions. Ebullient in coming to office and confident of a new level of support from trade unions, the Labour government was committed by election pledges (which, despite all, are taken very seriously in the UK) to a bold expansion of the public sector and a radical industrial strategy to democratize industry and weaken the hold of multinational corporations (MNCs) and their domestic counterparts. This was the most radical approach to government of a Labour leadership since 1945, and if the Labour Party was not quite prepared to wield parliament as a "sword at the heart of private property," their strategy in principle went far beyond the tepid modernizing norms of the 1964 Wilson government.

Unfortunately, the government never quite appreciated the situation it faced. Viewing its problem "not as a national consequence of an international crisis, but as a set of national economic difficulties intensified by world recession," the government could not hold the initiative.[16] Failing to recognize the dimensions of the problem, it was consistently trapped in a reactive posture. This was uninspired classical "political business cycle" politics: modest nationally based Keynesian (and labor-monetarist) strategies in the face of a post-Keynesian international world order which buffeted the tiny, declining, decidedly post-hegemonic UK. Helpless before economic forces — speculative runs on the pound, business unwillingness to invest — the Labour government squandered its considerable political capital with its extra-parliamentary trade union allies. More and more centrality was given to a less and less palatable, politically enervated, and negatively redistributive Social Contract. Still, the annual summer exercises of intra-labor arm-twisting went forward, as a succession of 12-month incomes policies marked each passing hour of government futility. How much longer?

With inflation running to 26 percent, Phase One, initiated in July, 1975, called for an across-the-board limit of £6 a week on increases (a measure that would reduce pay differentials as well as control wage demands). Introduced in June, 1976, Phase Two set a 4.5 percent wage limit with a £4 maximum, to remain in effect until July 31, 1977. The strategy foundered early, however, hurt by the precipitous decline in sterling in 1976 (it dropped 50 cents against the dollar). Unemployment approached 1.5 million and inflation substantially outstripped wage increases. By May, 1977, inflation had been brought down to 17.1 percent but with no official challenge to the 4.5 percent limit from any union, the rate of increase in wages was limited to 8.8 percent. This left a gap of more than 8 percent between the movement of prices and earnings, the largest such gap in the postwar UK.[17]

Phase Three, the government prophesied, would finally bring the charm. If wage hikes for the coming year could be held to 10 percent, inflation would at long last dip down into single figures.

As with the first two phases of the agreement, the government's side of the Phase Three bargain was less precisely defined. Gone were the heady promises that had led Jack Jones to the messianic brink. In return for TUC endorsements, Callaghan vowed to keep down prices and reduce unemployment — bold social reform was no longer mentioned. The trade unions were restive.

IN PLACE OF HARMONY

By July several industrial unions, led by the miners, had announced their opposition to the proposed 10 percent ceiling. Unofficial action picked up, as skilled workers — who had suffered reduced differentials and seen their potential syndicalist force arrested for 2 years — pressed their claims at Leyland, Ford, the British steel works at Port Talbot in Wales, and Heathrow airport. Struggle on industrial fronts reflected the complex maze of loyalties and interests within the labor movement. The 8-week strike by toolmakers at British Leyland was directed not only at management, but also against the Amalgamated Union of Electrical Workers (AUEW) — which would not take up the toolmakers' case for increased differentials — and against the TUC, which sanctioned a pay policy reducing those differentials.

Meanwhile, a previously obscure film-processing plant at Grunwick in North London focused the heterodox pressures fragmenting the trade union movement. When a number of workers — mostly Asian women — were dismissed in the course of a union recognition campaign, national union support and volatile rank-and-file sentiment were mobilized. Highly charged factory-gate confrontations over the efforts by supporters to prevent plant deliveries became the stuff of daily national headlines. Grunwick showed British syndicalism at its rough-and-tumble best (and worst): on the one hand, hundreds of northern miners picketing Grunwick with bold and heralded class solidarity for their dismissed comrades, some at least oblivious to the issues of race and gender, announcing to all and sundry that they were ready "to help the lads at Grunwick"; on the other hand, the TUC refusing to support the secondary boycotts of electricity and, notably, the delivery of mail (essential to Grunwick, a mail-order house) that would have been necessary to transform a hollow show of support into a strategy that might win. In the end, management withstood all the pressures. The newly formed National Association for Freedom trumpeted the virtues of the open shop. More significant, the Conservatives were able to rehearse issues of alleged trade unionist attacks on democratic rights which would play so well in May, 1979 — and the workers remained sacked. The TUC, as nearly always, played the de-politicizing role enshrined in the events of 1926, and rank-and-file solidarities were squandered.

Grunwick, like the campaigns against Phase Two, showed again the curious capillary vigor, cross-cutting interests, and organizational infirmity of the British working-class movement. There was something glorious about the Grunwick battles: the fury and sincerity of support for a cause which for once allowed trade unionists to proclaim pure classwide goals above self-interest, despite the everyday sexist and racist predilections of many among them. Unfortunately it was a different, more typical, story with the Leyland battles. This was a struggle by those with narrow "craft" privilege and attractive differentials downing their tools (literally, perhaps, since they were "toolmakers"), and in so doing, threatening mass lay-offs and the rundown of an already failing industry.

LABOUR'S DIVISIONS

It is in this context that the TUC support for incomes agreements became stretched very thin. Even Jack Jones, perhaps Callaghan's most unswerving supporter in the TUC, was forced by a decision of his own TGWU to denounce Phase Three. Callaghan withdrew the incomes policy, while he gamely tried to stockpile as much support as he could muster from individual trade unions. As his experience at the Durham Miners' Gala illustrates, successes in these efforts proved to be ephemeral, while the divisions within the labor movement proved far more enduring. The loss to Thatcher was the immediate consequence, but deeper expressions of the contradictions of Labourism preoccupied and polarized the party — from the constitutional crisis which spawned the Social Democratic Party (SDP), to the Alternative Economic Strategy

(AES) developed by the Labour Left to ensure that any post-Thatcher Labour government would not repeat the sorry performance of the Wilson—Callaghan years.

Long before Callaghan left the podium at the Durham fairgrounds, the forthcoming scene of fragmentation and defeat could be foretold. For a start the government, in principle, was going to have to "go it alone" on Phase Three. For the most part the Prime Minister and the Chancellor succeeded in keeping wage settlements within the 10 percent range. The threat, and in some cases, the practice, of blacklisting firms from government contracts if they allowed excessive raises had the desired intimidating effect. They also made the most of the TUC's 12-month rule, declaiming their willingness to resist firmly any public sector strikes in defiance of the pay policy. Besides these deliberate strategies there was the perverse luck of a still-dismal macroeconomic picture: increasing dole queues provided an inhibiting logic of their own. Also, to be sure, reduced inflation dampened any "insurrectionary" industrial—unionist resolve. Finally, with the miners as a notable example, the loophole expedient of potentially lucrative "self-financing productivity agreements" kept base pay claims to 10 percent (down from the 91 percent claim in their case), whatever the potential of wages drift later through incentive bonuses.

Despite a rising crescendo of unofficial work stoppages and growing divisions between rank-and-file (and shop steward) expressions of militancy, Phase Three proceeded with surprising calm. There was only one official national strike. Firefighters walked out in support of a 30 percent claim, but with the crucial refusal of the TUC to authorize national support, the 8-week strike resulted in a settlement which fell within the pay norm. All the heretics won was the stipulation (given routinely to other public sector workers such as doctors, university staff, and police) that their next round of pay bargaining would be exempt from the constraints of any incomes policy.

The only big winners in Phase Three were the highest paid in the public sector who made quick capital of a government-sponsored comparability study of private and public sector white-collar and upper managerial salaries. The balance sheet for Phase Three — 14.2 percent average increase in wages against 7.8 percent increase in prices — represents an inconclusive pause in the strange tale of Labour Party/labor movement peril.[18] It indicates the reversal from the previous year, when real incomes had declined by just over 8 percent, and suggests that government advantage and trade union acceptance was slipping. But inflation was down, the IMF mollified, and — at least in principle — the government might have achieved some space for maneuvering and reconsideration of the earlier, more radical view for a Social Contract. But, if there ever was such an opening, Callaghan didn't know it — or wouldn't permit it.

With Phase Four everything came undone. In a disastrous, aggressively uncalculating move, the government insisted on a 5 percent pay norm. Even when it backed off after a series of defeats at every institutional matrix of labor movement power, Callaghan's government could not remove the mark of this defeat. If 10 percent had brought resistance the year before, why go to 5 percent? Affronted, the TUC overwhelmingly rejected any "arbitrary pay limit" at its September conference, despite the belief cultivated by Callaghan that the announcement of an early election was only days away; union bloc votes subsequently commemorated this defeat at the Labour Party conference in October.

Worst of all, both rank-and-file and official strikes, fueled by a seemingly endless series of leapfrogging pay demands, erupted into a "winter of discontent" which battered the government in its last pre-election season. The catalogue of industrial action tells a story in itself. The strike season began with a 9-week shutdown by Ford workers, but action was concentrated where it would hurt the government the most, in the public sector where the government paid the wages: tanker and lorry (truck) drivers; train drivers; civil servants; local government workers; public utilities workers; ambulance drivers and health support staff. There was irony to the demise of the Callaghan government, which hasn't gone unnoticed. As Coates put it:

[I]f the backcloth to the Labour government's arrival in office in 1974 had been the successful miners' strike against the incomes policies of Edward Heath, the backcloth to the government's departure in 1979 was a pay revolt of even greater scale. The number of workers involved in strikes in January 1979 was the largest of any month since May 1968, and the number of working days lost the greatest since February 1974, at the height of the three-day week. . . . Four years of wage restraint may have given British capitalism a breathing space in industrial costs, but they gave the Labour Government in the end industrial unrest and electoral defeat.[19]

This defeat was not the result of a fortuitous electoral swing, but a deeper expression of the contradictory vision and structured incapacities of British social democracy. It brought in its wake a split in the Labour Party and the crude restoration of antedeluvian anti-laborist politics.

THE STRUCTURE OF DEFEAT

The era of the 1976—1979 Social Contracts was marked by the combination of inner structural divisions in the Labour Party and the outer structural forces of the international political economy, coming together with formidable power to overwhelm UK social democracy. In this context the "constitutional crisis" within the party is only a formal epilogue to the ravaging that had already occurred, and the breakaway of the SDP is merely an afterthought.

Perhaps the Labour Party can best be defined by reference to its structural divisions. It is a tripartite organization comprised mainly of constituency ("grass roots" or local) parties, trade unions, and members of parliament on the labor side (the Parliamentary Labour Party or PLP). It is a party governed by its annual conference where — before the 1981 constitutional changes — the trade unions cast just under 90 percent of the votes in blocs proportional to the size of their membership as a fraction of the party membership. (Accordingly, the Engineers and the Transport and General Workers between them cast 30 percent of all conference votes.) But Labour is also a party of government. Therefore the program voted by the TGWU, the AUEW, the NUM, all the other unions and, more or less incidentally, by MPs and constituency members, must be the substantive source of a claim to govern. As democratic theory and "catch-all" party strategy requires, it is a claim made not only to trade unionists and their allies but to all of the UK. Like the coincidence of philosophical wisdom and the will to rule, the identity of corporate trade unionist and broader national interest cannot be taken for granted.

Typically, the paradox is resolved by a practical — it could be called cynical, even hypocritical — division of responsibility. Out of office the trade unionist/conference orientations determine honest socialist principles; in office the PLP invariably dominates and the Cabinet sheds conference principles as necessary in the course of trying to run a government and an economy. Behind this expectation of seriatim exchanges of "real power" in the party lies an irreconcilable division of purpose, and one that transcends and complicates the tripartite constitutional division.

Is the Labour Party socialist or merely social democratic — oriented to a tranformative purpose or reconciled to the (albeit more humane) administration of capitalism? Can the party wield a sword to strike at the heart of capitalism? Or is it there simply to deliver a consensus and to craft pragmatic acceptance for a mainstream capitalist UK?

Add to this the final division between the trade union leadership — which casts the bloc votes at Conferences *and* orchestrates the corporatist exercises in incomes policies — and rank-and-file trade unionists. Here the message of the Durham Miners' Gala is important. Rank-and-file workers may be narrowly focused on financial reward or less often inclined to take seriously issues of control at the workplace and social policy in the national arena; they are unlikely, however, to appreciate the annual exercise of incomes policies imposed from above. The weakness of the TUC, which neither bargains effectively with government nor controls member unions, hardly improves the overall institutional coherence of the British labor movement. So multiple divisions are structurally cast: tripartite organizational division in the party; PLP vs. trade union/constituency domination of policy; corporatist elite strategies vs. rank-and-file interests; socialist vs. social deomcratic vision.

In the 1970s push came to shove, as incoherence became incapacity. The new brutalization of the British economy — the ineptitude of Keynesian demand management in the face of rising inflation and unemployment; the UK's diminished international competitiveness which squeezed profits at home and prodded capitalists to seek disproportional investment abroad — exacerbated to the breaking point the old divisions and inconsistencies of British Labourism. The "irony" which Saville attributed to the Labour Party (socialist phrases out of office but capitalist administration in office) resurfaced as a far crueler contradiction. A new international economic order (not the one of optimistic North—South dialogues) destroyed the social-democratic vision, the totemic unity that enabled the strange rituals of British Labourism to proceed.

The 1974 government campaigned on the pledges that it would further industrial democracy; improve incomes and benefits for the working classes; raise pensions; increase public ownership; expand welfarism; introduce industrial policies in partnership with the trade unions to help reverse the pattern of decline. In short, the new government would achieve a "fundamental and irreversible shift in the balance of power and wealth in favour of working people and their families." This was the programmatic basis for social democracy (or even shallow socialism) in principle, even as it lay the groundwork for the typical reversion to the pragmatics of capitalist administration later in office.

The setting was reminiscent of the 1945 general election, in which the manifesto boldly declared its "ultimate purpose" to be nothing short of the "establishment of the Socialist commonwealth of Great Britain." This pledge, sounding more like the passage from a socialist hymnal than part of a legislative program, was not wholly redeemed. But, as Beer observes, "the general election of 1945 was one of those rare instances in which programmatic party government launched a transformation of the social and economic order by means of an electoral victory."[20] Critical industries — coal, steel, electricity, and railroads (seven in all) — were nationalized; the National Health Service was set up and health care became free to all users and universal to all residents; social welfare benefits were vastly increased. If the 1945 victory did not represent the passage to Shangri-la envisioned by Labour zealots, it did inaugurate a period of decisive reordering of capitalist prerogative and state responsibility. It marked a determined transition to social democracy. The election of 1974, despite comparable promise, turned out to be a very different kind of watershed.

While the 1974 manifesto signaled a new march forward in the spirit of the 1945 government, events soon trumpeted an historic retreat from social democracy, let alone any more robust socialist vision. The thinness of Labour's advantage in the House of Commons throughout its time in office explains in part the timorousness of Cabinet ministers in the face of international and domestic economic influences. But there was something else far more crucial: the international economy slammed shut the window to change that World War Two had opened. Radical pressures following from the UK's decline — galloping inflation, periodic and cruel runs on the pound, serious reversals in the balance of trade — quickly turned the government from the political side of its program. Hence a Social Contract became an incomes policy.

THE CALLAGHAN/HEALEY LEGACY

Caught between the pressures of restive domestic allies and imperious international forces, the 1974 Labour government neglected its friends and befriended its enemies. What Michael Rustin noted about Wilson (in both his 1964 and 1974 governments) is equally true of Callaghan to the end:

> [T]he previously left-of-centre Wilson set his constitutional prerogatives as Prime Minister above any other claims on him, and asserted the powers of Government over the claims of party. "The government must govern," he proclaimed, and this turned out to signify not the independence of government *vis-à-vis* the International Monetary Fund or the United States, but *vis-à-vis* the trade unions and the Labour Party Conference.[21]

This Wilsonian independence, robbed of crafty ambiguity by Callaghan/Healey and taken to its full expression in the great IMF credit blackmail of 1976, destroyed the calculated ambiguities of British Labourism which had papered over the cracks in party unity for so long.

Labourism meant the charade of manifesto pronouncements

followed by governmental retreats, the reasonable (but partly disingenuous) expectation that the next government would really implement the next conference's more ideological agenda. In 1952 Tony Crosland wrote sincerely of a "post-capitalist society" in the UK, with the Labour Party as the natural party of government. The new society was distinguished from the old by a broad list of changes: greater equality of incomes and opportunity through governmental intervention in economic affairs; an increased level of social services; full employment; an improved standard of living; class struggle "softened" by the "rise of the technical and professional middle class"; and a shift in ideological emphasis from "the rights of property, private initiative, competition, and the profit-motive . . . to the duties of the state, social and economic security, and the virtues of co-operative action." Thus, Crosland's new society — what he called "statism" but what has entered tradition as a seminal expression of UK social democracy — is a rich hybrid. As Crosland explained, it is "non-capitalist to the extent that market influences are subordinated to central planning . . . [and] the power of the state is much greater than that of any one particular class;" socialist in its distribution of income; and, "a pluralist society."[22]

So long as Crosland's social-democratic vision represented the cautious, but still politically impassioned, mainstream of Labourism, then the more fundamentalist vision of socialism — through ownership and control of the commanding heights of production, radical redistribution of resources in society, and "workers' control" — could be contained within the party. Fundamentalism and Crosland-inspired revisionism could effect an intra-party electoral alliance and keep trade union, constituency, and PLP elements from the full expression of their centripetal divisions. The left could say: "this far, but no farther: at least through our vigilance the welfare state will be strengthened." All the while the right could be assured that any less temperate promises would be neglected by Labour governments. And outsiders could rest easy knowing that whatever the ideological preferences, and indeed whatever the vicissitudes of party fortune, the result would be a shallow welfare-statism. Labour under the revisionism of Hugh Gaitskell and the Conservatives under the modernizing of R. A. Butler forged a mainstream — "Butskellism" — which seemed likely to be the controlling influence of the high politics of the UK for some time. But the international economic crisis of the 1970s, which impelled Wilson and Callaghan to play the IMF card, ended all that and destroyed the uneasy coexistence of irreconcilables within the party.

Tony Benn, the most influential fundamentalist voice among recent Labour ministers and advocate of the potentially trans- formative AES, made the point bluntly in a 1980 interview:

> [T]he revisionism that was preached by Gaitskell and Crosland was killed, not by the left, but by the IMF, which simply said to the 1976 Labour Cabinet, "We are not allowing you to do that any more. Whatever you choose to do, we are not having this high level of public expenditure because we regard it as undesirable." Tony Crosland died six months after his social-democratic option had been killed for him by the IMF, and the IMF polished off revisionism fairly effectively. In 1976, I had hoped, when the IMF forced the choice between a socialist solution and a social-democratic defeat, that a Cabinet majority might be created for a more radical response. But that was not what happened.[23]

What happened, rather, was a slide from social democracy into a Labourist monetarism. The IMF demands became a convenient external discipline which enabled the Callaghan administration to pull PLP politics decisively away from constituency/trade unionist conference sentiments. As the government lived under the scrutiny of IMF inspectors and the strictures of an official Letter of Intent — which assigned limits on public sector borrowing, specific dates for debt repayment, and exacting targets for output and inflation — the cruelist truth of the politics of decline in its Labourist variant could no longer be concealed.[24] The pound could be stabilized and inflation rates controlled, as was the case in 1977 and 1978, but these improvements could only be bought at decisive political cost. As David Coates notes, "What recent Labour Governments have repeatedly found is that, at this stage of late capitalism at least, it just is not possible to strengthen the competitive position of a national capitalism and the power of its labour movement simultaneously."[25]

International circumstances make the interests of national capital and labor not only different — they are incompatible. There is no longer a "national interest." Before the imperious forces of international capital and finance, the declining hegemonic power can maneuver only by displacing the costs of decline strategically. Callaghan chose to sacrifice the immediate interests of labor in order to bolster capital in the name of the nation-state. The choice was more historic than he knew: it signaled a counter-revolution. As Ken Coates explained:

> [T]he most fundamental onslaught on the corporate powers of labour . . . came about with the IMF counter-revolution, which involved a Labour Government in reneging on its fundamental postwar commitment to welfare, and in major concessions to monetarist prescriptions. This was the practical defeat of social democracy of the Crosland stamp. The argument of this revisionist school had been coherent, and rested on the assumption that full employment was itself an "irreversible shift" in effective working class power. The reversal of this postwar shift nullified the Butskellite consensus, before Mrs. Thatcher's rise to office and before the birth of the modern Social Democrats, who have abandoned all pretensions to full employment, leave alone "socialism."[26]

The decision to retract minimalist social democratic programs in a highly visible campaign to win IMF approval — to terms that some close to the IMF considered harsher than "necessary" — destroyed the tenuous basis for cohesion within the party and signified the end of Keynesian society in Britain. Thatcherism was soon to follow.

3

From Toryism to Thatcherism

If Crosland's classic vision of social democracy died with the invasion of the IMF inspectorate, it is equally true that in the end the revisionists in the Labour Party pulled down their most progressive and sympathetic adversaries with them. When classic postwar Labourism expired the Tory modernizers were also endangered. These conservative moderates, like James Prior, Thatcher's first Employment Secretary (who was banished to the Northern Ireland office for his independence in Cabinet) and a politically chastened Edward Heath, were "one-nation" Tories. Tories in their inviolate "commitment to authoritative leadership as a permanent social necessity,"[1] they are nevertheless integrationists who support the KWS principles of political inclusion and the harmonization of diverse interests.

These Tory traditionalists believe in a hierarchical society but one organically constituted. Familiar divisions of labor should be preserved in families as in society, but the Burkean permanent interests of society — not self-interested particularism — should guide governmental actions. These Conservative moderates, derisively labelled "wets" by Thatcher (a rough equivalent to Lyndon Johnson's epithet, "nervous nellies" for those opposed to the Vietnam War), accept the postwar settlement. They are prepared also to apply the new steering capacities of the state within a broadly Keynesian and welfarist mold. In the end, these wets have been swamped by contemporary directions in British politics.

They had a problem long before Thatcher, but one only fully revealed in the social democratic debacle of the Callaghan years and the ascendancy of Thatcherism. Modern capitalism made them politically redundant, for whatever these one-nation Tories can do in a welfarist mold, by all rights the Labour Party revisionists can do better. If the Conservative Party was the natural party of government in the age of empire, these mainstream Tories were, despite their frequency in office, a natural opposition in the period of the Keynesian welfare state, as they are an opposition from within during the current period of right wing dominance. The negotiation of incomes policies and the management of national-ized industries are not taught at Winchester and Eton. While contacts with the City and the self-reliance, social camaraderie, and grace of a power elite may still be learned on the playing fields and practiced in government, there is no new empire to win. Perhaps more serious, public school virtues are no longer the stuff of an effective majoritarian appeal in today's harsh economic climate when electoral politics must be oriented to self-interested and practically minded constituencies.

THE EROSION OF THE CONSERVATIVE CENTER

During the period of apparent stability following the end of World War Two, the position of mainstream Toryism became increasingly untenable. Martin Jacques observed this transformation of the inner Tory dynamic.

> The fifties saw the Conservative Party resume what had been its traditional mantle in post-1918 politics — as the main governing party, inextricably linked with the establishment and the national tradition, albeit on a basis of an acceptance of many of Labour's post-war reforms. Such a role was no longer possible in the same way in the new phase; the old assumptions no longer worked and Labour's modernism to some extent deprived the Tories of the centre ground. In response to this situation the Tory party began to shift to the right.[2]

As Heath was to find during his premiership between 1970 and 1974, Tory centrism was increasingly incompatible with a politics of decline which seems to invite radical responses to the formidable problems which abound. By the 1970s public officials no longer saw the world they understood and could master. It had become

an economic world without growth and a political universe of
growing dissensus; a fragmenting society beset by racial antagon-
isms, the psychic burdens sustained by the absorption and erosion
of traditional communities, and increasing strains within the multi-
nation state. Powerful and new discontented constituencies —
youth, racial minorities, women — and increasingly restive core
constituencies struggled to achieve a larger share of a fixed social
product. The campaign slogan of the victorious Conservatives in
1959 — "Life's better under the Conservatives: don't let Labour
ruin it" — would never be seen again. Life never seems better any
more for a sufficiently broad electoral constituency and, besides,
the Conservative's "instrumental appeal to the working class"[3] as
the party of prosperity, good government, and sound economic
management above class and ideology has dimmed considerably.

From a model of stability and harmony celebrated by the
adherents of liberal democracy, the UK soon became the symbol
of a new, more troubling trend in Western societies. The Conservative modernizers who had ridden the first model to glory, lost
the most politically by its decline. As Krishnan Kumar wrote:

> It can hardly have escaped anyone's attention that what Carlyle
> called "the condition of England" question is with us again. But
> what a difference. When commentators wrote about the condition
> of England in the early nineteenth century they were discussing the
> social consequences of England's pioneering leap into industrialism,
> her revolutionary turning of the course of world history.[4]

In the 1970s, as Kumar observed, with few exceptions the
nineteenth-century observers like Marx and Tocqueville who
marvelled at UK industrialism and saw in the UK the very image of
development, had been replaced by a pantheon of foreign
detractors who found abundant evidence in the UK for a far less
sanguine diagnosis.

> [Then] growth, not stagnation, was the cause for concern of moralists
> and sociologists. Now the situation is precisely the opposite. The
> country's problems seem to be the product of illness and senescence,
> rather than youth and vigour. An acute case of the "the British
> disease" is pronounced. . . . Its symptoms are economic inefficiency,

antiquated attitudes and institutions, national complacency, a general and deep-seated inability to pull ourselves out of a growing pit of declining standards in all areas of society.[5]

Samuel H. Beer had written in 1965, "Happy the country in which consensus and conflict are ordered in a dialectic that makes of the political arena at once a market of interests and a forum for debate of fundamental moral concerns."[6] Reflecting on transformative changes in the interim, in 1982 Beer wrote of the "fragmentation of political life" and the "political contradictions of collectivism" which had turned the UK against itself, and now seemed to point toward a radically different system.[7] The homeostatic propensities which have always kept the UK, more than most states, oriented toward a coherent national interest have been arrested, the logic of the party system challenged, and the weakness of a divided society pretending to organic union exposed. As the inner rationality of British society changed, so too did the ideological and electoral appeals of party politics.

The authoritarian voice which acknowledged decline and fostered division in order to wrest electoral advantage from sectionalism and anomie overwhelmed the quieter, more gentle voice of universalism and political (as well as social) integration. Robbed of the relative prosperity and growth that made the unusual harmony of the Keynesian society possible, and lacking in any vital ideological justification, social democracy no longer seemed sensible. The ideological core of Labourism no longer held together, and the non-ideological Tory variant seemed hollower still. Suddenly, in this world, the choice between Thatcherism and Butskellism seemed foreordained — although it is in practice nothing of the kind — and Thatcherism prevails once, twice, until a new tradition of divisive politics assumes for many a "common sense" status.

A NEW POLITICAL MORALITY BUT AN OLD PARTY

As Herbert Marcuse once observed,

The people recognize themselves in their commodities, they find their soul in their automobile, hi-fi set, split-level home, kitchen equipment. The very mechanism which ties the individual to his society has changed, and social control is anchored in the new needs which it has produced.[8]

While the in-between strata of skilled manual, office, and lower professional—managerial workers could still acquire their commodities — they could afford also to accommodate the redistributive pressures (more ideological than real) of the welfare state. With declining fortunes came narrowed horizons. A new yearning not for "embourgeoisment" (What class am I really?) but for "suburbanization" (How can I acquire the things that make life worth living?) transformed the arena of national politics.

Soon after Harold Macmillan accepted the leadership of an ailing Conservative Party, confounded and humiliated by Suez, he spoke with an aristocrat's disdain for the "'suburban' middle class" whom he "so disliked" and little understood. "I'm always rather depressed by the rootlessness of modern Britain," Macmillan told Anthony Sampson in 1958, "particularly in the south. To think that within twenty miles of this room there are eight million people living suburban lives."[9] These are lives far more familiar to Thatcher than to her paternalistic forebears in the Conservative Party and they are curiously important to her and to an understanding of post-1979 British political life.

To go no further here, the "suburban vote" gave her the first election. Even more important, suburbanism — the xenophobia of the private housing estate, the pragmatic conservatism engendered by the inevitability of mortgage payments, the "narcissism of minor differences"[10] expressed in gardens and clothes and automobiles — became the touchstone of her political morality. Suburbanism is the experience and reality behind the catchphrase "Victorian values" — it is hard to imagine a successful campaign orchestrated around the theme "suburban values" — and suburbanism is the spiritual source of Thatcher's innumerable paeans to enterprise and initiative. The "new Victorians" of shopping malls and package tours, of modernized pubs and videocassettes, have come of age. Thatcher's ascendancy marked the suburbanization of the Conservative Party. Toryism was transformed as the party's ethos shifted from the playing fields of Eton to the housing estates of Grantham.

The process of suburbanization underscores the almost imperceptible series of changes by which the Conservative Party of Butler and Macmillan — the consensual modernizer and the paternal pragmatist — acquired a new ideological character and a surprising electoral base by the late spring of 1979. For unlike its Labour counterpart, which is organizationally wrought by internal centripetal pressures, the Conservative Party is constructed for unity. It was never bedevilled by the divisions of interest and fragmented sovereignty of Labour. On the contrary, it enjoyed a complacent division of responsibility and segregation of standing and duties. The "'high-Tory' leadership characterized by such figures as Macmillan, Eden and Home and enjoying close connections with the City, big capital, and the traditional 'upper classes'" had to share its party with a "cadre force drawn from the middle classes, the petty-bourgeoisie, and sections of the working class."[11] But there was no equivalent to the wrenching power struggles in Labour between party and union over policy, or between cabinet and conference over the meaning and direction of Labourism.

The Conservative leadership had little cause or occasion to share the governance of the party or negotiate the setting of policy. This was the *Conservative* Party, with a Burkean fear of the mob, and a relish for the principles of indirect representation for the many by the few who had the permanent (for which read: property) interests of the country at heart. It was only 30 years ago that the Conservative Political Centre published *The Tory Traditions*, and R. A. Butler wrote an admiring preface to a work which insisted that a "largely hereditary class system is morally right" because the UK requires a "governing class" with a "specialised preparatory training" to promote "generous self-confidence, not forgetful of the lesson of *noblesse oblige*."[12]

A party which prefers hierarchy and *noblesse* to participatory (or even representative) government for the nation, can hardly surprise observers by its anachronistic adherence to Burkean democracy within its own organization.

In the good old days, the Conservative Party made no attempt to pretend that it was democratic. It thus avoided all those modern irritations — rules, elections, debate, accountability. Its leaders 'emerged' by an ill-defined process of consultation about which little was known except that geriatric peers counted for more than young MPs. Tory leaders, having emerged, had complete control over the party's national bureaucracy — Conservative Central Office. Local constituency parties possessed complete autonomy. Their shared, but unstated purpose was to sustain the party leadership; but, formally, the local membership had no obligations towards the leader of Central Office; and the leader and Central Office had no obligations toward the local membership.[13]

This is not a glib exaggeration of Tory Party doctrine: no obligations means no obligations. In fact the organizational separation between the leader (and central bureaucracy) and the constituency parties is legally enshrined. In 1981 the Inland Revenue tried to levy a corporation tax on the party on the grounds that it was an "unincorporated association." The Court of Appeals ruled against Inland Revenue, accepting the argument of Tory lawyers that the Conservative Party failed to meet two legal conditions of association: members of the party were not bound by "mutual duties and obligations" and the party was not an organization "which had rules which identified in whom control of it and its funds were vested and on what terms." As Peter Kellner observed in the *New Statesman*, the "system was, of course, anachronistic and undemocratic. But it undeniably contained a powerful internal logic for a party of the ruling class that sought to preserve the status quo. It preached deference, and practiced what it preached."[14]

By the 1960s the anachronistic structure had to admit a trace of internal inconsistency, but only a trace. However limited, the democratic intrusion nonetheless had severe, perhaps lasting, consequences. Twenty years ago, Macmillan resigned in the wake of the Profumo uproar, the extraordinary cold war passion play which allegedly involved a prostitute employed both by a Soviet naval attaché and the British War Minister. Two years later the fourteenth Earl of Home, who had "emerged" to succeed Macmillan, also followed him into retirement from office after leading the party to defeat by Wilson and the Labour Party in 1964. Increasingly, by the mid-1960s, Labour effectively represented itself as the natural party of government in a "post-industrial" age where technological acumen and modern management technique made the high-Tory virtues outmoded. Vanquished at Suez, humiliated by a scandal which besmirched its image of rectitude, and defeated at the polls, Conservative elites were ready at last for some measure of organizational change and strategic redirection.

But there is more at issue here. A broader trajectory of decline — the same process which later, when more pronounced, threw Labour into constitutional turmoil and ruptured its social democratic vision — forced high-Tory compliance with the minimal norms of twentieth-century party democracy. The Tory's "image as the party of nation and national institutions" had been fatally weakened, and its claim as "the party of good government and the national economy" seemed increasingly dubious. Andrew Gamble traces the symbiosis of Conservative Party and imperial fortunes, hence the closing universe — and shifting terrain — of Tory options in the period of decline.

> The party developed in the era of the mass electorate as the party of the union, the Empire and the Constitution. It was as the party of the State, the Establishment, and the Land, rather than as the party of Capital that the Conservatives competed for votes, and this enabled them at times to play a mediating role between capital and labour, though rather less often than party mythology suggests. The Empire, however, has now gone . . . and the Union is unsteady. . . At the same time, the full integration of the Labour Party into the state since 1940 has weakened the Conservatives' claim to be the sole defender of national interests.[15]

In 1965, for the first time, a leader did not emerge. Rather, Edward Heath was elected by Conservative MPs after an energetic campaign. The change in organizational procedure, as well as that of the politics and style of the leader, are significant in charting the Conservative evolution. One observer noted approvingly, "A brand-new candidate, Ted Heath, was now presented as the Tories answer to Harold Wilson, with the same working-class background and technocratic command."[16]

But the significance of Heath's election can also be traced by reference to what it *did not* represent. For one thing the election of a leader did not inaugurate a period of substantial party democratization. More than 20 years later the Conservative leader still selects the party chair and the Central Office operates as her personal fiefdom, not as an organizational bureaucracy. Local (constituency) parties remain independent, thus inconsequential; there are, of course, no significant cross-cutting affiliations — to unions or extra-parliamentary organizations — which party leaders need fear. There is no inner tension of contradictory loyalties and far less pluralism within the party to fragment elite control.

Thus, the party changed because the leadership wanted it to reorient itself in a new political posture. The Tories chose modernism and Heath willfully. The choice was not (as with Labour's periodic lurches to left and right) the result of the play of paralyzing interests within the party, nor merely an automatic consequence of governmental disorientation.

The Conservative Party was and remains a more unitary party than Labour, a party of consent not consensus. Even more crucial, Heath's leadership strategy for the Conservative Party did not represent a successful alternative to Labour social democracy. Try as he might, Heath could not turn the Tories into the first party of state management or technological rationality. As a result the failure of his premiership greatly enhanced the historical process of Tory decline — far more than if he had simply been another Home. In fact, without the demise of "Selsdon Man" the current stage of Thatcherism would probably not be upon us.

HEATH AS PRIME MINISTER

The nature of Heath's failure is itself revealing. Edward Heath chose (as it turned out) the unfortunate venue of the Selsdon Park Hotel to work out the party's economic strategy for the 1970 general election, promising a bold departure both from the "paternalistic interventionism" of Butler and Macmillan, and from the creeping social democracy of British Labourism. After an "elaborate network of consultation with experts from government, business, and the universities which reflected the technocratic tendencies that were running strongly in both parties,"[17] Heath promised nothing short of "a change so radical, a revolution so quiet and yet so total, that it will go beyond the programme for a parliament."[18]

With a wonderful verbal riposte, Harold Wilson unearthed a sinister portent in the name of Heath's strategic hideaway, quickly dubbing his opponent "Selsdon Man." Thus saddled with vaguely prehistoric associations, Heath — and his Chancellor, Anthony Barber — could never transcend the constraints imposed by the closing circle of options available to British state managers. In an era marked, for the first time, by the previously inconceivable combinations of increases in wages/prices and reduced growth (stagflation), Heath's not inconsiderable attributes — technocratic wherewithal, the commitment to modernization, a forthright determination to pursue a coherent and exacting program for recovery — were no longer enough. As weak-willed social democracy was to fail under Callaghan and Healey, the free market (but never Thatcherite) approach of Heath would also succumb to fortunes which were at least partly beyond governmental control. Heath, to his credit, rejected cynical profiteering (what he called the "unacceptable face of capitalism") and, true to his "one-nation" approach, never used unemployment as a stick to beat unions into submission. The main problem was not that Heath got so little credit where credit was due to him — the left ridiculed Heath cruelly by drawing up pamphlets which figured the Prime Minister's head on the cover above the slogan "the unacceptable face" — but that his management strategy for capitalism proved unworkable.

Upon taking office the Heath government immediately reduced taxation in what would now be called a supply-side strategy to enhance savings, increase consumption, and swell entrepreneurial investment; it manipulated monetary policy in a "dash for growth" strategy which in the short run meant windfall profits for developers and those with City interests (the "Barber boom"); it even allowed Rolls Royce to go under — before a belated policy reversal — in an effort to back up its laissez-faire, free market assertions with bold non-interventions.[19] But, all too soon (at least from Heath's point of view), politics asserted its primacy over political economy. Conflict and rejection first clouded, and then defeated the government's plans. Core constituencies (both natural allies and increasingly restive enemies) rebelled, each in its own characteristic manner. There were strikes by workers and strikes by investors. Enjoying no honeymoon period, the government was greeted by a national dock strike which it met by convening a Court of Inquiry, then declared a state of emergency and recalled troops from Northern Ireland to ensure order at home. Making bad matters worse, the government prompted a strike of 125,000 local authority (municipal) workers by choosing an extremely inappropriate time to introduce the "$n-1$ norm," a policy of paying each group of public sector employees 1 percent below their previous annual settlement.

In the end the government was defeated not exactly by the miners, as is often said, but by a failed economic strategy which was forced by poor strategic judgement to its necessary political conclusions. Having broken the $n-1$ norm with a rank-and-file dominated strike in 1972, the National Union of Mineworkers (NUM) returned to the picket lines soon after the Christmas holidays, at the start of 1974. Despite the presence of sufficient coal reserves to permit industrial and commercial business as usual, Heath raised the ante by putting the UK on a 3-day work week. Calling an election on a "who rules the country" theme — the bloody-minded and never-had-it-so-good miners or the duly elected Tory government — he was to learn to his everlasting regret that in this unequal battle, and whatever the electorate's division and ambivalences, it was not to be Edward Heath.

In sum, Heath's government was marked by an ephemeral economic boom, followed by a lasting political bust. Even by contemporary standards, Heath's government spanned a tumultuous 4-year period, punctuated by a dramatic about-face half-way through it. In 1972 Heath inaugurated a notorious U-turn, re-orienting his government from an anti-interventionist stance to a familiar (albeit pro-capitalist) corporatist direction. In the end, aside from gaining credit from those who prefer pragmatism to any expression of ideological conviction, Heath gained little advantage from his reversals.

The government's Industrial Relations Act, which virtually outlawed the closed shop and held unions liable for compensatory damages in any strike-related breach of contract, failed miserably. The TUC opposed it. More to the point, a proliferation of agreements in many shops between unions and management to opt out of the law (via the loophole of "non-registration") rendered it inoperable. Between July, 1970 and July, 1974, more than 3 million work days were "lost" in strike actions against the Industrial Relations Act, and 1.6 million against the incomes policy (first voluntary, then statutory) that most clearly marked Heath's corporatist reversion late in 1972 and for much of 1973. Heath could withdraw threats to privatize parts of the nationalized sector (by "hiving off" the chemical and constructional engineering divisions of the British Steel Corporation); Barber could announce in his April, 1972 budget that public expenditure plans for 1974 would be raised by £1200 million; the government could even reintroduce the classic UK device for tripartite bargaining, the National Economic Development Council (NEDC or Neddy). But the Heath government could not effectively rationalize capital or solve stagflation or mobilize even grudging consent from a trade union sector threatened by the Industrial Relations Act and a working class bruised by increased unemployment.[20]

Most frustrating for Heath, he could not marshal the resources to motivate his allies. As he told the Institute of Directors in a bruising speech near the end of his stay in office:

> When we came in we were told there weren't sufficient inducements to invest. So we provided the inducements. Then we were told people were scared of balance of payments difficulties leading to stop—go. So we floated the pound. Then we were told of fears of inflation: and now we're dealing with that. And still you aren't investing enough![21]

Never the capitalist's capitalist, but very much by the time of his demise a figure reviled by the left and the trade unions, Heath drained modern Toryism of much of its appeal. Trapped by a process of internationalization of British fates and the growing political rigidities of class and corporate interests, Heath had little room for successful maneuver.

Neither right nor lucky, even Heath's ostensible victories deepened the prospects of future failures. His most lasting achievement, the integration of the UK into the EEC, weakened the classic appeal of mainstream Toryism by reducing its claim to be the defender of the nation and the national economy against the foreign "other." In the end Heath had done for mainstream Toryism what Callaghan was to do for Labourist social democracy. They exhausted the inner options of party and programmatic alternation within a Keynesian mold, placing the radical alternatives of a harsher politics of class, interest, and ideology closer to the center of British politics than most people had expected ever to find it.

I suggested earlier that a unity of opposites within the Labour Party between fundamentalists and revisionists, and among constituency, PLP, and trade union sections was predicated on the vitality of the social democratic vision. The pressures of decline, represented so forcefully by the visit of the IMF inspectors, occasioned a final retreat from even the minimalism of typical Labourist programs and shattered the balance of forces within the Labour Party. There is also a strange symbiosis between Labour and Tory mainstream, another unity of opposites which defined the Keynesian heartland — and restricted the degree of alternation — of British party politics. Heath's defeat in the quasi-corporatist phase two of his government on the occasion of a miners' strike prefigured Callaghan's defeat 5 years later after the "winter of discontent." Moreover, the defeat of Labour's social democratic vision in the 1974—1979 period, on the heels of Heath's defeat, makes the re-emergence of Tory modernism after Heath's demise unimaginable without a cataclysmic reversal in Thatcher's fortunes, and not altogether likely even then.

THE CONSEQUENCES: 1979

In this mood of double defeat and centrist torpor, the 1979 election was fought and won by Margaret Thatcher and a different Tory Party. Now, in Thatcher's second government, after a violent year-long miner's strike and a spate of urban disorders in 1981 and again in 1985, it takes an effort to still feel the shock one felt then at the raw edges of the campaign. It is even harder to recall, now that her metallic virtues have been cast on the high seas and the Labour opposition has shown itself often in disarray, that Thatcher's leadership qualities were a critical issue against her in 1979. She was, of course, gender-suspect and despite Callaghan's failures he was by far the more acceptable (though not terribly popular) candidate, a good bet to triumph were the contest a presidential, rather than a parliamentary election. But of course the campaign took a very different direction.

The issues of economic decline and the winter of discontent dominated the campaign, but only partly by anyone's design. The Tory manifesto "took the 'highground' and presented the party's style and philosophy rather than a shopping list of proposals."[22] Thatcher stuck to this approach, insisting that a new government would reduce public expenditure, cut taxes to increase investment, reduce inflation through stricter control of the monetary supply, and reduce trade union power by restricting secondary picketing, financing postal ballots in advance of strikes, and then reducing benefits to strikers.

Labour fought back as best it could, assailing figures that were not really there and appearing bombastic and rhetorical as a consequence. Shirley Williams, Callaghan's Education Minister, demonstrated on a blackboard just what would be lacking in educational provision if the Tory-projected cuts went through. Denis Healey noted that finding specifics in the Tory manifesto was like "looking for a black cat in a dark coal cellar" and added that Thatcher's macroeconomics was more radical than any policy advocated by the Communist Party, since they were merely trying to eliminate private property, whereas she had banished arithmetic. Callaghan, affecting an odd self-defeating pose for an incumbent, seemed to forget to defend his government's own policies and instead hammered away at Thatcher, insisting on the details: "How many jobs would be lost by Conservative policies? Where was the money coming from to pay for their tax cuts? How were they going to keep prices down?"[23] Thatcher's credibility on economic policy was thus assaulted — but the memories of the winter just passed were not assuaged. Many a Conservative campaigner echoed the words of Lord Hailsham, nearly always to good effect:

After complimenting us on our excellent phrases, [Mr. Callaghan] said that what [Conservatives] really stood for was a purely materialistic view of the world, the law of the jungle, and the weakest going to the wall . . . and Mr. Healey in his usual robust language said "Devil take the hindmost."

Do they really think we have forgotten last winter? We have seen the grave diggers refusing to bury the dead. We have seen the refuse accumulating in the streets. We have seen the schools shut in the face of children because the caretaker has walked off with the key. And now we see the teachers making them do without their lunches. We have seen cancer patients having to postpone their operations because hospital laundry is not done, floors not swept, or meals not cooked . . . These are facts. What is theirs but the law of the jungle? What is it due to but a selfish and materialistic view of the world? What is this but the weakest and the most vulnerable, the old and the sick and the poor going to the wall? What is this but women and children last and the devil take the hindmost? You would think Mr. Callaghan and Mr. Healey had been in opposition for the last five years instead of orchestrating this shambles of industrial confrontation.[24]

As the results were to show, in this exchange of moralizing epithets, against a backdrop of strikes that *had been* but cuts and lay-offs that only *might be*, the incumbents were at a serious disadvantage.

HOUSING AND THE IDEOLOGICAL SUBURBS

It was a campaign in which the side issues and the concealed appeals proved highly significant. For one thing the Conservatives pressed the issue of housing to decisive advantage. In the policy document which represented Thatcher's first statement of the new Conservative doctrine called quite correctly, *The Right Approach*, the Tories staked out their turf — the ideological suburbs:

> Housing is one of the many areas in which present policies simply do not make sense. Most people want to become home-owners. Yet we devote the overwhelming majority of our resources to public rented housing. . . . [T]he Labour Government have pursued the traditional Socialist vendetta against the private sector.[25]

The Tories were doubtless right in their approach, at least when it came to judging the aspirations of many of their potential voters. The Conservatives promised half-price sales of council houses to all residents and increased the salience of this appeal as "canvassers reports showed it was popular, particularly in some large council estates, especially in the Midlands and in New Towns."[26] This was a highly ideological (if financially dubious) proposition, based on an unerring instinct. A promise of home ownership would lure voters by linking their private aspirations to the Conservative's program. Those attracted by the appeal could feel good about themselves: they were not simply abandoning socialist community for individual interest but participating in a broad inter-class modernizing movement. There was also the "time-bomb" side of the privatization of housing campaign: each public council estate which was transmuted into a suburban housing estate might re-socialize a generation of youths, turn them into Tories, and help break Labour's virtual one-party rule in the industrial north.

In this — perhaps the most brilliant campaign offering — the Conservatives were typically blunt in their ideological appeal. By making the issue one of freedom (rather than simply the desire to acquire) they justified politically the private hopes of residents, blending the honest voice which spoke of family comfort and aspirations into the redolent cry of the New Right. By subsidizing council rents, suggested the Tories, Labour had brought the "serfdom" of social democracy that much closer. The resonance with Frederick von Hayek's *The Road to Serfdom* was as unmistakable as the argument that council housing was a restriction of freedom was incoherent. But it worked.

> There is a fundamental difference of principle between Socialist housing policy and our own. Obviously, we do not regard higher council rents as being something good in themselves. But without a fair and realistic distribution of housing costs there can be no real choice for very many people. For largely political reasons, Socialists actually *want* to limit choice, to keep thousands of families trapped (at great public cost) in what has been called 'the serfdom' of municipal estates. We offer the much more attractive prospect of a choice — a free choice between ownership and a less restrictive kind of tenancy.[27]

It was a choice which many took despite (for some, perhaps, because of) the harsh tone with which the Thatcher camp addressed council residents. There is a defeated air to an electorate or perhaps, worse, a self-loathing in those who, seeing themselves accused, nevertheless accept a candidate's message. The following reply was sent to a query from a council house resident:

I hope you will not think me too blunt if I say that it may well be that your council accommodation is unsatisfactory but considering the fact that you have been unable to buy your own accommodation, you are lucky to have been given something that the rest of us are paying for out of taxes.[28]

Written by Thatcher's correspondence secretary, the message certainly was blunt, and Labour made sure it got around, distributing a million-and-a-half copies in a leaflet of its own. One can't know the consequences of this flap, although it is tempting to suppose that Thatcher lost little by this publicity campaign at Labour Party expense. There is no doubt, however, that Thatcher won and won big (as we shall see) in the "in-between" areas where voters could view themselves either way — as council house beneficiaries of Keynesian society or future home-owning suburbanites. But the contrived and callous nature of Thatcher's housing appeal pales in the face of the just barely covert prejudice of the law and order/immigration campaign within a campaign which helped win her the election and certainly spoiled the victory for some.

"IMMIGRATION" AND GREATNESS

As in Nixon's US, "law and order" issues took on a noxious racist air, here made all the more virulent by their combination with lightly coded discussions about "immigration." Amidst promises of increased police pay and expanded powers, Thatcher offered an unambiguous law-and-order tone about the worst of crimes. "This is not a question of votes," she insisted. "It is a question of my deep belief. I think the vast majority of people in this country would like to see the death penalty restored."[29]

The rawest edge of the campaign, however, concerned "immigration", not capital punishment. Official Thatcherite policy balanced the naive with the pernicious. Conservative policy asserted, on the one hand, that "relations between different communities have been remarkably harmonious" and assured any doubters that racial discrimination and violence are "wholly abhorrent to our British way of life and must be unequivocally condemned." On the other hand, Tory doctrine insisted that "the present level of immigration is much to high" and maintained that "racial harmony requires . . . an immediate reduction in immigration . . . [and] a clearly defined limit to the numbers of those to be allowed into this country."[30]

Not content to leave unstated the implication in such policy that "immigrants" (more on the use of this term, later) are by their presence to be blamed for racist discrimination and violence, Thatcher chose, as she often does, a popular television program to reveal even more baldly the racist principles of her immigration policy. In January, 1978 during an interview on "World in Action", Thatcher explained the logic behind Tory policy (and made the scurrilous link between law and order and immigration):

> If we went on as we are then by the end of this century there would be four million people of the New Commonwealth or Pakistan here. Now I think that is an awful lot and I think it means that people are really rather afraid that this country might be rather swamped by people with a different culture, and you know, the British character has done so much for democracy, for law and order and so much throughout the world that if there is any fear that it might be swamped, people are going to react and be hostile to those coming in. . . . So if you want good race relations, you have got to allay people's fear on numbers.[31]

As David Butler and Dennis Kavanagh rightly note in their election compendium,

> Immigration was hardly debated, although Mrs. Thatcher in television and radio interviews stressed her sense of the importance of the problem, and defended her use of the word "swamped" in relation to the feelings of some of the indigenous population.[32]

David Steel, the energetic Liberal leader, was one of the few to publicly pull the veil on Thatcher's "immigration" stand. "I had hoped," remarked Steel acidly, "we might get through this campaign without making the colour of people's skins an issue at the hustings. Can she not imagine how the word 'swamped' must sound and feel to an unemployed teenager?"[33] Indeed she could imagine it, and that is exactly the point. Thatcher could also anticipate what feelings might be tapped among voters in East London who had witnessed weekly confrontations between supporters of the National Front and the alliance of black residents and leftist supporters who tried to block their highly provocative marches. Thatcher might have suspected, also, that her remarks would sit quite well with potential supporters in the Midlands who wanted some scapegoat group on which to pin the UK's decline. Some, no doubt, were delighted to find the leader of the UK's most respectable party echoing publicly their own half-admitted private hatreds. The signs were unmistakable. Thatcher's popularity jumped 11 percent in the opinion polls immediately after the "World in Action" remarks; a Gallup poll indicated that more than 70 percent of the questioned sample approved of the Tory immigration policy; 61 percent agreed with Thatcher's statement that the UK was "in danger of being swamped by people of different cultures."[34]

It all came together: the yearning for a better life, the imperial nostalgia, the subliminal racism of the campaign. The occasion was Thatcher's final major address. Butler and Kavanagh explain that "idealism not polemic dominated her final broadcast" on Monday, April 30. But this observation misses the point, as Thatcher's closing words of the campaign reveal:

> Somewhere ahead lies greatness for the country again. This I know in my heart. Look at Britain today and you may think that an impossible dream. But there is another Britain which may not make the daily news, but which each of us knows. It is a Britain of thoughtful people, tantalisingly slow to act, yet marvellously determined when they do. It is *their* voice which steadies each generation. . . . Its message is quiet and insistent. It says this: Let us make this a country safe to walk in. Let us make it a country safe to grow old in. And it says, above all, may this land of ours, which we love so much, find dignity and greatness and peace again.[35]

Perhaps Butler and Kavanagh are right that the speech was idealistic. If so, it represented the ideals of whites in East London (or South Boston) who feel swamped at the sight of black children outnumbering white, and who resent the children in a playground, spouting an unfamiliar "foreign" patter — and it foretold the "marvellous determination" of the Falklands War. Neither the unemployed black teenager nor the Midlands loyalist would have had much difficulty breaking the code. They understood whose land it was for Thatcher, what groups made her feel that it was not safe any longer (for whom?) to walk the otherwise peaceful streets. Enough people heard her instinctual appeal to clan and race and nation; and so the campaign ended and Thatcherism proper began.

4

The Seeds of Division

Not simply the extent of the victory but the remarkable quality of the returns was pure Thatcher. It is not enough to note the raw superlatives of her claim to office: she was beneficiary of the largest swing between Labour and Conservative since 1945 (6.4 percent); likewise, winner of the largest plurality of seats over the primary opposition party (7.0 percent) since 1945; she was the architect of a daunting 71-seat advantage over Labour and a 43-seat edge over all parties.[1] More important, the results indicated that the seeds of division had been artfully sown in a responsive and volatile electorate. Thus there was a macabre cast to Thatcher's first public remarks as Prime Minister when she announced upon entering 10 Downing Street: "Where there is discord may we bring harmony."[2] Discord was the name of the game, and the radical divisions in the electorate were the first consequence of her strategies.

VOTING TRENDS: REGION, RACE, AND HOUSING

The division easiest to see was regional. Not so celebrated a distinction as in Spain or Italy, the North—South divide in the UK is still an abiding (if more or less subliminal) force in British society. Regional accents matter, and even the homogenization of popular culture — there are national beers and newspapers, uniform styles in dress and decor in discos — has not eroded the sense of difference. To the Southerner the Yorkshireman (or woman) is gruff, ill-tempered, and bad-mannered; to the Northerner, Londoners are snobs and toadies. Few take the road to Wigan

Pier, and even Orwell was not free of class-regional effrontery. More to the point, the UK's regions reflect widely uneven material circumstances: the North remains a depressed region, reliant on obsolete capital investment in declining industries and mining, and the per capita income in Wales is scarcely more than 60 percent of that for London. UK patterns of disinvestment reflect the broad EEC conditions of peripheral decline. The ten worst-off regions in the European Community have slipped badly. In 1970 the ten poorest had incomes per capita which were one-third those of the ten richest. By 1979, the year of Thatcher's victory, their income per capita had slipped to one-quarter of the richest.[3]

For once the election showed this North–South variation: the North of England swung[4] to the Tories by barely more than half (4.2 percent) the swing the Conservatives enjoyed in the South (7.7 percent).[5] Even more dramatic, outside London Labour won only six seats below the Humber–Mersey line which divides North and South.

Race

Other divisions in the electorate and trends in voting were linked more directly to the themes of the campaign. These were harder — perhaps because more troubling — to detect. Of the contested issues, race was clearly the first among equals in importance. The swings to Thatcher in the London constituencies which had witnessed the most sustained National Front (NF) organizing, notably north-east London, were astonishing. Barking (14.0 percent); Dagenham (13.4 percent); Hackney South (11.6 percent); Islington Central (10.8 percent); Stepney and Poplar (12.9 percent); Peckham (11.5 percent).[6] Indeed, these six were among the ten constituencies with the highest swings in the UK. Drawing inferences as to the motivation of voters from data of this kind always represents an uncertain exercise, but there is a clear logic to the results this time. Why, if not because of the pronounced salience of the race issue, would constituencies in north-east London swing so dramatically to the Tories, when constituencies with comparable attributes (in occupation, historic loyalties, demographics, and settlement patterns) experienced the lowest swings of all more generally?

The Economist estimated that the race and immigration issue accounted for 16 seats.[7] One NF leader indirectly concurred, explaining that "Mrs. Thatcher's apparent anti-immigration stance was the central cause of NF's electoral decline."[8] The NF's share of votes fell from 3.1 percent in October, 1974 (after a high of 3.6 percent in 1970) to 1.4 percent in 1979.[9] In every constituency to which they returned, having run a candidate in October, 1974, their tally of votes declined. The explicit transfer of votes linked to race from the National Front to the Tory Party, which in large measure legitimated their transmutation of the issue of race relations to the "immigrant problem," cannot be unambiguously demonstrated from the data; but grounds for confident inference remain.

A look at the constituencies where racial issues had been placed to the fore by the NF and communities which were, at least potentially, the most polarized reveals the full measure of the racist vote behind Thatcher's victory (see table 4.1). In every constituency in which the NF polled at least 4 percent in October 1974, and stood a candidate in 1979, the Conservative Party improved its share of the vote — and two constituencies (Hackney South and Barking) registered among the ten highest swings in the nation. The figures were impressive. In these racially contested constituencies the Tory share of the total vote increased on average 9.6 percent (compared to an 8.2 percent national average) and Conservative gains compared to their October 1974 tally represented a huge 40.5 percent increase (compared to the 22.3 percent national average). When one considers the NF penchant for choosing to contest constituencies with relatively high concentrations of citizens with New Commonwealth roots, and accepting the veracity of survey data which suggests that Labour got 80—90 percent of New Commonwealth votes in 1979[10] — the Conservative increases in these constituencies were all the more notable. It is hard to ignore the implication that Thatcher's final electoral message and her "World in Action" remarks which legitimized the white UK's unstated fear that the country might be "swamped" had served her purposes well.

Table 4.1 Conservative success in "National Front" constituencies: comparison of general election results october, 1974 and 1979

	National Front vote (in percentage figures)				Conservative vote (in percentage figures)			
Constituency	Oct. 1974	1979	Change in total vote	Percentage loss	Oct. 1974	1979	Change in total vote	Percentage gain
Blackburn	4.4	1.5	−2.9	65.9	32.1	36.6	+ 4.5	14.0
Rochdale	4.1	1.4	−2.7	65.9	16.4	19.3	+ 2.9	17.7
Leicester East	6.4	2.7	−3.7	57.8	36.5	41.3	+ 4.8	13.2
Leicester South	4.1	1.8	−2.3	56.0	41.0	42.6	+ 1.6	3.9
Leicester West	5.1	2.7	−2.4	47.1	30.4	35.4	+ 5.0	16.4
London. Barking*	4.9	3.0	−1.9	38.8	15.6	32.4	+16.8	107.7
Enfield. Edmonton	4.6	2.8	−1.8	39.1	32.5	42.6	+10.1	31.1
Hackney. South*	9.4	7.6	−1.8	19.1	14.9	28.2	+13.3	89.3
Tottenham	8.3	2.9	−5.4	65.1	24.3	32.0	+ 7.7	31.7
Wood Green	8.0	2.8	−5.2	65.0	25.9	39.8	+13.9	53.7
Islington Central	5.3	3.1	−2.2	41.5	21.1	35.6	+14.5	68.7
Lewisham, Deptford	4.8	4.2	−0.6	12.5	22.6	32.5	+ 9.9	43.8
Newham. North East	6.9	4.2	−2.7	39.1	22.2	30.5	+ 8.3	37.4
Newham, South	7.8	6.2	−1.6	20.5	11.2	22.5	+11.3	100.9
Southwark, Bermondsey	4.8	3.9	−0.9	18.8	13.8	24.9	+11.1	80.4
Bethnal	7.6	6.1	−1.5	19.7	10.5	19.5	+ 9.0	85.7
Battersea North	4.5	2.7	−1.8	40.0	21.8	33.2	+11.4	52.3
West Bromwich, East	4.3	2.9	−1.4	32.6	31.4	42.4	+11.0	35.0
West Bromwich, West	5.4	3.4	−2.0	37.0	22.8	36.3	+13.5	59.2
Wolverhampton. North East	4.2	2.7	−1.5	35.7	24.2	37.4	+13.2	54.6
Wolverhampton. South East	4.7	3.1	−1.6	34.0	26.7	34.5	+ 7.8	29.2
Average	5.7	3.4	−2.3	40.5	23.7	33.3	+ 9.6	40.5

* One of ten highest swings
Data from: David Butler and Dennis Kavanagh. *The British General Election of October 1974* (London: Macmillan, 1975); David Butler and Dennis Kavanagh. *The British General Election of 1979* (London: Macmillan 1980).

Housing

Thatcher's housing platform also seems to have been successful in tapping the volatility of the UK's electorate, and especially in forging her intra-class support. As Michael Jones observes:

> It was electorally crucial in dividing a working class movement, deeply disillusioned by the apparent inadequacies of the Welfare State and politically embittered by the economic policies pursued by the Labour government after 1976, by its populist appeal to the anti-bureaucratic, individualist and self sufficient ideology of home ownership.[11]

The Labour Party elites and members of the broad left were divided and uneasy in their response. Should less than satisfactory public housing be defended? Should potential buyers be considered disloyal to the KWS vision? At the same time, the "right to buy" was serving Tory electoral interests well. In the South-east, the Conservatives won the Greater London Council election in 1977 fought on the "sale of the century" theme, and in May, 1978 Conservative successes in Wandsworth and Hillingdon at the Borough elections foreshadowed Thatcher's success with housing in the general election one year later.

Table 4.2 suggests the crucial political role housing policy assumed in Thatcher's victory. In the 37 English constituencies in which council tenancy exceeded 50 percent, Conservatives gained a net increase in support (against all parties) of 9.5 percent from their October 1974 showing (an extraordinary 39.4 percentage points gain) (see table 4.2).

Although Labour dominated in general, constituencies with a high concentration of council housing moved closer to the Thatcher—Tory camp. Significant inroads were made even in the solidary working-class North. In Gateshead the Tories registered a 5.5 percent gain; in Jarrow 6.8 percent; in Houghton the Tories more than doubled their tally; in Sunderland South they gained 7.9 percent. All of these increased tallies significantly exceeded the 5.2 percent North of England two-party swing. Clearly the Tories had found in housing an issue which targeted Northern constituencies well, just as "immigration" had done for the vast suburban middle of the country.

Table 4.2   Comparison of October, 1974 and May, 1979 UK general election results (English constituencies with at least 50 percent council housing)

	1979	Change October, 1974 to 1979
Conservative	33.6	+9.5
Labour	54.0	−5.1
Liberal	10.0	−4.5
Other	2.4	+ .1

Data from: David Butler and Dennis Kavanagh, *The British General Election of October 1974* (London: Macmillan, 1975), David Butler and Dennis Kavanagh, *The British General Election of 1979* (London: Macmillan, 1980).

THATCHER'S INTER-CLASS APPEAL AND THE
QUESTION OF WELFARE

With housing and race the most catalytic issues, Thatcherism emerged from the campaign — like Gaullism at its height in France — with exquisite inter-class appeal. This is the core significance of the 1979 election and the strongest possible clue of what was to come.

One observer explained, "Labour lost the election because of an immense shift of working class support to the Conservatives."[12] As table 4.3 shows, the Tories gained handsomely among both skilled and unskilled workers. A fragmented working class, disillusioned with Callaghan's ineptitude and worn out by the failures of social democracy, divided itself into smaller self-interested aggregates. Some wanted tax cuts, while others wanted to buy their council houses at the promised 30—50 percent discount from market rates. Too many were drawn to the racially suspect paeans to the UK's pre-immigrant grandeur, when the citizens of the New Commonwealth were still the subjects of the old Empire. The upper/professional classes held Tory, skilled workers moved in large numbers to the Conservatives. Even among the unskilled laborers of the

Table 4.3   Occupational trends in UK voting, 1974—1979

Party	Professional/managerial (A,B) office/clerical (C1)		Skilled manual (C2)		Semi—/ unskilled manual (D)	
	1979	Change from October 1974	1979	Change from October, 1974	1979	Change from October, 1974
Conservative	60%	+9%	35%	+11%	35%	+13
Labour	23%	−2%	50%	− 5%	51%	− 9
Liberal/Other	17%	−7%	15%	− 6%	14%	− 4

Data from: Adapted from Bo Särlvik and Ivor Crewe, *Decade of Dealignment* (Cambridge: Cambridge University Press, 1983), pp. 80—85. British Election Studies CBES) October 1974 Election Survey; BES May, 1979 Election Survey. Useful comparison may be made to Market and Opinion Research International, *British Public Opinion: General Election 1979* (London, 1979) which indicates a far more modest swing to Conservative in A, B, C1 category.

UK, the Labour Party lost significant ground (9 percent of its October, 1974 tally) and barely held a majority.

Many have seen in these results the final demonstration of "social convergence" or "class de-alignment" in electoral behavior and some (usually others) have seen in the returns from the general election of May, 1979 a rejection of the welfare state. Some such elements are apparent (and will be discussed below). More to the point, however, these returns may indicate an instrumentalism and performance orientation within the electorate. Among the working classes, it seems, Thatcherism attracted those softened up the most by declining standards of living. They were fed up with a Labour Party that allowed the cost of decline to be borne unequally by the least advantaged. Hence they were prey to race and immigration appeals and cheap housing give-backs that overnight might make unexamined and half-forgotten dreams come true. This voting appeal is not so much the result of convergence (as in an embourgoisement, "we're all part of a post-industrial society now" theory) as anomie; not so much a rejection of the welfare state as a call by each and every one for a greater share in the good life — the unfulfilled promises of the welfare state. Whether the provisions were located in the public or the private sphere mattered rather little, but someone should provide good, clean affordable housing, houses that felt like homes, that buoyed the spirits. Social democracy in its shabbiness and torpor failed to replace pride in ownership with pride in community.

These failures gave Thatcher her opening, not only on housing issues, but in the construction of an electoral base — as we will see with Reagan, below, in chapter 6 — which began negatively, as a rejection of KWS principles, and never positively evolved into a coherent domestic coalition. If this is true, as the electoral data and polling information imply but cannot prove, then Thatcherism is based on an *arithmetic* politics. It relies on the sum of diverse particularistic appeals — on housing, race, anti-Labour or anti-union sentiments, entrepreneurial ethos — but does not represent a unified coalition such as that which lay beneath the Butskellite program of the KWS.

Such electoral volatility is not surprising, particularly among the non-traditional (perhaps first-time) Tories — the demoralized council-house dwellers cum suburbanites, the unemployed skilled workers who watched Labour orchestrate their predicament. Why shouldn't they want more and less at the same time: more for themselves even if that means less for others, more services (or more efficient provision of services) with less taxes. Polling data provide strong indications of curious ambivalences within the electorate that allowed Margaret Thatcher, the unregenerate outsider, to become a mainstream politician and made her one of the more imposing Prime Ministers of the century. As Butler and Kavanaugh note:

> The polls showed that voters had a good idea of the policies which a Conservative government would pursue: cuts in direct taxes, increases in VAT, and a reduction in spending on welfare and on industrial subsidies. There was overwhelming support for tax cuts, and yet when voters were asked specifically to balance tax cuts against reduced expenditure on health or education or pensions, a very different picture emerged.[13]

According to Gallup and BBC/Gallup polls, 34 percent of respondents said taxes should be cut even if health, education, and welfare provision were to suffer and yet 34 percent — a pollsters' dream! — said the opposite (that these "big three" services should be expanded, even if that required an increase in taxes). By election day the results had shifted significantly, although it must be admitted that one of the questions had also changed considerably. Now, only 30 percent registered their "cut taxes" view as preponderant and fully 70 percent agreed that health, education, and welfare expenditures should be "kept up" (but note the change from "should be extended") even if that meant no tax cuts (note also the change from "some increases in taxes").

On the face of it these are extremely puzzling results. It is commonplace (and more or less mandatory for professional election watchers) to assume that general elections are never referenda on particular issues. In this they are like Rousseau on politics. "Did individual interests not exist," he wrote in his *Social Contract*, "society would become automatic, and politics would cease to be an art."[14] If elections were referenda on single issues, then their interpretation would be automatic, and commentators would cease to be involved. Nevertheless, it is too much to suppose such apparent inconsistency between ethos and electoral choice on an issue as fundamental to our age as the status of welfarism versus the level of direct taxation. The problem is that in this case inconsistent results are so easy to find. An April, 1979 MORI poll showed a 75:17 majority in favor of reducing government spending (the opposite of the election-day results). Yet there may be a relatively simple way out of the paradox.

For a start, it may help to accept that respondents are simply an aggregate of individuals who, plausibly enough, avoid fiscal rectitude by permitting themselves muddled thinking. Living on monthly wages, and given the opportunity, who hasn't balanced a checkbook by buying with a credit card? The polling results and electoral preferences reflect the desires to cut taxes *and* maintain or improve services — views that are nonetheless sincere for being incoherent. "All this suggests that the public is human," writes David Lipsey. "Faced with a choice between tax cuts and services, it ducks the issue and just assumes that the money can be found by eliminating waste or bashing scroungers."[15] Or it can't be found and the government runs up a deficit. Here the perceived analogy with household finances ends. A deficit has little meaning for a voter, while health care and unemployment insurance manifestly do.

What welfare backlash?

But there is another critical issue revealed in a study of the Thatcher electorate's attitude toward government services, where preferences are gauged against the expectation of reduced taxation. What really mattered to them, it seems, was the government provision of services which they received or reasonably expected to receive some time during their lives. The welfare state was not the issue, but their own welfare was. It seems economic decline teaches pragmatism, and diminished expectations inclines one toward a prudent interest for the self. The results of an SSRC-financed survey in Kent in 1981 suggest the specifics of the welfare backlash which accompanied Thatcher's rise to office.

As table 4.4 indicates, respondents differentially support particular welfare programs. The major expenditures (for health, education and pensions) got solid approval since everyone might reasonably expect to benefit at some time. The ambiguous support for single-parents' benefits, unemployment, and council housing reflects the loss of the redistributive instinct behind welfarism, a "concern about indiscriminate handouts to the undeserving or simply a low level of general enthusiasm for meeting minority . needs."

The findings which related to support for the universal provision of particular benefits show the most clearly the decline of the welfarist ethos, which is by its nature a call for universal provision at least potentially for redistributive effect. Apart from child benefit (which is the only universal benefit in the UK much like the tax deduction for each dependent child in the US), the declining support for universal provision as one works down the columns from education (96 percent approval) to unemployment (28 percent approval) corresponds simply to a rank ordering of the respondent's expectation that she/he will be a beneficiary.

As one of the survey researchers noted bleakly, "The wider social policy aims of redistribution over the family life-cycle or between wallet and handbag, were not echoed in what men and women said."[16] It is a curious sign of the times that the researcher

Table 4.4 Opinions about welfare state provision

	Support for		Spending should be		
	State Provision (%)	Universal Provision (%)	In- creased (%)	Main- tained (%)	Cut (%)
Education	NA	96	40	51	9
Sick benefits	98	75	50	47	3
Old age pensions	98	65	26	68	6
National health service	NA	58	48	41	11
Single-parent benefits	85	49	35	60	5
Council housing	NA	43	20	63	17
Child benefit	68	32	8	58	34
Unemployment benefit	92	28	18	72	10

NA = Not asked
Source: Peter Taylor-Gooby, "Public belt and private braces," *New Society.*
April 14, 1983.

neglected even to note that the responses suggested little support for the signal policy aim of welfare in its original implementation, namely, redistribution between the most and the least advantaged.

Thus, the Thatcher victory signaled a mixed message to which, after a few false starts, the new Prime Minister was to prove extremely responsive: government provision of social services within an anti-welfarist ideology, benefits but no beliefs, welfare but no welfare state. She gave the public what they wanted, although probably (in the matter of the National Health Service, for example) less of it. What her adherents wanted was a self-interested and ideological repudiation of the principles of the welfare state — redistribution and universalism — as the basis for believing in the rightfulness of government. The civilizing concern for the less advantaged would no longer be the index of progress, the rallying cry for popular support. Rather, a market logic would prevail, an economic Darwinism which implies species advancement through individual combat, and assumes that the more advantaged deserve to be that way.

"Tennyson's most famous biological line — his description of life's ecology as 'Nature, red in tooth and claw' — does not apply in all or most cases," remarks Stephen Jay Gould. "Darwin's 'struggle for existence' is a metaphor and need not imply active combat."[17] Of course, contrary to the common maxim, dogs don't eat dogs, but the political economy of decline operates by (and encourages) a more rapacious logic. Before the 1979 election a decade of social democratic and mainstream Tory mismanagement was witnessed by generations of Britons who personally lived the decline — or vicariously experienced through older relatives and friends and the sentimentalizing of the pulp press — the precipitous drop in national fortunes, power and prestige. Queen Elizabeth II, who gained the throne with an empire still of impressive extent, enjoyed her silver jubilee amidst growing expectations of devolution — and fear of worse — in Scotland and Wales. Security could not be assured for a visit during the Jubilee year to Northern Ireland (she visited nearly every nation of the Commonwealth), so she parked at sea and helicoptered into a university compound for a brief visit, narrowly avoiding explosives which had been left behind just hours before. There were jokes that by the time Charles got his chance only England might be left (indeed, there were local variations on this, with the Geordies, fierce regional "nationalists" of the North of England, leaving him only the South of England).

Whatever the dimensions, the signs of social democratic defeat and geopolitical and economic decline abounded, and pressures of austerity and diminished expectations inclined the Thatcherite electorate to affirm individual rights over social justice. In instinctual libertarian fashion they embraced the minimalist state — a "monopoly of the legitimate use of physical force" but with "power stripped of all redistributive functions."[18] Common sense in hard times, when social democracy has failed and the sense of collective fates has eroded, seems very much like the argument of neo-Conservative libertarians such as Robert Nozick. People are ready to hear the claims of the individualist: that moralizing and sentiment aside, there is no reason to assume that redistribution downward — rather than the Thatcherite obverse of support for the more advantaged sectors — enhances the common good of growth and economic vitality.

THATCHER'S DE-INTEGRATIVE PROJECT: THE WELFARE FRONT

Democratic theory assumes an evolutionary trend which governmental practice in the golden age of Keynesian society consciously re-enforced. Working-class interests, women, minority races, non-hegemonic ethnic and religious groups become integral and conscious participants in the affairs of both the polity and the economy. Alternation of government includes in office the representatives of diverse interests which previously assumed no role in governance. As Kirchheimer put it, politics becomes the "cooperative enterprise of all social classes."[19] While participation and, more so, political power, were never so broadly distributed nor so casually disaggregated as this model suggests, it was certainly the case that Keynesian society presupposed a model of an integrated society. Few "outgroups" were too far off the mainstream to influence policy directly — or at least have their needs negotiated for them by others. Surely tripartite bargaining over industrial policy among unions, business associations and government agencies represented a model of fairness and harmonization (whatever the practical realities). As an image of democracy, tripartism-corporatism was for the period of the KWS what the idea of a representative assembly was to the Enlightenment.

In a sense, managers of the KWS should not be held accountable for what the last 250 years of capitalist, racist, and gender exploitation within democratic society have done to their public relations effort. Nothing taxed their imaginations more than the effort to harmonize interests, convince outgroups that they have a stake in society, mobilize at least pragmatic acquiescence among potentially disruptive sectors, and maintain sufficient popular support to implement policies and gain their government's re-election — all the while managing a declining economy and distributing the consequences of that decline.

There must be better ways to run a country, or so thought Thatcher and enough other people to put her in 10 Downing Street. Hence monetarism replaced Keynesian demand management as economic doctrine, enterprise and initiative supplanted fairness and equality as legitimating maxims; and virtues of self-interest, corrected by police force when necessary, replaced

concern for the less advantaged and the positive goals of social harmony. The Thatcher regime has consistently replaced welfarist/ integrative *ideology* with a competitive "them-and-us" rhetoric of a xenophobic and crudely Darwinist capitalism. The government's practice, of course, has fallen far short of a dismantling of the welfare state and, as we shall see, the resulting contradiction between the ideological representation of the government and its practice represents a signal feature of Thatcherism.

The history and meaning of the cuts

In the UK, the majority wanted taxes cut and services (particularly universal and life-cycle benefits they might need) kept up. The Reaganite base in America was more coherent in its preferences: two out of three preferred lower taxes *and* less services.[20] The two governments responded accordingly. Reagan cut virtually all health, welfare and other social programs, offloading 40 percent of the cutbacks onto the poor as the administration pursued a strong tax-cut policy until Congressional support gave out.[21] Thatcher managed the anti-welfarist campaign with more subtlety, as the ambivalences of UK voters raised on 30 years of NHS medical care and more extensive unemployment and pension benefits required, and previous cuts by the Callaghan/Healey government permitted.

A "presumption against public spending . . . has always been politically opposed to the socialist vision of public services as collective provision for social needs," notes David Hall, former research officer for the Society of Civil and Public Servants. "From 1974 onwards this conflict became a central political battle. A massive wave of propaganda was unleashed to support attacks on public services."[22] Some Labour Party and trade union elites endorsed the notion that Britain's 'de-industrialization' followed from the crowding out of private by public investment, and the reduction of manufacturing in favor of public sector employment. None of this sounded very fresh since criticism of the public sector and the inefficiency of bureaucracy is as old as socialist plans to limit the prerogatives of capitalists. Colonel Blimp and the cigar-chewing capitalists versus the "idle, bloated parasites" of state bureaucracies: this is a familiar setpiece in the Manichean iconography of British politics. As Hall noted, however,

The major new contribution came from the doctrine of monetarism. This won widespread support for its central theme, that both inflation and poor industrial performance were due to excessive borrowing by governments, and that the aim of maintaining employment by expanding public spending was doomed to make things worse — a "natural" level of unemployment was unavoidable. The public sector borrowing requirement (PSBR) shot to prominence as the root of all evil and anything that reduced the PSBR was a good thing.[23]

With Labour's White Paper of February, 1976, which announced cuts of £4600 million (in 1976 terms) for the next 2 years (in the end the figure was closer to £8100 million for the 1977—1979 period), cuts in spending on public services (apart from social services) began in earnest. Alongside budgetary restrictions in a whole range of services, the cuts eliminated jobs in the civil service and local councils, not insignificantly a critical area of female employment.

Cash limits

At the same time the government introduced the new "cash limits" system in public sector accounting. Except for social security payments and a few minor items all central government spending would be constrained by an exact figure set in advance and local government spending would be limited also by cash limits.[24] The consequences of operating public spending this way, without regard to plans or targets or changing needs, are significant in practical terms, and symbolically enormous:

Because cash limits are set before the start of the financial year to which they relate, they depend on prefixed assumptions about the rise in pay and prices. . . . It is these assumptions which effectively set an incomes policy for public service pay. They also effectively fix what can be spent on services. . . . Whatever the actual rise in prices, whatever the actual need for services and workers to provide them, no more money will be forthcoming. The political conflicts between the real level of services and public sector pay, on the one hand, and the amount of finance available from taxation or borrowing, on the other, are thus automatically resolved in favour of finance: the workers and the public have to fit in as best they can.[25]

So, all was in readiness for Thatcher by the end of Callaghan's government: the pre-eminent importance of controlling the public sector borrowing rate (PSBR) had gained popular currency; the public sector pay was viewed by many as a source of inflation; "full" employment had been abandoned as a goal of macro-economic policy; the cash limits system of restrictions on public spending was in place; and, apart from social security benefits which had risen 18.5 percent because of increased unemployment, non-defense spending on public services had already been cut 8.6 percent from the 1975—1976 level.

In aggregate terms, during the first 6 years Tory policy in government spending was not so much a reversal of Labour policy as a hardening of the inherited soft-core monetarism of the Callaghan/Healey years. Aside from a fairly dramatic reversal in defense spending — from an average annual decline in real terms of 1.4 percent in the last 3 years of the Labour government to an average 2.7 percent rise under the Conservatives — the results seem to indicate continuities. Certainly the change in the average rate of decline in non-social security benefits (from −2.7 percent per year between 1975—1976 and 1978—1979 to −2.3 percent per year between 1979—1980 and 1983—1984) seems unremarkable. Likewise, the social security expenditures seem to show a fairly steady pattern. Social security (income support) expenditure rose an average 5.8 percent per year during the last 3 years of the Labour government and a more modest 4.4 percent per year under the Conservative government.[26]

The decline at first seems not terribly significant: one would expect some decline with the change to any Conservative government. The true spectre of Thatcherism only comes into focus with an understanding that the unemployment benefits and supplementary benefits which, alongside pensions, constitute the majority claims on social security expenditures had to be stretched to cover the families of more than twice the number of unemployed persons in 1982—1983 and thereafter than in 1978—1979 (more on this later).

Despite the continuities with the defeated social democracy of Callaghan, there were from the start of the first Thatcher government considerable innovations — and these would become more significant in her second government. From early days, social security benefits (akin to AFDC in American terms) were systematically eroded in value, and contributory benefits such as sickness and unemployment benefits were reduced significantly. New controls over local authorities forced the Lothian council in Scotland to make cuts under direct order of the Secretary of State. In a celebrated and highly symbolic victory for Thatcher the House of Lords upheld Parliament's new statutory control over local authorities, and forced the Greater London Council (GLC) (against the highly articulate voices of its committed leftist councillors) to raise the fares on the underground rail system and the buses of the London Transport system. The cash limits system, which now required parliamentary on top of Cabinet approval for any excess spending, was wielded with new power as the battle against local councils — which was to culminate in the abolition of the GLC and a set of powerful metropolitan county councils in March, 1986 — was begun in earnest.

Deliberate underestimates of inflation and a ruling by the Treasury that a breach of cash limits would be considered an instance of "financial maladministration" have forced the provision of services below "planned" levels and intimidated responsible administrators. Thus in 1981—1982 public services were forced by inflation and the undercalculation of inflation to absorb a real cut of nearly 3 percent and administrators in a panic underspent cash limits in non-defense spending by a further 3.3 percent — for a total net decline of 6.3 percent of hidden cuts. A more invisible hidden cut in the cash limits scheme occurred when increases were not made to accommodate higher taxes that government agencies have to assume in their normal operations. Accordingly, when the new government increased Value Added Tax (VAT) in 1979, the National Health Service had to "save" £40 million in wage costs and services to pay VAT to the government.[27]

It is not that social service expenditures in the UK were uniformly slashed, nor that the least advantaged have been hit as hard as they have been in the US in terms of social welfare provision. It is probably closer to the truth to say that social service expenditures have been cut by hidden accounting techniques as they have been publicly reduced by highly visible and ideologically targeted attacks on the redistributive and egalitarian principles of the welfare state.

A STRATEGY OF DIFFERENTIAL CUTTING

Programs have been cut differentially in relation to the salience of a particular service program within Thatcher's highly ideological anti-integrative campaign. Responsive to the voters' ambivalent sympathies — which her politics have strategically formed and manipulated — Thatcher has highlighted for destruction programs that divide the population, leaving the classic universalistic or life-cycle programs (like the NHS or old age pensions) diminished but more (OAPs) or less (NHS) intact.

The assault on public housing, since it is by its nature sectoral and voluntary, can be far more radical — with public expenditure in 1983–1984 less than half that of 1974–1975 — than the attack on the NHS. Even the suburbanized Tories who represent the best hope of Thatcher's property-owning democracy, may take suddenly ill — and they are expected to grow old — but by dint of will they may be expected to avoid the "voluntary" conditions of poverty. It is here, in the means-tested programs, that the raw edge of Thatcher's de-integrative strategy is fully revealed.

Health care

Thus a comparison of how health care and supplementary benefits have fared under Thatcher's government indicates the balance in the attack on the welfare state between the ideological representation and the highly material practices of Thatcherism. The National Health Service, the "jewel in Labour's crown," remains — with universal provision and extremely low user's fee — a highly visible institutional symbol of welfare ideology with full institutional effect. Moreover, having stood the test of time (it was inaugurated in the heady postwar boom of social democracy in 1946), it has become a habit for more than 90 percent of the population. Of course, the NHS is the only way of life for a growing proportion of the electorate who are NHS babies and now adults, for whom "socialized medicine" doesn't seem socialist at all, but a minimal condition of civilization and convenience — like social security (old age pensions) in the US.

During the ideological days of the last Labour government, the debate about health care was over pay (private patient) beds and the ability of paying customers with private doctors to "jump the queue" and use NHS hospital and laboratory facilities ahead of NHS patients for non-emergency procedures. Thus the public—private controversy in health has had a very different orientation in the UK, compared to the US, where discussion limps forward (and now jumps back) on the question of whether or not any publicly financed insurance scheme ought to be introduced to supplement the privately dominated (and highly remunerative) system in effect.

Thus it is fair to say that health care was not a fertile ground for anti-welfarist rhetoric in the 1979 campaign, and official Conservative policy in the run-up to the election was cautious. Labour was criticized for the decline in capital expenditures and for an increase in prospective patients waiting for admission into NHS hospitals, and this pro-NHS partisan criticism was balanced with moderate expressions of support for increased user and prescription charges.

Mr Patrick Jenkin, Conservative Shadow Cabinet spokesperson on Social Services, told a meeting of Health Service Treasurers at York in March, 1977: "In the longer term, I believe that we should seek ways of transferring more of the cost of the Health Service from taxes to insurance."[28] In October, 1977 in a speech to the Conservative Medical Society, Jenkin asked whether it was "so unthinkable that people might be expected to pay towards the cost of their keep when they are in hospital? I recognize that there are administrative problems, but they should not be insuparable. It seems to me that this is a proposal which should be examined."[29] This is hardly the stuff of welfarist counterrevolution.

Nevertheless, with the growing assertiveness of the second Thatcher government, the situation has changed significantly. In fact, signals of a more radical approach were not so long in coming. Steve Illife wrote in July, 1980:

The goal of the present Government is clear: they wish to see market forces dominate the development of health care as far as possible. Within the ideology of Conservatism, responsibility for health is to become personal rather than social.[30]

Iliffe could not know then that in 1982 the Tory Cabinet would receive a think-tank proposal in which "abolition of the NHS was the centerpiece of their suggestions for dealing with the problem of public spending."[31] But already a radical approach to health care was coming into focus. As Iliffe explains:

> The Conservative strategy, as far as it can be assessed, is directed at stabilizing the private sector, diminishing the scope of NHS activity through cuts and cash limits, and shifting certain (profitable) areas of health care into the private sector. The Government will take a "firm line" on industrial relations within the NHS, aiming to weaken trade unionism and solidarity generally by limiting trade union rights and turning one group of health workers against another. The medical profession (and professions like nursing) will be given more influence in planning development and allocating resources, and doctors will be encouraged to act as the link between private and public services. Finally, declining standards in NHS care that have been caused by cuts imposed by this (and previous) governments will be used as evidence of the failure of state intervention and the superiority of private enterprise.[32]

Currently the NHS has shifted resources into chronic care, a shift fully justified by the poor quality of such services and the expanded need which follows from demographics. Nevertheless, NHS policy increasingly represents a subtle form of *implicit* privatization.[33] Very likely, in the end, the NHS will be diminished and ideologically assaulted but only undermined materially: cuts, fewer jobs, less equipment, an erosion of confidence in socialized medicine, and a commensurate swelling of private sector initiative. Thatcherism in the provision of health care represents, oddly, a cautious appraisal of the public ambivalence about welfare expenditures. Universal provisions are cut, but some services which are especially important for the less advantaged — for example, staffing in emergency rooms or nursing care for patients bed-ridden at home — are the more constricted. For now, the majority that want taxes cut but universal benefits maintained will be satisfied that most of the benefits they use are still available.

Nevertheless, cuts mean an overloading of services and a growing incapacity of the NHS to respond to demands which may be expected to grow as unemployment and poverty adversely affect heart disease, infant mortality, and psychological health. As provision by the NHS and belief about provision by NHS decline, frustration by staff and patients and desires to opt out of the system increase. All consultants may now, for the first time, take private patients (even if they are ostensibly paid for full-time commitment to NHS), and there is evidence that part-time nurses are increasingly drawn to the private sector.

For now, the "jewel in Labour's crown" is only tarnished. In the medium term the logic of the cuts may lead, as one observer puts it, to "the creation of two health services, one public and one private, working in parallel and in conjunction and finding their own balance of influence and responsibility for provision of care".[34] For the time being the ultimate long-range solution — the elimination of the NHS and its replacement with a US-style health system based on insurance coverage and private health care provision — has been shelved. The material cuts are still constrained by the habits and needs of the populace, but each day's cuts, and the growing weariness and resentment which infects the users, diminish the jewel and build ideological bridges to the yet-too-radical approach of total reprivatization.

Means-tested programs

By contrast, the government's treatment of means-tested programs — what "welfare" means to the moderately advantaged when they rant about "welfare scroungers" (UK) or "welfare chiselers" (US) — demonstrates unambiguously what Thatcher's vaunted attack on the welfare state is and is not. The "welfare state" has not been dismantled — only individuals not institutions have been torn down. As *The Economist* observed in one of its June, 1983 election features: "When the Tories were elected in May 1979, about 4.5 million people depended on supplementary benefits — the means-tested handout that the Beveridge report in 1942 intended only as a safety net for the poorest. In 1948, only 1.5 million people depended on it, making up about 3 percent of the population. By the end of last year, 7 million people clung to that net, about 12½ percent of the population."[35] The unelaborated figures tell the tale. During the course of Thatcher's first term in office, the ranks of the marginalized have increased by at least 60 percent. The point is not that the government can be blamed for all the increase in poverty. During the period of the 1979 government the number of those receiving supplementary benefits above pensionable age increased by 46,000 and those receiving single parent benefits have increased (between late 1979 and late 1982) from 358,000 to 501,000. The policies of Thatcher are only partly to blame. Clearly, decreasing British fortunes within an international context reduce the capacity of any government to administer economic successes and there are causes beyond poverty itself — longer life and increased divorce — which influence the numbers of people dependent on these two forms of supplementary benefit.

When it comes to unemployment related supplementary benefits, however, we see Thatcherism short and sharp. Not only are a vast mass of people knocked (some permanently) out of the working classes — they are then kicked when they are down. In 1983 an unemployed person got £25 a week for a year (and a couple got £40.25). Thereafter, the dole stopped and the unemployed person — no longer officially listed — could seek supplementary benefit. If under 60, the jobless then received £32.70 (single) or £52.30 (for a couple).[36] The £7.70 (single) or £11.95 (couple) wedge between the dole and the post-dole benefit, a policy continued from Labour, shows the meanness of a system which presupposes that if there were an extra £7—12 payment from the start, too many would prefer not working to working. This says a lot about the continued Victorian attitudes of the middle classes toward the poor, and it tells us something about what the pay must be like in marginalized jobs. (In fact, the number of working poor — those with jobs who may claim supplementary benefits — more than doubled during the first 3 years of Thatcherism.) But it tells us nothing of what it must be like for a couple to pay the bills on £52.30 a week.

Apparently, however, for Thatcher's government this was still too generous a set of safety-net provisions. In 1980 the government raised many supplementary benefits by 5 percent below the inflation rate (and only restored the cut directly in advance of the

1983 election). Next, it ended earnings-related dole payouts. Then in July, 1982 unemployment benefits became taxable, and they were subsequently withdrawn altogether from those engaged in strikes.

THATCHER'S DE-INTEGRATIVE PROJECT: RACE AND CLASS

A mere financial accounting in pounds and pence, however illustrative the figures, cannot fully reveal the political dimensions of Thatcher's de-integrative strategy. For this it is necessary to turn to two crucial issues of state policy under Thatcher: race and immigration, and industrial relations.

Race and immigration

The record of preceding governments makes such troubling reading that it is difficult — although, as we shall see, not impossible — to detect the special anti-integrative dimension which sets the current government policy apart. Worse, the racism in the UK is now of such dimensions that no government is likely to muster the resolve to improve the situation considerably.

Nevertheless, important distinctions can and must be made. Racism may be a permanent attribute of divided societies, but its historically constituted forces and effects are fluid and subject to considerable manipulation. As Stuart Hall writes:

> Though [racism] may draw on the cultural and ideological traces which are deposited in a society by previous historical phases, it always assumes specific forms which arise out of the present — not the past — conditions and organisation of society. The indiginous racism of the 60s and 70s is significantly different, in form and effect, from the racism of the "high" colonial period. It is a racism "at home," not abroad. It is the racism not of a dominant but of a declining social formation.[37]

The last point is essential. The postwar period has witnessed the gradual erosion of the black experience in the UK prior to Thatcher. It has been linked, it seems inextricably, to the UK's global decline. Blacks have suffered from a casual consensus over a program of cultural isolation of New Commonwealth residents within the UK, and a calm acceptance by others of their increased physical harassment. At the same time there was a bipartisan continuity in the gradual transformation of black citizens into trespassing aliens, a change expressed through a series of immigration and nationality laws.

The postwar legal history of nationality and immigration statutes represents a tightening of the rights of settlement of black citizens, much as the social history indicates the growing insecurity of black residents. Beginning with the 1962 Immigrants Acts a growing body of law has served to keep blacks out and invidiously distinguish Commonwealth citizens within, as Tom Rees observed.

> Because of the large number of citizens of Commonwealth countries who, prior to independence, were entitled to citizenship of the United Kingdom and its colonies under the British Nationality Act of 1948, pressure built up to distinguish, in law, between those United Kingdom citizens who in some sense "belonged" to the United Kingdom itself, and those United Kingdom citizens whose closest ties were in some territory within the Commonwealth.[38]

The UK created a new kind of citizen, "stateless in substance, though not in name."[39]

Thus the 1962 Act passed over strong Labour Party opposition removed from most colonial citizens not of recent UK descent (and from all Commonwealth citizens) the right to enter and settle in the United Kingdom without restriction. This was the last significant moment of partisan fury or Labour Party resistance to the unending stream of racially suspect exclusionary policies. After the settlement of several tens of thousands of ethnically Indian, Kenyan UK citizens (following the Africanization policies of the Kenyan government in 1968), the Labour government firmly enshrined the principle of patriality with the Commonwealth Immigrants Act of 1968. Thatcher's British Nationality Act 1981 simply tightens the restrictions and formalizes the hierarchy of citizenship levels, but the principle of patriality, once in place, follows its own insidious logic. Citizenship need not confer rights of settlement and these rights are subject to arbitrary statutory instruction, ministerial prerogative, and prejudicial design. We know perfectly well that Thatcher isn't feeling "swamped" by Canadians and Australians.

Patriality is the legal veneer and "Paki-bashing" the hard surface of UK racism. As Michael and Ann Dummett sourly note: "Not even the most racist of American whites has ever tried to deny that black Americans are as American as apple pie."[40] Not so in the UK, where patriality drives a wedge between the state and (to consciously apply the odious concept of Nazi vintage) the *Volk*. Blacks may be British citizens, but the whites won't let them be part of the English nation. Thus immigration and nationalization have served as a lesson in racial division; the problem is not "our racism" but "their" entry.

It was, in some sense, a necessary lesson. The Dummetts note:

> The majority [of white Britons] has been composed of people whom we shall call 'crypto-racialists'. These are people who have, side by side, within them, both deeply rooted racial prejudices and an awareness of the shamefulness of racial prejudices.

Immigration and nationality law has served as an important socializing mechanism, pushing the "silent majority" of crypto-racists into the anti-immigrant camp. "The country, which, even in 1967, was merely in danger of becoming a racialist society, is now definitely one," note the Dummetts, "and is recognized as such both by the black people, living in it and by the world at large."[41]

The psychic defeats and material discomforts suffered by the British are the costs of imperial decline, just as (if the whites could only see it) the enrichment and revitalization of the UK by entrants from the old empire may be a considerable benefit. But a society haunted by decline in geopolitical power and prestige abroad, and reduced economic standards at home, may make sense of things in an odd way. As Solomos *et al.* note:

> There is no one-to-one correspondence between the 'crisis of race' and the economic crisis. Yet race is always present whether the issue under discussion is the growth of unemployment, the role of the police in inner-city areas, or the recent 'riots' in a number of major cities.[42]

As the "romantic revolt" of the 1960s became the attack on "the nation" and "order" in the 1970s, positions hardened. Anti-state movements (anti-Vietnamese War, student movements, subcultural currents like Punk, and anarchist collectives like the Angry Brigade) and rank-and-file movements in trade unions contributed to a sense of anomie and the breakdown of order. The British Army began to serve as an occupying force within Northern Ireland, the economy got out of hand, and urban violence increased. At even a more general level, the women's movement attacked family norms and patriarchal values, and "the categories of crime, sexuality and youth were the raw materials from which the image of a violent society was constructed."[43] In the end

> the battle lines between "society" and its "enemies" were more clearly drawn by the end of the seventies than they had been for decades. This was because responses to crisis had taken a specific course, with hegemony being secured on the basis of ever more loose definitions of the enemy within. The cause of the crisis was constructed through ideas about externality and criminality which supported a view of blacks as an "outside" force, an alien *malaise* afflicting British society.[44]

This demonization of the blacks in the UK antedates Thatcher, as do the sources of conflict which accompany political decline and economic crisis. But only in the current phase have British blacks borne so heavily the deplacement costs of decline, measured in material privation and racist attack. Until Thatcher — although in declining proportion in the waning Callaghan years — governments introduced social welfare and urban policies which were designed to treat the "problems" — education, employment, social services — associated with the black presence. While ideologically pernicious in transmuting problems of poverty in stagnating capitalism into problems of race, there were nevertheless some material benefits. Likewise, despite the weakness of race relations boards and the hollowness of accompanying legislation, at least lip service was paid to integration and a small set of grievances were positively resolved.

But as the 1970s wore on, increased police powers, not improved social services, became the focus of governmental interest in improving "race relations." Thatcher inherited a most congenial emphasis on the "control and containment of forms of black resistance against racial domination."[45] But in the end, only Thatcher has molded public demagoguery and the threat (and subsequent practice) of declining public services into an electoral strategy which guarantees blacks both unequal material privation and an increased tempo of social victimization. Responses to the urban riots in the spring and summer of 1981, and especially in the fall of 1985 — the references to "tinderbox ghettos" and "gangs of criminals"[46] — implies only more of the same.

At last the meaning behind Thatcher's stirring call after the British capture of Port Stanley, that the "spirit of the Falklands" be turned to the tasks at home, becomes clear. Strategic racism makes the blacks in the heart of the empire, their uprisings against repression and their calls for cultural autonomy — their mere presence on "this crowded island" — an affront to white English sovereignty and the nation within. Likewise, the Argentine capture of the Falklands was an assault on those principles far away in the South Atlantic. How much more threatening the struggle at home? Every Brixton is a potential *Belgrano*, and there are no "exclusion zones." Threats must be met with brutal and unmistakable force.

Thus, not simply racism but the strategic application of racial prejudice — as police suspicion, as electoral tactic, as economic policy, as the categorical division of the population into "them" and "us" — is pure Thatcher. It is the intended and successful culmination of a complex de-integrative strategy which is also expressed with unmistakable political force in the hard class edge of Thatcher's industrial relations strategy.

Industrial relations

Throughout the period of the rise and fall of the KWS until Thatcher, British governmental efforts to reduce industrial strife, canalize the political power of trade unions, and increase productivity by limiting wage increases have been mainly of two kinds. On the one hand, governments have sought to implement statutory restrictions on trade union rights (for example, in the 1972 Industrial Relations Act of the Heath government). On the other hand, efforts have been made to expand TUC integration in the conduct of macroeconomic policy and therefore to involve trade union elites in the enforcement of wage restraints (most notable in the series of Social Contracts negotiated by the 1974–1979 Labour government, initially, with the TUC and later with particular trade unions). In fact, both Labour and Conservative governments have tried each approach — legislative restriction and political integration — with only fleeting success, and the alternation of the two approaches represents only one instance of the UK's notorious "stop—go" policy upheavals.

There are strong indications that the Thatcher government has altered this pattern — by application of a decisive de-integrative strategy. Huw Benyon and Peter McMylor have observed that:

> From the beginning, Thatcher had been anxious to break the old consensus . . . . The old class compromises were not for her, neither were collective forms of life and relationships. With all *corporate* forms apparently in crisis, the powerful articulation of individualism was made to seem both fresh and plausible. In this way of thinking, the phrase "right to work" became deflected from its original social-democratic meaning of a *public* commitment to full employment, towards a citizen's right to sell, unhindered, one's labour as *individual* in the market-place.[47]

This ideological shift has prefigured a fundamental change in the meaning of labor—management disputes. They have become, under Thatcher, an opening for defeating trade unions, reducing their industrial and political influences, and restructuring the balance of forces in society: from the public to the private sector; from the trade unions back to the private owners and managers. Thatcher's industrial strategy, like that of the KWS governments, involves legislation, but direct confrontation replaces the second tack of political integration.

The first element of these strategies involves to date three pieces of legislation — the Employment Acts of 1980 and 1982, and the Trade Union Act of 1984 — which legally "individuate" trade unions and substantially reduce the rights with which British trade unions have been collectively endowed since 1906. Taken together, these Acts (among other things): hold union officials as individuals financially and legally responsible for a wide range of illegal activities (including large-scale picketing, strikes to protest at government activity, and secondary strikes); severely restrict the institution of the "closed shop"; expand the ability of owners to dismiss strikers and union officials; and remove legal immunity from unions (and officials) who authorize otherwise legal industrial action without meeting particular balloting procedures.

Thatcher's second industrial relations strategy began, in a sense, even before the election of her government. Here the memory of the defeat of her Tory predecessor Edward Heath in 1974, when he used the occasion of a national miners' strike to call an election the Conservatives subsequently lost, has figured prominently in Thatcher's policy. Soon after becoming leader, but before the 1979 general election, two internal Conservative Party reports commissioned by Thatcher apparently influenced her thinking considerably. In the first, Lord Carrington — Heath's energy minister — dispelled the belief, widely held by senior Tory officials, that Heath's failed showdown with the miners had been a consequence of weak leadership. Instead, argued Carrington, society was being challenged by strategically powerful and self-interested groups of workers, particularly in the energy sector. The society was at a disadvantage in such industrial disputes due to extreme economic dependence on electricity, and the fact that neither miners nor electricity-generating plant personnel could be replaced by the armed forces during a strike.

The second report, a widely leaked document written for Thatcher by Nicholas Ridley, laid a blueprint for a political plan to overcome the technological and organizational problems identified by Carrington. Referring to the likelihood of a "political threat," the Ridley Report urged a carefully orchestrated set of confrontations with energy sector unions beginning with the weak and divided and working up to an ultimate challenge to the National Union of Mineworkers (NUM) who had "defeated" the last Conservative government.[48]

The miner's strike of 1984—1985, it is widely agreed, was triggered by government threats to reduce substantially the size of the NUM workforce and — in an application of pure Ridley strategy — to challenge once and for all the political power and industrial clout of the NUM. It is a very rare postwar European government that would intentionally invite bitter and unregenerate class struggle in an effort to restore a political balance in class forces that was last seen in the UK in the 1920s, if then. It is a measure of Thatcher's radicalism, however, that with increased confidence and a second term in office, the deepening of her de-integrative strategy has come to absorb so crucial a part in the government's political agenda.

5

American Decline Management

Imperial decline means, above all, reduced options and riskier consequences. At different points in the arc of decline the range of choices available to post-hegemonic powers varies considerably, and the political legerdemain of ruling elites reflects the very different options they have left to pursue. Thus the UK and the USA greeted post-boom capitalism in radically different circumstances.

A middle-rank power in the postwar international order, the UK had long since lost the ability to control international events. Suez demonstrated what de Gaulle's rejection of British entry into the European Community confirmed — and Wilson's futile efforts to save sterling all belabored — the obvious fact that Britannia ruled no more. Worse, decisions made in Washington or Bonn — or by the controlled anarchy of international bankers — could defeat British economic strategies and harm domestic political fortunes. Thus the very drama of Wilson's long campaign to save the pound helped obscure for a time the inevitability of devaluation and the structural erosion of British economic performance and global influence which the decline of sterling represented.

Such self-deception by British elites had profound consequences. Not realizing that stagflation, the newest American import would scuttle any "dash for growth" strategy and direct considerable UK investment overseas, Heath engaged in increasingly brittle, high-risk (and in the end unsuccessful) confrontations — verbal taunts at the City, financial attacks on public sector employees, direct political assaults on the trade unions and, in particular, the miners, perhaps the strongest and most politicized among them. His integrity intact but his judgement reviled on all sides, Heath brought down with him the best hopes of one-nation Toryism. Likewise, never understanding the full measure of its impotence, the Callaghan government squandered its considerable capital with Labour's working-class base. Playing the IMF card and cutting wages while prices rose, the government succeeded only in advertising the apparent futility of the Keynesian laborist formula. At a stroke it destroyed the historic vision of a society motivated by social justice and secured by artful compromise, a vision which it had taken a fragmented and uncertain labor movement 75 years to construct.

The trajectory of decline has a different logic in the US from that in the UK, and the US case occasions a different periodization. In the UK decline is expressed in the gradual transformation of political parties, and by the discrete shifts in the center of gravity in each major party. Labour replaces Conservative as the natural party of governance in the postwar and post-hegemonic order only to lose its place decisively with the collapse of the Keynesian social democratic vision on a grand scale during the period of the post-1973 recession.

In the United States, by contrast, parties seem almost beside the point and administrations become the natural focus of attention. To be sure, the construction of the meaning of epochal events by foreign policy elites may influence geopolitical postures which span several administrations. Thus, the "Pearl Harbor paradigm" encouraged aggressive interventionism until a new "Vietnam paradigm" (expressed in Nixon's Guam doctrine) absolved the United States of primary responsibility for the defense of all allied territories.[1] Likewise, existing institutions, like those inaugurated at Bretton Woods, will limit the range of options available to any administration so long as the fundamental rules which govern the conduct of the international economic order endure. Nevertheless, each administration must choose its own path for stabilizing the uneasy alliance between domestic Keynesianism and the international liberalism of Bretton Woods, free trade, and multilateralism. Equally significant, pre-eminence has conferred on the US the signal privilege of imposing a set of self-interested designs on the rest of the world.

As the scale of its pre-eminence declined, US macroeconomic and fiscal policy — from Kennedy's New Economics to the Nixon

Revolution, from Volcker's strategy at the close of the Carter years to the deficit-building of Reagan — have represented hard-nosed American efforts to displace the costs of decline and maintain maximal geopolitical influence at minimal cost. At each step the US has tried to use its leverage to "export its disequilibrium."[2]

The story that follows suggests how difficult that task had become by the close of the 1970s. Declining competitiveness accompanied by watershed foreign policy reversals — Vietnam, the fall of the Shah of Iran — shattered the uneasy coexistence between international liberalism and mild welfarist Keynesianism. The two central conditions, growth as the solvent of domestic disputes, and US control of a Western bloc — in military, foreign policy and economic terms — had been significantly eroded. Hence Carter's assertion of the United States' loss of confidence in the future was consistent both with a President's genuine sense of loss of mastery in a post-hegemonic international order and with a politician's fear that an aging growth coalition which made an internationalist and welfarist agenda possible was irretrievably lost.

At the close of the war, however, there was little concern given to potential weaknesses in American economic performance or to the possibility that US military and geopolitical influence would not always remain unchallenged. It is often said that the structure of an international monetary order reflects the degree of leverage that the most powerful nation can exert over its rivals.[3] This was never more true than in the system of agreements for fixed exchange rates and ready convertibility of gold which the US coercively extracted from its grateful allies in the backwoods of New Hampshire in July, 1944.

HEGEMONY NOT YET LOST: THE ERA OF BRETTON WOODS

In fact the deal that was cut in Bretton Woods was no deal at all, certainly not the "New Deal in international economics" touted by an official in the Treasury Department. Throughout the war Keynes, serving as an adviser to the British Treasury, and Harry Dexter White, the most influential and technically gifted economist working at the US Treasury, considered designs for the postwar monetary system. They shared much common ground, although in the end differences of interest forced some significant divergence, and Congressional and business pressure on White forced dramatic reversals. As Alan Wolfe observes:

> Hoping to reorganize the international system to prevent depression and war, both men put their faith in international liquidity. Their idea was that an expansion of the global economy would give each national economy more wealth, thereby providing a "floor" that could prevent a vicious cycle leading into depression.[4]

From there, however, national interests determined different points of emphasis. Representing a state in certain decline, Keynes proposed generous credits to assure liquidity in times of need. He battled strenuously for a clearing house which could be "a genuine organ of international government,"[5] dispersing funds of almost unlimited size — $32 billion in liquidity — and with no power to require revisions in domestic macroeconomic arrangements or social welfare policies as a condition for the receipt of funds. Whatever else it might mean — and how diffuse its meaning was in the US context will soon become clear — Keynesianism represented a strategy to restore full employment through government spending during times of decreased private investment. At the least Keynes wanted the fund to have sufficient resources and independence to permit weak economies to pursue counter-cyclical spending strategies and to pressure stronger countries to reduce their balance of payment surpluses. At the worst he wanted a UK which would be dependent on international credits to suffer as little as possible. Thus he preferred the automatic provision of credit through an active agency representing the multilateralism of an open international order to an intrusive vehicle of American parochialism.

Despite White's sympathy for Keynes' views in his own early drafts of the plan and the early appearance of compromise, however, the institution which was finally created at Bretton Woods reflected US national interest. In the end White's overriding concern was that Republican financial and isolationist interests not have sufficient opportunity to seize on specific points of the agreement in order to defeat Congressional approval.[6] At Bretton Woods, White dismantled the Keynesianism of the proposal piece by piece: the liquidity was reduced to $9 billion; drawing rights became conditional on domestic economic concessions; and pressures on balance-of-payments surplus nations were eliminated. Indeed, the whole meaning of the IMF had shifted toward the institutionalization of *Pax Americana*. As Wolfe notes:

> Rather than protecting vulnerable economies from a depression, which had been the original idea, the fund was becoming a device to ensure the dependence of poor countries on the market. The IMF that came out of Bretton Woods, like domestic macroeconomic planning in the United States, was counter-Keynesian, designed to do the opposite of its original reformist intention. Keynes himself agreed to these changes only with the greatest reluctance, knowing that America had the power in these matters and that the choice was between a fund on American terms or no fund at all.[7]

The remaining 42 nations acquiesced to the terms. What else could they do, particularly once the UK had submitted? "They looked to us for their military salvation and for their economic salvation," noted one American participant, "and any proposal within human reason put forward by representatives of the United States would in the nature of things be acceptable."[8] The inaugural meeting of the International Bank for Reconstruction and Development, in Savannah, Georgia in March, 1946, deepened British foreboding about the intentions of the Americans to make the most of their supreme position. On each issue still at odds — the location, the duty of the directors, their pay — the US demanded and obtained its hegemonic prerogatives. An editorial in the *Manchester Guardian* reflected UK opinion on the bitter fruits of the Anglo-American alliance on monetary matters.

> [T]he conference appears to have been a most unhappy experiment in post-war monetary co-operation. The American Treasury which in these matters seems at present to take the lead over the State Department, massed its voting powers and ran the conference in a rigidly domineering manner. Every proposal put forward by the American delegation was pressed through with steam-roller tactics, and the delegation seems to have made no secret of its belief that

the United States, which pays the piper, has a right to call the tune. In fact, the worst fears of those who had always warned us that this was what the United States meant by international economic co-operation were borne out at Savannah.[9]

Keynes may have expected that with the agreement through Congress, and thus the political pressure abated, White and his Treasury colleagues would return to the New DEal internationalism of their early proposals. But if he had such sanguine hopes he was to be disappointed. As Richard Gardner observed, "Keynes was shaken by the results of the Savannah conference"[10] — and for good reason. Against the majority of the directors of the Bank of England who objected to the Bretton Woods agreement, Keynes had defended the Americans boldly, most notably in an impassioned address in the House of Lords, where he affirmed the United States' "honest purpose" and assured doubters of their responsible intentions.[11] Now, "at Savannah, it seemed as if all his fine protestations on behalf of American goodwill and co-operativeness were belied," Roy Harrod, Keynes' biographer noted poignantly, "His castles were falling around him."[12]

The dream of an organization that would pursue policy above national political designs and offer generous benefits and loans *automatically* to promote economic recoveries and full employment policies was now gone. Politics, and jingoist power politics at that, only thinly leavened with internationalist sentiments, held sway. An American financial columnist accurately noted that each decision by the Bank or the Fund would be "as political as a troop movement."[13]

Hard-nosed decisions in New Hampshire and Georgia set the tone and the substance of 25 years of American international economic policies, and this in turn crucially shaped the whole physiognomy of domestic US politics. David Calleo has noted that "[t]he World's monetary system is generally a metaphor for its political system."[14] Bretton Woods institutionalized and served as a metaphor for the first and longest phase of US imperial rule, from the close of the war to Nixon's NEP announcement in 1971, when at its height hegemonic multilateralism abroad delivered the goods for a growth economy and a Keynesian domestic policy at home, in fact if not in name.

There were, to be sure, crucial differences in the way successive postwar governments earned support and framed their macroeconomic strategies, as there was wide variation in the foreign policies they pursued and the constituencies they served. But from Eisenhower, the first who administered the postwar calm, to Johnson, the last who combined Keynesian and multilateralist elements in a hegemonic design, they all were motivated by a common belief. For them it was axiomatic that American military and technological pre-eminence set the terms for a new world order in which growth accompanied geopolitical power and domestic Keynesianism perfectly complemented international liberalism.[15]

THE SLOW DAWNING OF A NEW ERA

This vision was no less pervasive for it being naive or self-serving. It was no less powerful as a call to arms for almost every postwar American administration simply because it mistook transitory circumstances for permanent truths and ignored the cracks which were threatening to wreck the structure of the international economic order.

The problem with the new system was that it was both too visionary and outdated virtually from the moment of its inception. Calleo has noted:

> The arrangements decided at Bretton Woods proved highly premature.... After the terrible destruction and dislocation of the War, European powers could not sustain the exchange rates of their currencies against the dollar without tight exchange controls.[16]

It was too early in the cycle of recovery to make operational the Bretton Woods principles of liberal convertability: European economies were too weak in the short run to float their currencies against the dollar without substantial exchange controls. Yet it was already too late to assume the degree of American pre-eminence in the world economy that was required to make the system work.

For the US dollar to effectively fulfill its dual function as national currency and international reserve currency backed by gold, the

US had to supply the world with sufficient dollars to permit steady growth and accumulation. But, as Cohen and Rogers note bluntly:

> [F]looding the world with dollars effectively meant that the United States had to run balance of payments deficits, or deficits on the overall account of its trade and capital flows with the rest of the world. And such imbalances between what an economy takes in and what it puts out, cannot continue forever.[17]

Ironically, the agreement whose passage expressed the full measure of American geopolitical leverage and economic authority, served in the end to foster US decline.

An overly strong dollar makes imports relatively cheap compared to domestic commodities, and pushes US investment abroad. Accordingly, for a time, the prosperity of the multinationals and the size of the trade surpluses tended to obscure a growing decline in American competitiveness. Industrial productivity and the growth rate of total fixed capital stock lagged significantly behind that of Japan and Germany almost continuously throughout the postwar period[18] as the real value of US direct investment abroad grew at well over twice the rate of gross domestic product.[19] The US share of total manufacturing goods in the capitalist West fell from an amazing 60 percent at the time of Bretton Woods to roughly 30 percent 30 years later, and in the 20-year period from 1956 to 1976 the US share of worldwide exports declined from 25.5 percent to 17.3 percent.[20] In the end it would take the shock of a dangerous run on gold reserves and the first absolute deficit (when at last trade and investment surpluses could not offset capital deficits) to trigger Nixon's revolutionary withdrawal from the principles of Bretton Woods. As Block observes, US officials schooled in the gospel of American pre-eminence had difficulty acknowledging the danger signals of decline.

> American policy-makers were slow to recognize that the US balance-of-payments deficit was a reflection of more basic contradictions in the world economy. They continued to see the deficit as a relatively superficial problem for some time after the drain on the US gold stock first became an issue in 1958. Those policy makers assumed that the deficit would be solved simply by pressuring the Western

European nations to modify their economic behavior because the American policy-makers thought of American international dominance as undiminished.[21]

While this comforting myopia continued, American economic management remained, for better or worse, relatively uncomplicated. For the first quarter-century of the postwar era, the full effect of the contradictions of the US position at the apex of the international economic order could be forestalled. Domestic Keynesianism and the international liberalism of free trade and ready convertibility of currencies were never the natural allies that policy-makers supposed, but the postwar cluster of administrations from Eisenhower to Nixon (before August, 1971) oriented macroeconomic policies within these familiar parameters.

KEYNESIANISM IN AMERICA

At least one side of the hegemonic dualism — Keynesianism at home, liberalism abroad — requires some immediate clarification. There is much dispute about the meaning of Keynesianism, not least between economists and those directly viewing the social consequences of economic policy, but also concerning the applicability of the term to the United States. For a start, it is best to admit that it is the politics of Keynesianism, and the transformation of the world of macropolitics and social policy in the age of Reagan and Thatcher, that tilt the balance in the definition here.

What "Keynes really meant" is not the issue — but what the "Keynesian era" signified for British and American governing strategies. Prime Minister James Callaghan, in summarizing the rise and fall of Keynesianism in England before the 1976 Labour Party conference, makes clear what Keynesian meant during the period of the KWS in Britain:

> We used to think that you could spend your way out of a recession, and increase employment by cutting taxes and boosting government expenditure. I tell you in all candor that the option no longer exists, and in so far as it ever did exist, it only worked on each occasion

since the war by injecting a bigger dose of inflation into the economy, followed by a higher level of unemployment as a next step.[22]

Callaghan's remarks, coming as they did during the period of his government's capitulation to the IMF credit terms, indicate the dimensions of the Labour Party's conversion. By 1976 they had come to consider inflation to be a co-equal evil with unemployment, and had withdrawn from the programmatic basis of classic British Keynesianism.

In the US, Keynesianism has not involved such a unitary focus on the problems of employment, and may be gauged instead by reference to a new social vision and a different set of assumptions about state management of the economy. In the US, Keynesian society was an exercise in coalition building — the political integration of previously marginal social groups and the harmonization of diverse constituencies — in the singular American sense, set against the backdrop of a very shallow welfare state.

During the same 25-year period a new way of doing macroeconomics dominated state economic management. It was a pragmatic vision which considered unemployment only one of many economic problems, and finally rejected the socialist implications of Keynes's famous remark at the end of his *General Theory* that "the outstanding faults of the economic society in which we live are its failures to provide full employment and its arbitrary and inequitable distribution of wealth."[23] It also, however, rejected the dogma of budget balancing at all cost, and accepted that the modern postwar order required a state which, in its macroeconomic policy interventions, might intrude on the sanctity of private capitalist prerogative to order and autonomously allocate a society's economic resources. Herbert Stein notes clearly the dimensions — and the open questions — of the new consensus Keynesianism in postwar America.

> By the end of 1949 the country had reached a consensus on fiscal policy which was a long way from traditional ideas of annual budget balance and from the early post-Keynesian ideas of compensatory finance. We would not try to balance recession budgets by raising taxes, or by cutting expenditures. In recessions of some exceptional degree of severity we would do more than accept the automatically resulting deficit and take affirmative steps to enlarge the deficit. In

contrast to earlier thinking about deficit spending, these steps were more likely to be on the revenue side of the budget than on the expenditure side. And we would in general look to some version of balancing the budget in prosperous conditions as a norm. We would not expect positive fiscal measures to respond to and counteract every actual or forecast departure from the high-employment target, but would accept the principle that in fiscal policy, as in many things, striving for the best may be the enemy of achieving the good. Also in contrast to earlier "new" economics, we would give a considerable role to monetary policy as the partner of fiscal policy.[24]

However mild it was in the US, the Keynesian revolution was nonetheless significant. Perhaps it was especially important in the US where social democratic visions and economically activist governments cut against the grain, and the international conse-quences of macroeconomic policy are so widespread. American Keynesianism represented a shift in elite perceptions and a coherent era in social and economic values which came and went and which, to a surprising degree, fostered a common arc of policies in an otherwise disparate set of American administrations.

At least until the Vietnam War signaled the end of an era of unchallenged geopolitical influence, Keynesianism provided the suitable domestic balance to particular images of dominance abroad. Thereafter the trade-offs between domestic policy ends and international geopolitical designs became increasingly hard-edged. In this sense Eisenhower's equal caution in domestic and foreign policy marks the last easy confluence of the inner and outer dimensions: mild Keynesianism without the ideology at home, pragmatic internationalism and mild anti-Sovietism abroad.

By the Kennedy years *Pax Americana* was already coming undone, and no excess of youthful New Frontierism could deliver the policy package of international liberalism and domestic Keynesianism without a growth economy. Then, oddly, Carter's trilateralism and defeat confirmed politically what Nixon's NEP demonstrated in the international economic order — that in the end more limited hegemonic ambitions follow naturally from the acceptance of declining economic capacities. Their defeats, in turn, proved that in domestic American politics an acceptance of decline may have serious repercussions. It remained for Reagan to re-unify domestic and international policy, and to arrest the decline in presidential control over a post-hegemonic order by denying the very fact of US decline. This is an extraordinary task, and one very different from that which greeted American policy-makers at the end of the war.

LESS IS MORE

In the early days of the postwar world, "[a]ltruism and self-interest worked hand in hand,"[25] and this was never more true than during the Eisenhower administration, when the untrammeled growth of US corporate investment anchored American profits but also encouraged unparalleled growth in the capitalist west. But cynicism and jingoism were never far from the surface. After all, through the Central Intelligence Agency the Eisenhower administration toppled Mohammed Mossadagh in Iran and Jacobo Arbenz in Guatemala in its first 2 years in office. Nevertheless, it must be said that, for a general and an American President, Eisenhower's cautionary approach to the use of military options to secure foreign policy objectives is noteworthy, and his record is more remarkable for what did not happen.

After the Soviet's atomic test of 1949 illustrated dramatically that the US would not long maintain a nuclear monopoly, Truman had ordered the National Security Council to assess Soviet capacities and intentions. The result, NSC-68, symbolized the emergence of the "growth consensus." The report urged a vast increase in the military budget and saw this necessary build-up linked to an expanding economy, pushed forward through government demand stimulation.[26] Early in Eisenhower's second term a report to the NSC by the Security Resources Panel of the Science Advisory Council — the Gaither Report of September, 1957 — included the same message of cold war militarism and drastic growth. This formula represents, in fact, another expression of Keynesianism in America. NSC-68 and the Gaither report were eloquent pleas for military Keynesianism,[27] with bipartisan and powerful domestic support and extremely able political brokerage behind them. After the Korean War Eisenhower, however, declined these options and apart from modest increases in military spending in 1958—1959 to "cushion the effects of a recession,"[28] he rejected the military Keynesian high-growth model.

Instead the Eisenhower administration offered a modern label for the old Republican inclination to ignore the world when possible, particularly if it helped balance the budget. Insisting that the retaliatory might of the US arsenal was sufficient to forestall Soviet aggression, the administration offered what it called a "New Look" foreign and military policy — and as late as 1957 proposed a 10 percent cut in defense spending.[29]

Eisenhower had a "complex on inflation"[30] and a healthy concern over the growing balance-of-payments problem endemic to the US role in the Bretton Woods system. But he had no complex on the Soviet threat, and would not sacrifice his fiscal orthodoxy needlessly. Indeed, Eisenhower's consensus Keynesianism permitted an unusual symmetry in the inner and outer worlds of domestic and foreign economic policies.

> [T]here were similarities between Eisenhower's hostility to urban public works projects and his support for the New Look. In both areas, Eisenhower was suspicious of using growth to reconcile political differences. Distrustful of big government and high taxes, Republicans in both domestic and foreign policy sought solutions that were fiscally orthodox. Eisenhower seemed happier mouthing homilies than cultivating an image of problem-solving toughness. . . . The new look was a bit complacent, unmoved by perceptions of an immediate crisis.[31]

Of course there was no immediate crisis, just the first signs that political elites recognized the end of unfettered growth and unchecked geopolitical influences. Eisenhower maintained a steady course, guided by pragmatism and the tacit acceptance of Keynesian precepts. The administration accepted the idea that the economy required government action to increase stability and that "the fiscal instrument was one of the most powerful the government could use" to effect that end.[32] It is also worth remembering "Eisenhower's fat legacy" to Kennedy, a GNP still displaying modest rising trajectory and the recession of 1958 firmly survived, if not forgotten.[33] On balance it was a healthy economy and, even better for the new administration, it was just sluggish enough and sufficiently underutilized that it was marvellously poised for expansion.

KENNEDY

John F. Kennedy admitted with the kind of bravado only Camelot myths inspire that he had a hard time remembering the difference between monetary policy and fiscal policy. So, when in doubt, he remembered that the head of the Federal Reserve, William McChesney Martin, had a last name starting with "M" like the "M" in monetary policy.[34] As untutored in state economic management as this story suggests he was in the early days of his administration, by 1963 Kennedy had clearly become a "convert" to Keynesianism, American style.[35] In this sense Kennedy's "new economics" is, as Walter Heller observes "the completion of the Keynesian revolution," and as Ronald Frederick King concludes, "The story of the Kennedy administration's economic policy is . . . that of the education of and by our first Keynesian president."[36]

With Kennedy the big brassy contradictions of *Pax Americana*, like everything else about his administration, emerged with new drama. A sluggish economy with room to grow had helped elect Kennedy, and 2 years of conventionally mild and studiously balanced stimulants — investment tax credits and increased depreciation allowances on the supply side and increased transfer payments in social security and government financing of public housing on the demand side — hardly amounted to a new frontier in economic strategy.

By 1962, however, Kennedy's economic program began to assume its characteristic direction. With Kennedy distressed at the growing deficit which flowed from defense expenditures in response to the "missile gap" and the Berlin crisis, Walter Heller, who chaired the Council of Economic Advisers, and others devoted to the Keynesian virtue of countercyclical government spending, made their move. As Calleo put it, "His advisers gave the President a crash course in Keynesian demand management and thereby rescued the country from a balanced budget."[37]

The particular fiscal instrument for the education of John Kennedy is in itself unremarkable, but the way it was justified has had considerable consequences. The policy was a tax cut, an idea first floated seriously in 1962, but the curious feature was its sophisticated Keynesian aspect. Fiscal orthodoxy called for tax cuts to stimulate investments during recessions, but 1962 was a growth year with GNP rising at 5.8 percent. The Kennedy team argued from a new premise; namely that fiscal calculations should presuppose an economy operating at full employment (whatever the actual capacity utilization or level of production). Counter-cyclical measures were needed, therefore, not only during actual recessions, but whenever the economy operated below capacity. Increased spending or decreased revenues were called for under those circumstances, to ensure that later in a cycle of recovery as growth increased government revenue would not act as a "fiscal drag," constraining the economy from growth spurred by private investment. Kennedy was won to the distinctive Keynesian logic: assuming a "full-employment budget" and full employment *later*, it's all right to cut taxes and further unbalance a budget *now* during a period of sizeable growth in GNP. Stein observed that "the idea of the fiscal drag was more firmly established in Kennedy's own thinking than any of the other fiscal concepts of his advisors."[38] True to this Keynesian credo, Kennedy replied with a convert's passion to a question in October, 1961, as to whether the administration would raise taxes to produce a balanced budget. "We don't want to," replied the President. "[W]e don't want to provide a tax structure which already is very heavy — and brings in tremendous receipts at full employment — we don't want it to result in waste of resources and manpower. So that's the judgment we must make."[39] Signed by Lyndon Johnson in February, 1964, the Kennedy tax cut represented a significant new direction in fiscal management. From this point, at least until the Reagan candidacy, deficits became the unquestioned rule in periods both of recession and of growth. In fact, from that day until this, only once has the US budget not registered a deficit.[40]

For the time being Keynesianism was secure, as a strategy of countercyclical demand management to wrest every fraction of growth and utilization out of an increasingly troubled economy. Keynesianism provided Kennedy with the "scientific" authority to purchase a glittering package of expensive domestic and foreign policy advertisements for the New Frontier, from the Manpower

Training Act and Medicare to the Peace Corps and the Alliance for Progress. Keynesianism was the theory behind the growth obsession, and the theory became undone only with the full unraveling of America's imperial design, a process much aided by Kennedy's restless ambition to push the US beyond all limits. The Kennedy global strategy was a gaudy display of contradictory impulses; but it was wrapped so effectively in appealing motives that it is difficult, even a quarter-century later, to reject as pure manipulation Kennedy's ambitious plans: to promote Third World development with US assistance; to foster European integration by pressing the UK's entry into the EEC; to support the ongoing development of a European trading bloc which would exclude the US.

For many a moral certainty about the United States' worldwide role unified the anomalous features of the Kennedy program. One observer of the Kennedy years notes:

> According to the fashionable doctrine of the sixties, after a certain stage, development could become self-sustaining and favorable to democracy. Communism was a childhood disease, to be held off by force, if necessary, until development had proceeded to "take off." Liberal faith in progress thus combined with Hobbesian faith in power. Hence, two characteristic innovations of the Kennedy Administration: the Peace Corps and the Green Berets.[41]

Imperial altruism was backed by the marines to preserve and extend the American field of geopolitical maneuver.

Growth would take care of the rest. In 1962 Kennedy created a cabinet-level committee on growth, and Walter Heller, in an unusual display of dialectical reasoning, explained that economic growth was "both an end in itself and an instrumentality, both the pot of gold and the rainbow."[42] As instrumentality it would, as Paul Samuelson another economic adviser noted, provide "healthful outlets for ambition, energy and adventure" and reduce the "discontent, frustration, irritability" that the opposite might bring.[43] More important, a non-zero-sum game of distribution would help the administration achieve the dream of Keynesian activists: civil peace, labor harmony, and even relative business confidence.

The political implications of growth even outweighed the economic, and the obsession with growth was at the core of New

Frontier imperial ambitions. Kennedy believed that economic performance would be the measure of victory in the global competition with the Soviet Union. American growth and the distribution of its benefits would demonstrate that despite the asymmetries of private ownership of production, all social groups would gain from prosperity. Beyond the economic payoff, therefore, growth would promote concord at home and encourage countries abroad to accept US leadership in the cold war struggle for international dominance.[44] Unfortunately for Kennedy and his successors, the domestic and international activism of the administration forced open fissures in the Bretton Woods system which modest growth could not obscure.

Under Truman and Eisenhower, NATO rearmament and the positioning of US forces overseas, US multinational investment abroad, and Marshall Plan and subsequent foreign aid packages had placed the US in a perilous balance-of-payments deficit. By the time the full convertibility provisions of Bretton Woods came into effect in 1958, "America's overseas liquid debts already exceeded its monetary reserves."[45] Thus Kennedy's insistence on an extensive overseas presence by US forces seriously aggravated the endemic balance-of-payments problems, making the connections between international economic liberalism and domestic Keynesian even harder to reconcile. Kennedy's more robust plan for US global influence fit very badly with his ideologically determined policy of trade liberalization which was enshrined in the 1962 Trade Expansion Act and the Kennedy Round of tariff negotiations. The dollar lost ground in overseas markets and US policy-makers worried about the prospect of the kind of speculative run permitted by Bretton Woods and intimated by the 1960 run on the London Gold Market. The Federal Reserve was bound by the agreement to provide gold for dollars on demand to foreign central banks, and American markets remained subject to short-term speculative assaults by private holders of currency. Even though US trade surpluses regularly offset capital deficits, there were growing problems. The costs of *Pax Americana* were considerable: overseas military expenditures, direct capital investment by US corporations, foreign aid.[46]

This was an imperial deficit, and aside from palliatives like unilateral agreements to stabilize the market price of gold, any cure would be worse than the disease. The welfarist vision of Keynesian society would be sacrificed to the demands of the empire. There are signs that Kennedy recognized the trap, but he could only gloss the consequences. In July, 1963, the President attempted to assure any doubters that he would not permit the balance-of-payments problem to force him to choose between his domestic and internationalist ambitions:

> Rejecting a choice between two equally impalatable alternatives — improved employment at home at the cost of a weaker economy and nation — we sought a new course that would simultaneously increase our growth at home, reduce unemployment and strengthen the dollar by eliminating the deficit in our international payments.[47]

It was not quite true, however, that he would refuse to choose; and it was impossible, in the end, that he or successive Presidents could avoid the consequences of his New Frontierism for ever. Defense and related costs amounted to nearly three-quarters of the increase in government expenditures during the Kennedy years, and the increase in welfare outlays during the 1962—1964 period amounted to only about 5 percent of the rise in GNP in the closing years of the Kennedy—Johnson administration. In the second quarter of 1963 the US suffered a record deficit of $5 billion in annual terms,[48] and in the end the administration was forced to try capital controls as the only way left to improve the declining balance-of-payments situation, however contrary to the tradition of economic liberalism they were. Their effectiveness would, of course, be swamped by the growing war in South-east Asia.

The scope of Kennedy's vision exceeded America's still great, but nevertheless declining, geopolitical and economic capacity. In the end his grand designs, domestic and international, controlled Johnson as they haunted Nixon, and "[t]ypically, but perhaps inevitably, the outcome was inflation, war, and a collapse of the dollar."[49] The Kennedy years thus mark both the high point and the point of no return in the United States' imperial trajectory.

AFTER KENNEDY

In many ways Johnson's collapse, Nixon's NEP, and Carter's

trilateralism were extrapolations from Kennedy's mix of domestic Keynesianism and activist foreign policies. First Johnson sent the uneasy balance crashing. Kennedy's overseas posturing fostered a growing trade deficit and constrained domestic spending programs. The fundamental incongruity between domestic Keynesianism and international liberalism in economic policy (plus militarism in foreign policy) was becoming increasingly clear. With Johnson the incongruity became a radical impossibility. To some extent the Great Society programs of the Johnson years worked the integrative miracle of the Keynesian social vision and bought, if not a period of social calm, at least a period of pacification through fragmentation. The urban riots were quelled, student activism contained, the edges of middle class expanded. But the extraordinary overseas military spending of the Vietnam era deepened the balance-of-payments crisis and pushed the dollar further downward in foreign markets.

With the US losing much of its economic comparative advantage the economy could no longer pay for such an excess of guns and butter. It wasn't growth but paper that paid the bills for Johnson, as Cohen and Rogers note.

> On top of already high levels of spending, between 1966 and 1970 an additional $106 billion was poured into the defense budget to help finance the war. Even under conditions of careful wartime fiscal controls, such an acceleration of military spending would have placed a strain on government finances. Under conditions of sagging international competitiveness, a variety of competing domestic claims on the economy, and a refusal to cover the costs of an increasingly unpopular way by raising taxes, its inflationary impact was manifest. The buildup was paid for by printing money.[50]

This situation could not last long, and did not. The most expensive program of social Keynesianism combined with the most militarist foreign policy of America's postwar empire pushed Kennedy Round trade policy and Bretton monetary liberalism to the edge. By the time the Kennedy Round tariff cuts occurred, many US firms, caught in a liquidity squeeze, with productivity declining and credit tight, were more harmed than helped; and by 1967 the now endemic pressure on the dollar and a crescendo of speculative crises forced the US in practice to abandon its Bretton

Woods promises to back each overseas dollar with gold on demand. There was little left of *Pax Americana*; neither peace nor the benefits of economic liberalism. Richard Nixon, electoral beneficiary but long-term loser in his efforts to manage the Democrats decline, "inherited from Johnson not only inflation and a feeble dollar, but also a structural trade deficit."[51]

From this point onward the options of decline management within the Keynesian gambit were limited. The structural fix was set. The problems were beyond the remedy of Keynesian fine-tuning and the growth which was needed to sustain welfare and warfare, a Keynesian society and a restive imperial ambition, was no longer possible. Stagflation would replace simple inflation. Protectionism and state-centrism in economic policy — a kind of neo-mercantilism — would erode the US internationalist stance. Bretton Woods, long moribund, would now formally be declared dead.

Nixon and Carter, shallow consensus Keynesians and innovative architects in a new era of hegemonic restraint, tried their best to organize the retreat from imperial glory. In a grand political gesture Nixon personally announced his wage-and-price freeze and the official suspension of the dollar's convertibility into gold or foreign currencies in August, 1971 — packaging perilous economic weakness as a New Economic Policy. It is not really his fault that he could never quite transform military defeat and economic decline into political success, although he almost did, but for Watergate.

Likewise, Carter inherited a much-diminished United States: the budget now, it seemed, permanently in serious deficit, interest rates moving upward to prove any burst of growth ephemeral, foreign competition hurting US producers, and foreign governments increasingly recalcitrant in the face of US pressure. The new strategy for imperial management — trilateralism — is especially notable for being the first to acknowledge decline. Democracy was in crisis, traditional values in flux. In the words of Michel Crozier, one author of *The Crisis of Democracy* report of the Trilateral Commission, "The more decisions the modern state has to handle, the more helpless it becomes."[52] Worse, as the trilateralists and their President, Jimmy Carter, recognized, new strategies were needed to meet a "structural crisis" in US and world capitalism.

Still within an integrative mold, Carter cut domestic social spending to the Keynesian consensus minimum. As William Tabb observed about Carter, "He is embarked on an economic policy very different from the welfare liberalism of a Kennedy or a Johnson and which goes well beyond the conventional budget cutting and special-interest favoring of Nixon and Ford."[53] The plan — not successful and politically damaging — was to hold down wages and reduce union bargaining rights and powers to make American industry more competitive again, and to return the US to its rightful place at the top of the international division of labor. Paul Volcker, chair of the Federal Reserve, slowed growth through tightening the money supply to quell a dollar crisis, while wage controls slowed growth, and heightened inflation created unemployment and reduced the living standards of many traditional Democratic constituencies.

Foreign initiatives now required extraordinary gestures and the artful manipulation of client states like Israel and Egypt to make the Camp David accords. But temperament and power reduced Carter's options abroad as the administration's response to the Soviet invasion of Afghanistan and the Iranian hostage crisis suggest. American politics is not a morality tale, and Carter's restraint in Iran and Afghanistan, and his insistence that human rights be involved in foreign policy decisions, served him worse, no doubt, than Nixon's venality in Vietnam and dangerous deceptions to retain power in the last days of his regime.

Where Eisenhower had succeeded in his modest goals, Kennedy pressed to the limit the imperatives of Keynesianism at home, economic liberalism and cold war militarism abroad: a combined agenda which could no longer be satisfied. Just as Johnson destroyed the boldest visions of Keynesian society and the grand designs of empire, Nixon and Carter discredited each party's reduced visions of hegemonic constraint and weak consensus Keynesianism. The options were exhausted. With this unlikely pair of Presidents, the postwar epoch of Keynesianism and *Pax Americana* ended.

6

The Roots of Reagan's Triumph

With influence over the terms of the international order flagging in the wake of the Nixon Revolution, a "national mood . . . of self-criticism bordering on masochism,"[1] and declining competitive advantage against trading partners by the close of the 1970s, the United States' situation invited a radical departure. The world recession which began with the oil crises of 1973 underscored and accentuated a trajectory of decline. From 1973 to 1980 the average annual productivity increase dropped to 1.7 percent (from a 3.2 percent average between 1948 and 1965), and in 1979 (as in 1974) productivity actually declined.

The contrast with other industrialized nations was significant. During the same 7-year period following the 1973 oil shock, German productivity increased at an annual rate of 4.8 percent, French productivity by 4.9 percent, the EC averaged an increase of 3.8 percent, and Japan's productivity improved by an average annual rate of 7.2 percent.[2] At the same time the United States suffered increased import penetration, as the percentage of imported goods purchased by Americans increased during the decade of the 1970s from 7 percent to more than 22 percent.[3]

Despite the challenges of the 1970s, the United States remained the pre-eminent military force and the most productive world economy.[4] Nevertheless, the US was significantly squeezed in terms of economic competitiveness as it lost control over a world economy on which it was also increasingly dependent. Moreover the US, whose foreign policy elites had never recovered from the loss of the Vietnam War, had been beaten in turn by OPEC and Khomeini, and had been rebuffed by allies in a series of efforts to pressure the Soviets after the invasion of Afghanistan — an action, in itself, which represented a considerable foreign policy defeat for adherents of detente.

It was time for a change, certainly, not only in candidate and narrow partisan appeal, but in the construction of a political agenda and in the definition of a national image. Leaving behind the KWS domestic vision and dismissing the mood of self-doubt, Reagan re-asserted the United States' hegemonic destiny. With artful presentation he consolidated a new social and political geography, and the United States' old Keynesian—internationalist coalition, like Labour's social democratic consensus in the UK, was left on the political switchback.

In this sense Reagan's agenda, precisely because it flies in the face of the realities of the post-hegemonic international order, demonstrates the extent of the US decline. The economic implications of decline are considerable, but the political and cultural implications are perhaps even more significant. Above all else, Reagan is the electoral expression of a culture of defeat — Vietnam and Iran, the dollar, stagflation and unemployment — and fear — of reduced life chances, fear by men of women, fear by middle-aged, middle Americans of the fragmentation of society, and the lingering *Weltanschauung* of the 1960s.

In some sense the answer to the "why Reagan?" question is too easy. Economic stagnation and declining global influence broke a 30-year consensus. The era of economic liberalism abroad and Keynesianism at home was finished. In the United States, compared to the United Kingdom, the collapse of elite consensus on the core strategies of government transformed the prospects of parties less, but individuals and attendant ideologies much more. There is a *dealignment* in American electoral politics, as many have noted,

> associated with the near-collapse of the intermediary vote of political parties in shaping voting decisions in recent decades, and the resort by more and more voters to other cues (notably those provided by public relations imagery and television) to their vote — that is, if they vote at all.[5]

As an unemployed millionaire, Reagan was definitely suited to the 2-year pre-nomination marathon of self-promotion and presidential primary electioneering.[6] As an actor and simplistic ideologue and the supremely homey orator, Reagan was of course a master at manipulating the now essential media cues of American political success. There are deeper issues involved, however, in the Reagan triumph.

THE POLITICAL OPENING

The erosion of empire and the collapse of the Keynesian—internationalist consensus left a political opening for some radical alternative, and the structural weakening of the American economy tended strongly to push the opening to the right. While growth seemed possible, economic liberalism and domestic spending on social programs could be justified. While economic expansion was considered likely, the actual Democratic lead over the Republicans in acknowledged party identification of 45 to 25[7] and the permanent hint of a potentially resurgent New Deal/Kennedy coalition of blue-collar, ethnic, urban, black and Hispanic voters made the Democrats the "natural party" of government. When the Keynesian—internationalist system stopped paying dividends the stock of the Democratic Party fell considerably, and the New Deal ideologies were eclipsed. As Walter Dean Burnham observed:

> Conservatives and Republicans suffered for a very long time from their class and ethnocultural narrowness of outlook. The Democratic coalition enjoyed such long-term ascendancy as it had precisely because 'the nature of the times' seemed to permit Americans to have it both ways: to gain the benefits of the political-capitalist state without having to pay excessive costs, and to enjoy the pleasures of continually rising affluence and — for many — rising social status as well. In such a world, it seemed that only cranky ideological perfectionists and corporate oligarchs would be likely to decry the passing of relatively Simon-pure laissez-faire.[8]

When the world changed, Reagan's New Right coteries were finally able to capture the White House; for the changes in the macroeconomy had also transformed the United States' political culture.

New frontiers had given way to old fears and misgivings on the right and the left, in the corporate world and in grass-roots United States. Alan Wolfe has written of the much-heralded Report of the Trilateral Force on Governability of Democracies distributed in May, 1975:

> Pessimism and authoritarianism pervade the report . . . from start to finish. In both Europe and the United States all the traditional agencies of what political scientists call political socialization are seen as falling apart. People are no longer deferential, accepting as inviolate what established authorities tell them. The value structure of society has changed, and new expectations have revolutionized political life. . . . Cut loose from ties of obedience and traditional values, people begin to make political demands on the state. The result is an overload of inputs which cannot be met by government.[9]

Writing the European section of the report for the Commission, Michel Crozier did little more than paraphrase Jurgen Habermas's *Legitimation Crisis* — a leading mid-seventies work on the state by the "most influential thinker in Germany"[10] who inspired a generation of left social scientists in Europe and the US. So Crozier and Habermas repeated the pattern of surprisingly similar observations among intellectual opponents that Daniel Bell and Herbert Marcuse had begun a decade earlier. These prominent right and left thinkers accepted common themes despite basic political disagreements: in the sixties, the decline of ideological commitment, and, then, in the seventies, the erosion of belief structures which motivated participation in capitalism's economic hierarchies. The message was clear: the state is no longer able to accommodate the increased demands made on it. In some sense there was a dead heat between the trilateralists and the progressive intellectuals, as the *crisis of democracy* trumpeted by the right and the *legitimation crisis* heralded by the left equally inspired each set of academic rivals. Moreover, both — although here, very much unequally — contributed to a generalized media-hyped spirit of fragmentation, malaise, and anxiety for what was to come.

Apart from academic debates, however, there was really no contest. Not only was the right organized and funded, it had in Reagan and the shambles of the post-Nixon Republican Party, an exceptional vehicle for political unification and the successful promotion of a wide — and deep — set of instinctive concerns about the way things had been and could be again.

For many, student activism, poor people's campaigns, the anti-war movement, and what Beer calls the "romantic revolt" were what made the sixties.[11] And, to be sure, the women's movement altered in profound ways the psychic balance and challenged the deeply rooted norms of society in the seventies. Unfortunately for the American left, however, a robust and varied movement of a very different character was growing, more quietly but probably with greater force. Mike Davis summarizes well the pattern of middle-class, middle-American backlash which accompanied the hard squeeze in economic prospects, particularly for residents of the "frost-belt" states of the North and East.

> Grassroots political mobilization during the 1970s was on the whole an inverse mirror-image of that of the 1960s. If the latter decade was dominated by the mass civil rights movement, followed by the new student left and various cognate liberation currents, then the 1970s were, without quite so much sound and fury, the decade of the revanchist middle strata. In the mid-1960s thousands demonstrated in the South for school integration and educational opportunity; a decade later hundreds of thousands of Northern whites counter-marched, even rioted, to prevent the school busing necessary to accomplish this integration. If the nodal activist organizations of the 1960s were SNCC and SDS, those of the seventies were groups like BUSSTOP (Los Angeles) and the innumerable taxpayers leagues.[12]

Ideologies were back, fears were tapped, organizations were being built: and a President was being created. As Hugh Heclo and Rudolph Penner wrote:

> Reagan's candidacy represented the culmination of almost fifteen years of grassroots political agitation and organization across the nation. Following the Republican defeat of 1964, multi-faceted populism of the Right gradually evolved at the local level of American politics. It was a stream of political persuasions with many currents — of unabashed patriotism in a time of self-doubt about American power; of social conservatism alarmed at permissive "lifestyles"; of resentment against high taxes and high-handed bureaucrats. As the 1970s unfolded, it was a set of inclinations

mobilized and sharpened by new direct-mail techniques and heavy investments in conservative media outlets and think tanks.[13]

Reaganism was no accident. Each element of his appeal — the populist anti-state, anti-welfarist rhetoric, the Manichean cast of foreign policy, and the no-pain promises of supply-side economics — succeeded at least in part because of objective circumstances. As many have argued, "multinationally oriented, free trade conscious business groups comprised the hegemonic element in Jimmy Carter's 1976 campaign."[14] With the rate of real growth dropping from 1978 onwards, however, a dollar crisis mounting, the energy shortage of 1979 and the collapse of the Shah, American corporate elites "suffered something like a collective nervous breakdown," note Ferguson and Rogers.

> Spurred by the increasingly apparent inability of the United States to influence the unpredictable Khomeini regime, American business woke up to the threat posed by instability in the Third World generally. Many of the biggest firms involved in Iran — notably the big commercial banks and the oil and construction companies — were driven almost to distraction by the awful thought that something similar could happen in Saudi Arabia. . . . [T]he chorus of voices demanding rearmament swelled to an insistent roar.[15]

Carter's misfortune and the deepening scissors effect of the inter-nationalization of the American economy at last shattered the Keynesian-growth-internationalist consensus which had held together for a long 30 years.

In the end, Carter's moderation in the use and threat of military force was self-defeating. A reduction in military provocations and threats of war — like a more sustained detente between the Soviets and the Americans — made allies less dependent on the US for security.[16] They were thus more likely to challenge American efforts to parry military supremacy and economic influence into a set of foreign policy commitments, and US elites were encouraged in turn to raise the level of military raillery to force the allies back into line. This imperial heat-up accompanied the swift cooling of economic growth, and the decisive decline of Democratic Party fortunes. Even the trilateralists deserted Carter, switching camp in the eleventh hour, and leading Reagan from the nether world of Goldwater's 1964 defeat to a new mainstream in American politics.[17]

There was a double-edged genius to Reagan's campaign for hegemonic renewal. As one observer noted:

> The decay of empire and economy, taken together, has created optimal conditions for skilled conservative political entrepreneurs to offer the most consoling and least disturbing way out of the impasse. This quite literally involves a return to the "good old days" when the exactions of the state did not press so heavily on the individual, when the empire was strong and our position within it was unchallenged and when proper standards of social and cultural morality were maintained without question.[18]

Reagan's message was comforting, promising a return to the 1950s in geopolitical terms and to the 1920s domestically.[19] The election was, in comparison, unremarkable.

THE ELECTION

Reagan won the easy way in 1980 as Neil R. Peirce and Jerry Hagstrom observed,

> by scoring extraordinary majorities among normally Republican segments of the electorate, winning a majority of independents and cutting deeply into the traditional New Deal Coalition that gave Jimmy Carter his narrow win in 1976.[20]

Only the "party of non-voters" gave Reagan a run for his money. Reagan won because he had a constituency — in fact he had several, some distinct and some overlapping — and Carter had none or more accurately none mobilized or sufficient to the task. Carter held his 1976 support only among blacks, who gave him 82 percent of their votes.[21] By socioeconomic status, Carter's only plurality was among families with annual incomes below $15,000. He won union households 47 to 44 percent, but even there his support had declined 14 percent in four years. One observer asked reasonably enough:

Why, apart from considerations of traditionalism in party or group identification, should a working-class voter continue to support the most conservative Democratic President for his time since Grover Cleveland left office in 1897? If the election was in some important sense between anger at Jimmy Carter and fears of the great unknown which Ronald Reagan evoked, anger eventually won.[22]

Besides that, Reagan's urgent assurances that America could be great again, taxes should be cut, and the budget balanced, family life (and patriarchal dominance) reinvigorated, quelled perfectly rational fears. The themes of the campaign were family, economy, empire. The success was remarkably one-sided, and the effects, as one might expect, were decisive and polarizing.

Sexual politics and the family

More so even than Reaganomics, this was the heartland of the Republican appeal, as Rosalind Petchesky argues.

> Above all . . . what has given the New Right both ideological legitimacy and organizational coherence, has been its focus on reproductive and sexual issues. If there is anything "new" about the current right wing in the United States, it is its tendency to locate sexual, reproductive, and family issues at the center of its political program — not as manipulative rhetoric only, but as the substantive core of a politics geared, on a level that outdistances any previous right-wing movements in this country, to mobilize a nationwide mass following.[23]

Thus the New Right brought its full influence to bear during the 1980 Republican platform hearings on opposition to ERA and support for an anti-abortion constitutional amendment. These issues, in turn, oriented New Right organizing efforts throughout the campaign.[24]

While there is a skittishness and demagoguery to the New Right theorizing of Gilder and Schlafly, part of the New Right success must be credited to material realities which lay behind their raw appeals. Keynesian society *does* transfer some patriarchical duties of financial support away from the family. Hence "the man" becomes not the father/husband but, as is common in street slang, the state. Likewise, contemporary capitalism *does* erode patriarchical dominance in the family by making female wage-labor increasingly necessary, even as these changes in the family economy influence, as well, its inner political dynamic. New Right ideology legitimizes the raw fears of many men that the new world of the 1970s and 1980s erodes their privileges, challenges their control in the household, destroys their one-sided sexual prerogatives. This is the fear that worked so well for Reagan, it seems, and targeted a successful constituency for him among women, too.

It is important to remember that Reagan's electoral strategy was *analytic*, based on separating constituencies into their component parts, and then taking the greater. "I don't want everyone to vote," Paul Weyrich, New Right director of the Committee for the Survival of a Free Congress is quoted as saying during a crowd warm-up at a Dallas campaign rally just before the candidate's arrival. "Our leverage in the election quite candidly goes up as the voting populace goes down. We have no responsibility, moral or otherwise, to turn out our opposition. It's important to turn out those who are with us."[25]

The Reagan forces made the right bets across the board. Blacks and households with income under $15,000 could prefer Carter as long as most of them stayed home. ERA supporters could support Carter, but more women (many of whom were older) who were afraid of losing the lopsided security that patriarchical families apparently provided and who welcomed Reagan's fatherly support for the lives they had lived, would vote in higher percentages than their younger more feminist counterparts.

Understanding that the percentage of eligible persons who actually vote is shrinking, and moreover that the sociological profile of voters and non-voters varies in a fairly predictable manner, Reagan went after women *voters*. Nearly two-thirds of married women (but fewer than half of single women) tend to vote. Also, persons between the ages of 45 and 65 tend to vote in the highest proportions. Thus, by appealing to married women between 45 and 65 on a "pro-family" platform, Reagan maximized the electoral value of gender politics and family issues, notes Zillah Eisenstein.

> Many of the women in this age group are frightened by the ERA in that they fear it will deny them the security and protection they feel

(and may need) from the traditional patriarchal family, which still defines their lives to a large extent. The ERA, in their estimation, has come too late for them. At the age of fifty, after raising their children, they do not want to think about their "rights" within divorce. The women the Republican party courted are the women who are economically dependent on their husbands and therefore do still obtain security within the nuclear family.[26]

This is the *gap within the gender gap* the Republicans counted on — the division in age, experience, and circumstance which separated their constituency of women from the other. For these women anti-feminism may well have reduced the gender-salient concern for peace over war — the other gender gap — and improved Reagan's tally. There is no doubt that Reagan was willing to write off the poor and working-poor and women of color. For them traditional appeals to the "single-male-breadwinner" family model promoted by New Right propagandists must have seemed extremely remote.

How the family and sexual politics issues in all their subtle forms effected electoral outcomes is hard to gauge. Whether the Republican candidate won more men than the women he lost by these themes is hard to figure, although the positive multiplier effects for Reagan of the New Right and anti-abortion mobilization were doubtless considerable. This much, too, is clear: *women divided sharply on issues that divided them as women.* While a slim majority of the women respondents to the *New York Times*/CBS News exit poll on election day favored the ERA, the real story lay elsewhere. In the two-party context, women for the ERA gave Carter 63 percent of their vote, while women opposing the ERA supported Reagan massively, 69—31.[27] The de-integrative strategy of division within divisions — men vs. women, then women feminists vs. women traditionalists — anchored the Reaganite New Right approach to family and sexual politics, as it would orient the economic and imperial defense issues. They would all come together in the feminization and racial divisions in poverty that were to be the clearest expression of "Reaganomics" in practice.

War, peace, and money

On the questions of war and peace, and the subliminal appeal of Reagan's imperial renewal theme, a more conventional gender gap emerged with new force. The 1980 election occasioned the widest split between men and women on record: men supported Reagan 54—37, while women split 46 percent for Reagan to 45 percent for Carter.[28] There is strong reason to suspect that women were less put off by Carter's "image of humility and long-suffering"[29] and less inclined to permit Reagan's finger to control the button. When CBS/NYT researchers asked voters leaving the polls if they favored a more forceful position *vis-à-vis* the Soviets, even at the risk of war, women agreed 16 percent less often than men (62 percent to 46 percent).[30]

It seems clear above all that the election turned precisely on the theme of imperial decline. Are Americans doomed to watch the Soviets assume military mastery? Is the economy past the point of renewal? Can industries compete effectively again? Are "you better off than they were four years before?" "Inflation and the economy" were singled out by 40 percent of the voters as the crucial issue in the election (ironically, "balancing the budget" came in second at 26 percent). As Burnham notes, the

> Carter years were associated with the decay of the American empire abroad and the deterioration of the political economy (and many Americans' post-tax, post-inflation real income) at home. The visible symbols were the endless Iranian hostage imbroglio on the one hand, and rampant inflation and high unemployment on the other. . . . To an exceptional extent, this campaign was fought out in terms of a debate — much more implicit than explicit, but nonetheless central — between those who believe, with Reagan, that realization of "the American dream" in the 1980s is possible and those who with Carter believe that privation and a historically revolutionary decline in mass expectations are inevitable.[31]

It is perhaps no surprise that the 34 percent of the electorate who believed themselves to be "worse off" than 4 years before gave Reagan a huge 72—28 majority (while the "better-offs" supported Carter 59—41, and "the sames" split evenly between the two). The real "worst-offs" stayed home in unprecedented numbers: the "party of non-voters" won the election easily: 49.9 percent no-shows; Reagan 28.0 percent; Carter 22.6 percent, others 4.5 percent.[32] Reagan's appeal was formidable among those who could still imagine themselves part of the mainstream, beneficiaries of a renewed United States which could be "great again" or at least a little bolder and wealthier and confident of the future once again.

A NEW IDEOLOGICAL CONSENSUS

There are some speeches Reagan has repeated so often in his long series of campaigns that observers simply refer to them together and severally as "The Speech." There is one version which gained much favor during the 1964 campaign. It stressed the advantages of government withdrawal from the market, a tougher military posture against the Soviets, more power to states and communities, and protection against an all-consuming federal government.[33] The 1980 version added to this familiar recipe the ingredients for economic recovery. There was something in it for every Republican taste: for the monetarists a promise of better control of the money supply; for traditionalists a commitment to reduced spending and a balanced budget; for the new breed of supply-siders a pledge to reduce taxes to enhance investment prospects.

Programmatic clarity is hardly the point; nor intellectual rigor. "The Speech" didn't make that much sense, but it worked because supply-side theory offered, for the first time, an alternative to the discredited assertions of Keynesianism. Growth without pain. It was political magic, as Hugh Heclo and Rudolph Penner observe:

> The political attractiveness of this supply-side vision of growth is not difficult to understand. It seemed to allow the Reagan candidacy to escape the dismal prospect offered both by traditional Republican economics and by monetarism, a prospect of austerity and distributional conflict in the name of long-term solvency. Tax-induced "growthmanship" meant that there could be economic success without pain, as monetary policy held back inflation and faster growth in a private sector relieved of high taxes benefited

everyone. As far as treating an ailing economy was concerned, supply-side theory was the equivalent of laughing gas when compared to the monetarists' and orthodox conservatives devotion to chemotherapy. It is not difficult to convince people that the world would be a better place if their taxes were cut.[34]

Among those who voted (and worried about their taxes) the appeal went down very well.

The family, war and peace, finances, and empire — these themes galvanized Reagan's support; but there were other factors above and beyond Reagan, which added historic force to his considerable personal appeals. For one thing, labor market demographics and regional settlement patterns had shifted dramatically in his favor, adding a certain objective character to the Reagan logic. The tipping of the nation's population towards the energy-rich, union-weak sunbelt states, which had proceeded apace with the dissolution of the blue-collar working class, created the basis for a natural Republican majority. By 1980, white-collar workers had achieved an absolute majority within the labor force (52 percent) while blue-collar workers represented only 32 percent. Work in the service sector amounted to 13.3 percent and farm labor 28 percent. Regionally distinctive social structures have emerged, the North retaining a traditional base of mass-production workers, with the South and West "characterized by the more extreme segmentation of the labour-force into concentrations of technical—scientific professionals on one side, and very low-wage primary and tertiary sector workers on the other."[35]

Different social structure means a different balance of class forces and divergent coalitional possibilities. Davis notes:

> In most Northern urban areas, local capitalist "growth coalitions" had to engage in conflictual bargaining with politically influential inner-city populations. In the Sunbelt, by contrast, local power structures have enjoyed a virtually untrammeled hegemony supported by electoral gerrymandering and widespread disen-franchisement of non-Anglo working-class neighborhoods.[36]

With the exception of Hawaii, the Democrats were totally shut out in the Western sectors of the country. In the 19 states west of the nineteenth meridian the Democrats averaged only a 35.5 percent share of the two-party presidential vote.[37] Burnham rightly calls the "shift of a political Mason—Dixon line from its old North—South position to an East—West position," the "most striking" of all the observations about the political geography of the 1980 election.[38] The decline of the United States' "heavy manufacturing consumer durable sectors and the growth of Sunbelt economics based on the sectoral predominance of science-based industries (aerospace and electronics), primary products, and amenities (tourism, retirement, and recreation)"[39] has already had considerable political consequences, and 1980 may be only the beginning.

A new Sunbelt consensus has emerged to replace the old Keynesian consensus. Based on an ethnic — and labor — exclusionary model of white suburbanized politics, it reflects crucial demographic and geopolitical transformations of the United States' electoral landscape. Free of the integrative pressures of the Keynesian growth coalition, it is Reagan's spiritual home and, more significant, the objective base for the United States' rightward electoral swing now, and quite possibly for some time to come. In this context the boasts heard during the 1984 Republic convention, that with a little extra organization in the Congressional contests the GOP might become the governing party for the rest of the century, cannot be shrugged off as mere hyperbole.

For it is also true that the Republicans of the right are the beneficiaries of a major change in the intellectual currents which direct contemporary American discourse, and which influence electoral options in the US today. Thus the organized movement of the New Right represents the radical edge of a much broader force pushing American politics in important new directions. Interviewed by CBS News during the 1984 National Convention which re-nominated Reagan on a promise of "Peace, Prosperity, Patriotism," as one tabloid put it in huge block letters, Vice President Bush dismissed the leader of the New Right direct-mail campaign, Richard A. Viguerie, as an unknown man with a mimeo machine. The popular Vice President observed that his party didn't need the "crazies," many of whom weren't even registered Republicans. Andover- and Yale-educated, born to the squirearchy of Connecticut, the son of a former governor of that state, Bush cannot easily conceal the class antipathy and almost squeamish discomfort which New Right activists cause him. Entering the re-election campaign, even his supporters were reportedly worried that his "preppie" image would place him at a disadvantage against Geraldine Ferraro, his untested but redoubtable and far more sympathetic adversary.

Division within the Right: ideology,
the New Right and the neo-conservatives

The case of Bush is important not only for a consideration of post-Reagan prospects but for what it shows, indirectly, about the Reagan appeal. In both breeding and substance the Reagan image conceals serious ideological divisions within the Republican camp. The battle for the hearts and minds of the Grand Old Party is a battle with deep personal wounds which come out in Bush's brittle dismissal of the New Right and their equally caustic rejoinders.

> So deep is the New Right's antipathy for intellectual elitists that it has prompted them to turn their guns also on genuine conservatives who, by their cultural styles, appear to New Right primitives as enemies

observes Alan Crawford.[40] Thus William F. Buckley, Jr, whose *National Review* was a powerful vehicle for bringing together nascent New Right forces behind the Goldwater candidacy 20 years ago, has been more recently pilloried for his class and culture, as Crawford explains:

> Member of a rich and distinguished family, Buckley exemplifies much of what the New Rightists despise: Educated in England and at Yale, he is cultured and erudite, speaking with what many New Rightists suspect is an accent he has affected. Cosmopolitan in his attitude, he has been an iconoclastic journalist, controversial and unflapping. He plays the harpsichord and paints, has been known to swear on television, and writes in a prose style that is highly individualistic and often obtuse. He prefers to use the correct word, even if it is unlikely to be understood immediately by many of his readers.[41]

All this and, according to a conservative newspaper publisher quoted by Crawford, Buckley "spends too much time skiing with that Galbraith," besides.[42]

Clearly, real class differences and divisions in perspective separate homespun evangelical preachers and the Eastern Ivy League intellectuals. Hence, there is a real clash as the "rednecks and rubes" wrest the Republican Party away from the "preppies and elitists." Even more significant is the fact that the dichotomy in cultural ethos and class style which separates the Bushes and Buckleys from the Falwells and Vigueries represents a considerable division in world view and policy imperatives.

The New Right grounds its policies in social life and family, moving to economic issues and questions of foreign policy only, in a sense, inferentially.

> Sexual and family politics . . . beginning with abortion, becomes for the New Right intrinsic elements in a larger program that encompassed more traditional right-wing aims: anticommunism, antidetente, antiunionism, racial segregation and antifederalism,

notes Petchesky about the evolution of New Right perspectives in the 1980 election. Quickly, the Moral Majority moved onward to target constituencies on issues that are not "moral" in the usual sense: taxes, a balanced budget, gun control, military preparedness.[43]

Thus the New Right politics includes a "privatization" impulse which legitimizes the anti-integrative, anti-welfarist edge to their politics and the strident plea to save the family as the bastion of male privilege. But there is also in New Right demands the contradictory cry to *make public*, and thereby repoliticize, matters that American liberalism and Keynesian welfarism had left protected by a shield of Lockean freedom. A constitutional amendment to outlaw abortion would violate very deeply the freedom of choice which is at the core of liberal assertions of liberty.[44] Likewise, attacks on homosexuality, which have become increasingly hysterical with the AIDS epidemic, like demands for the return of prayers to public (state) schools, represent sustained efforts not to "get the state off our backs," but to move the state into bedrooms, bath houses and school rooms — places where it had not recently been invited. As moral crusaders more than as political thinkers, New Right activists have not been terribly concerned to sort through the inconsistencies in their programs.

They know what they want and that comes first: a powerful Christian America where white privileges and patriarchy secure in turn the social and family worlds they know, cherish, and see endangered by the modern world. But their ertswhile more intellectual allies are not so sanguine about the implications of New Right political theology.[45]

These "other conservatives" are themselves divided. There are the much heralded neo-conservative intellectuals of *Commentary* and *The Public Interest*, Irving Kristol, Daniel Patrick Moynihan, Daniel Bell and others. Many observers consider their writings deeply significant for the evolution of American views about politics. Referring to this neo-conservatism, which is clearly on the rise as New Deal liberalism is just as clearly on the decline, Peter Steinfels makes the point most directly: "I believe that neo-conservatism *is* the serious and intelligent conservatism America has lacked."[46]

There are also, however, traditional Republican conservatives in business and in government who combine in an unreflected way the hodgepodge American conservatism — a Burkean fear of the mob and a Lockean fear of excessive government intrusion. They were consensus Keynesians and they remain pluralists. Like their one-nation Tory counterparts, they are pro-business and individualist. There's is the patriotism of free enterprise but not the gushing jingoism of USA chants at Olympic games. By instinct and multinational motivation they are internationalists and compromisers on foreign policy, and disengaged (compared to their New Right competitors) on domestic issues. The public versus private split should be observed (or so they argue), individual liberties within market capitalism preserved, and outgroups should be integrated to the degree that privileges of merit, material circumstance, and patriarchy permit. They are elitists, but so was Jefferson. They undoubtedly find participation in a Republican Party, with its unleashing of Falwell's and Viguerie's minions, a disheartening and alien experience.

The intellectuals among them are increasingly influential outside the party. *Newsweek*, for example, observed recently that in "intellectual circles, the social thinkers who were once the driving force of Democratic liberalism — men like Arthur Schlesinger, Jr. and John Kenneth Galbraith — have been upstaged by a group of neoconservative academics."[47] But inside the party, the neo-conservative intellectuals and their traditional conservative allies among government and party officials are increasingly marginalized. Ironically, just as traditional Republicanism has been intellectually re-invigorated by born-again conservative intellectuals, party politics has been taken over by the very different forces of the New Right.

Divisions within the Republican Party

Fundamentalists have taken the party away from those Republican traditionalists rooted deeply in the Middle West and the rural outlands of the South and far West. Never ideologically driven, these descendants of the Taft wing of the party — fiscal conservatives and isolationists when pushed — were there for Reagan, to rescue him from a repeat of the Goldwater debacle of 1964. A. James Reichly, calling them the "stalwarts" of the Republican Party, notes their distinction from Reagan's true believers: "The stalwarts stand for an instinctive kind of conservatism: more pragmatic and less theoretic than that of the fundamentalists, less open to beguilement by faddish notions like supply-side economics, less combative in world affairs."[48] They are powerful in the House and Senate, including prominently in their numbers Senator Howard Baker, Republican leader of the Senate during Reagan's first term; Senator Robert Dole, who chaired the Senate Finance Committee and became the majority leader in 1984; Representative Barber Conable, the ranking Republican on the House Ways and Means Committee; and Representative Robert Michel, Republican leader of the House. These powerful political brokers and party leaders were in a position to make or break Reagan's economic program and to tie his hands in Congress. In a sense they did both, as Reichly explains:

> In 1981 the stalwarts loyally supported the administration's drive to reduce domestic spending, increase military expenditures, and achieve a record cut in federal taxes — though with private reservations, particularly over the tax cut. Facing economic recession and continued high interest rates in the summer of 1982, however, stalwarts in Congress, led by Dole, put together the tax package to reduce deficits. When cuts in federal aid began to cause

pain in state capitals, many stalwarts dug in against future cuts in aid programs. While favoring a strong national defense, the stalwarts' roots in the isolationist outlook of Robert Taft make them leery of the kind of overseas adventures that attract some of the fundamentalists.[49]

They were repaid well for their ideological recalcitrance and legislative restraint as they were cold-shouldered and marginalized in Dallas during the 1984 Republican national convention. Howard Baker was slotted into the first night's speakers list to get the hall jumping before the anticipated lackluster delivery of the official keynote address by Katherine Ortega, the Hispanic woman Treasurer of the United States, chosen to parade Republican rectitude on issues of race and gender. But as it turned out the delegates barely responded to Baker (who was widely reported, therefore, as losing considerable potential as the 1988 nominee), but embraced Ortega, whose obvious emotion gave her conventional patriotic rhetoric rare force. Dole fared even worse, his speech tucked away out of prime time and receiving very little attention, and having to reply to innumerable slightly condescending interviews about the prospects of an all-Dole 1988 ticket and whether the husband (ill-fated vice-presidential nominee in 1976) or the wife, Elizabeth Dole, current Secretary of Transportation, would get the top slot.

As the Reagan bandwagon speeds ahead, erstwhile allies are squandered, their powerful influence over legislative affairs partly taken for granted and partly ignored. While the fiscal policy becomes more traditional, the political and social direction of the Reagan movement shakes off the tag-alongs. Thus Reaganism reflects a curious conjuncture of neoconservative intellectual ferment at the elite level and carefully orchestrated New Right agitation at the base of the Republican world. These are competing forces that cannot easily be reconciled in part, for objective, historically constituted reasons. Sheldon Wolin has written of the tension between the conservative values — some New Right and some neo-conservative — and conservative business practices as they contribute to modernization and the evolution of capitalist industrial processes:

The progress of power in America has had a special piquancy for the conservative. While conservative politicians composed hymnals to individualism, localism, Sunday piety, and homespun virtues, conservative bankers, businessmen, and corporate executives were busy devitalizing many local centers of power and authority, from the small business and family farm to the towns and cities. They created the imperatives of technological change and mass production which have transformed the attitudes, skills, and values of the worker; and erased most peculiarities of place, of settled personal and family identity; and made men and women live by an abstract theme that is unrelated to personal experience or local customs.[50]

The two movements of conservatism in America cannot be reconciled. Modernization contradicts the Burkean impulse to conserve everything that has served the test of time even tolerably well. Alan Wolfe notes:

[E]ven in a period of relative stagnation, capitalism is still a dynamic economic force and conservatism a frozen political doctrine, creating a host of problems for modern conservatives. Defending business freedom on the one hand and tradition on the other, is an impossible task, as anyone who has watched what capital accumulation does to neighborhoods and families can testify.[51]

The task of reconciliation is thus doubly difficult. First, the modernizing consequences of capitalist development in general and conservative "free-market" practices must be reconciled with preservationist ideological assertions. Secondly, New Right social activism which welcomes a carefully drawn agenda of state intrusion upon the private/family sphere must share a party and a candidate with Republican traditionalists and neo-conservative intellectuals for whom the state which governs best is a state operating within parameters set by a Lockean view of liberty on the one side and consensus Keynesianism on the other. It is the modernizers versus the Slavophiles written into the drama of post-welfarist American politics and, at the moment, against all odds and contrary to precedent, the Slavophiles are winning.

IDEOLOGY AND INTEREST

In 1968 and 1972 Nixon had assembled a coalition, as it was described at the time, of "the unyoung, the unpoor and the unblack"; in other words, a coalition defined by its rejection of New Deal/Welfarist principles and the "new politics" which surged in the Democratic Party in the wake of the civil rights movement and the anti-war campaigns. Although Nixon never crystalized a positive coalition, the 1972 nomination of George McGovern by the Democrats helped create for him a "silent majority" and a landslide victory.[52] Nixon's support lacked a coherent ideological basis, but before the full economic consequences of the oil-shock and the NEP were felt and, especially, before the revelations of the Watergate scandals, it held together satisfactorily on pragmatic and performance grounds. Devaluation, a release from international monetary rules, and wage and price controls put the political business cycle on the upswing for the 1972 election.

Where Nixon's anti-ideological coalition relied on the stabilization of the United States' geopolitical position — through "peace with honor" and the Guam Doctrine — and pragmatic economics at home, Reagan's base of support remains highly ideological, but nonetheless fragmented. It would be wrong to look in Reagan's rhetoric or programs for a magic unity formula. As campaigner, Reagan did not have to reconcile the disparate rightist currents which supported Republican politics, nor theory and practice. He needed only to motivate a sufficient following to displace an ineffectual opponent who had already alienated his Democratic base. Each of his appeals — tax cuts, reduced social expenditure, a balanced budget, an end to federal support for civil rights initiatives, defense of the family and opposition to abortion, expanded military spending, reduced environmentalist constraints on business — was intended to mobilize support in a specific constituency.

Interestingly, the themes were both highly ideological and, in various combinations, either politically divisive among Reaganite supporters or mutually exclusive in objective terms. Tax relief was incompatible with expanded military expenditure without excessive deficits;[53] the business interests who welcomed a new era of laissez-faire entrepreneurship were ill at ease with government intrusions in matters of social morality. Thus the success of Reaganism is measured not in terms of ideological or programmatic coherence but *arithmetically*. For Reaganism does not create a true domestic coalition, an anti-KWS coterie of interests, with each participating group willing to trade particular advantages for admission to a collectivity which asserts some set of unifying principles. Flag and empire provide the factors of cohesion, but in domestic terms Reaganism, like Thatcher's appeal, pieces together a plurality through the addition of disparate self-interests.

In fact, the contemporary ethos of particularism is so abiding that even oppositional movements, like Jesse Jackson's campaign, ostensibly based on a rainbow coalition — a New Deal base broadened to include in a crucial way black and other people of color — often seemed to break down into particularistic appeals for support, in this case, from politically and economically marginalized outgroups. Jackson fought hard and well, in part for the principles of equality or the redistributive principles of the Keynesian welfarist vision. More often, however, he seemed simply to be trying to cut his people, on the street and in the black churches, into the deals.[54] They were to have jobs and better housing not because states should provide the necessities of commodious living to all citizens, but because they, too, had the power to get their piece of the action; they should have leadership roles in the Democratic Party not as a final universalization of the franchise outward from men of property and white privilege, but because the Democratic Party needed their blocs of votes. When Keynesian universalism is exhausted, it seems that only claims to self-interest and factional advantages can be heard. Appeals to principles above group interests — except for the very special appeal of national pride — seem like naive diversions from the steady force of *realpolitik* and *machtpolitik*. At these Reagan excels.

Reagan tends towards New Right politics on social policy and unconsciously moves from the highly ideological supply-side economics to more traditional Republican fiscal conservatism or economic policies, as his celebrated U-turn from 1981 federal tax cuts to 1982 tax increases starkly represented.[55] He works tactically outward from the areas of common ground which he plows for all they are worth: anti-communism, military preparedness, geo-political assertiveness, and devotion to traditional Americanism. The material facts of declining competitiveness, the United States' scissors crisis, and the "retreat and humiliation" of the Carter years provide Reagan with the perfect political and economic foils: leadership and renewed confidence can make the US great again, can obscure all New Right and neo-conservative differences, can (like Thatcher's appeal to "Victorian values") return the US to simpler and grander times.

The appeal to flag and empire gives the politics of New Right hucksterism and of business self-assertion a high moral tone. Even modest and quite peculiar "successes" — like the invasion of Grenada or the forced interception of the plane carrying the alleged hijackers of the *Achille Lauro* — enhance Reagan's apparent political invincibility. They add a layer to the Teflon coating and, with the institutional and economic policy mechanisms described below in chapter 7, these patriotic appeals and grandiloquent military gestures help secure for Reagan considerable room for maneuver.

As a consequence, even quite dramatic and uncalculated reversals seem relatively costless for the Reagan administration. Thus for the first 3 years in office the President tended to see all difficulties "in terms of East—West conflict, with a touch of Armageddon thrown in." The administration overstated the effect of Syrian—Soviet collusion on US strategic policy in the Middle East, and vastly exaggerated the international significance of Nicaragua in order to vent its anti-Soviet rhetoric. As mainstream establishment critic and former Defense Secretary, James Schlesinger, observed: "While the Sandinista regime is a geo-political nuisance which we wish would either disappear or moderate its behavior, it can scarcely be described as a major threat to the republic."[56]

Finally, the sudden announcement of the Star Wars proposal in March, 1983, which apparently caught both European allies and Department of Defense by surprise, signaled both a reversal in strategic military policy — deterrence would be scrapped — and a new stance toward the Soviet Union. By the beginning of Reagan's second term, arms control focussed East—West relations, and a distinctly less confrontational stand toward the Soviets, a wariness of Gorbachev, and plans for a Geneva summit changed the whole context of American foreign policy.

What remained constant was the effort to revivify US geopolitical dominance, if not by aggressive confrontation with the Soviets, then by Star Wars initiatives which may — if successful — enhance American efforts to reunify a hegemonic bloc by linking European allies economically to the extraordinary research and development and production implications of the American initiative. Where Carter's admission of loss of confidence invigorated opposition and obscured his administration's successes (as Camp David was widely considered), Reagan's brash assertiveness and tone of American (and personal) self-congratulation help unify disparate sources of support both within and outside a natural, and expanded, conservative camp. Wolfe notes:

> Bourgeoise democracy, so recently the enemy of reason and civility, was transformed by [the advent of socialism] into a bulwark against the dictatorship of the proletariat. Capitalism, ignoble in the recent past, was the best one could hope for in a world in which men were not angels. Modern conservatism in a word made peace with capitalism in order to wage war against socialism. . . . Contemporary conservatism, then, is an uneasy mist of its anti-capitalist and anti-socialist ingredients.[57]

Reaganism reflects this uneasy alliance of contrary instincts which are unified by a constant series of imperial defense initiatives. All Reaganite currents come together in praise of the free market and in shared outrage at Soviet ambitions abroad and "Marxist dictatorships" in Central America. Thus, Bush and Viguerie, Buckley and Fallwell can all take solace in Paul Laxalt's assertion in nominating the President for re-election that during Reagan's first term in office not one inch of territory had been lost to Communist aggression. This is the abiding basis for the Reaganite appeal as evangelical patriotism, celebration of the market, and unreflected anti-socialism/anti-Sovietism constitute the "America can be great again" coalition.

7
Reagan and the politics of economic policy

These ideologically determined and highly statist governments are different from mainstream governments which are nominally of the left or right to the degree that they can suppress and externalize criticism and reduce the "normal" capacity of groups in society to constrain their exercise of executive powers. For Thatcher the very *concentration* of state power — the unitary character of economic management, the reduction of the powers of local councils and the outright elimination of a set of particularly antagonistic ones, the introduction of a labor-exclusion model of industrial relations — has provided the leverage for securing her government from excessive intrusion by outside forces. For Reagan the state's institutional *fragmentation* and ostensible irresolution have provided a relatively equal measure of insulation, not only from interest intermediation, but also from legislative influences, and from the capacity of hegemonic class fractions to structure the choices available to government officials. I will consider this last point first.

REAGAN AND THE CAPITALIST CLASS

Theorists disagree, of course, about the extent to which financial and business elites exercise control over state initiatives. For some "while the state does act . . . *on behalf* of the 'ruling class', it does not for the most part act *at its behest*."[1] For others the "*direct* participation of members of the capitalist class in the state apparatus and in government, even where it exists, is not the important side of the matter" — because political power represents a "condensation" of class forces.[2] For still others the state acts to stabilize the economy and enhance the possibilities for accumulation, not because it is dominated by the capitalist class, but because political elites have an interest, themselves, in the defense of "capitalist class institutions" and in the health of the economy which provides the state with needed revenue.[3] Whatever the best analysis of class—state relations in capitalist democracies may be, it seems clear that the Reagan government cheats us of our normal expectations.

Reagan's administration has preserved an unusual ability to steer clear of the directive influences of capital in the formulation of economic policy. Whether they have violated their own interests or simply dodged elite pressures, the Reagan *apparat* has remained unusually insulated from pressures generated by the economy.

There are at least three elements in this very special set of circumstances. The first should by now be clear: hegemonic decline broke the Keynesian—internationalist coalition and invited a politics of imperial nostalgia. Reagan's ability to appropriate the flag gives him a political resource of considerable value. When spoken by this President, a plea for American renewal becomes a celebration of the most privileged themes of America — the free market, military pre-eminence, the sanctity of the family. Thus, Reagan captures the ideological high ground, and leaves to all others only the nondescript valleys of special pleading.

Trade unions which are struggling to preserve jobs and wages are dismissed as special interests, an attack introduced during Gary Hart's primary campaign against Mondale in which unions were dismissed as PACs (political action committees), the current derogatory label for self-regarding interest groups. Democrats who are concerned about the sorry plight of their New Deal and Kennedy-era partners — trade unionists, people of color, the poor — are whiners (as Senator Paul Laxalt told us in his speech nominating Reagan for re-election in 1984). Those who want to halt the arms race are naive, or not quite arduous enough in their patriotism.

Political opponents have little choice but to assail Reagan's policies, ignore the eminent advantages of his secure and unimpeachable high ground, and risk ideological oblivion. Business elites seem to know better and need ideological engagement less, so whatever their reservations about Reagan's policies — and we shall see that they are considerable — they bide their time, lower their profiles, and take care to criticize the sin but never the sinner. Thus, Reagan has created the first means of escape from the normal constraints of interest group and capitalist class intermediation by securing ideologically unassailable terrain. Imperial decline has provided the opening for Reagan's remarkable political renewal.

AN OUTSIDER'S ADVANTAGES

The second factor which enhances Reagan's sphere of independence involves his unusual base of support outside the party organization and traditional GOP constituencies. This representation of Reagan as anti-party populist — a citizen-leader reluctantly performing his civic duty and not a professional politician relentlessly pursuing personal ambition — has been the fundamental stock line of the Reagan candidacy for more than 20 years. Strangely enough there is some truth to the claim, and some important consequences for the evolution of a presidency which is at once highly ideological, outside the traditional Republican mainstream and beyond the reach of many typical moderating pressures.

The emergence of Reagan as the principled outsider began with his impressive performance in Goldwater's doomed 1964 campaign. It gained force throughout his efforts to displace Gerald Ford as the Republican nominee in 1976, the year of Carter's victory. At the time Reagan's association with the Goldwater fringe, and his failure to dislodge Ford, an unelected incumbent tainted with the Nixon intrigues, led many observers — party insiders among them — to underestimate his chances in 1980. The plot was one of ideological isolation and defeat, an outcome which comforted those who thought that the governorship of the most populous state might be an adequate reward for a retired actor seeking a new career option. But a very significant sub-plot was developing, and this would create the conditions for a *deus-ex-machina* in American politics of historic dimensions.

The peculiar trajectory of the Reagan candidacy has provided Reagan the President with an unusual capacity to distance himself from direct party pressures. Perhaps more important, as a consequence of his genuine outsider's history — and the insiders' ridicule which was long directed at the Reagan odyssey by the party regulars — Reagan is unusually indifferent to pressures expressed through congressional leadership from the President's party. If they couldn't intimidate him as a crank, why should he succumb to them as commander-in-chief?

Hugh Heclo and Rudolph G. Penner have recognized the significance of Reagan's unusual path to the Oval Office. As they recently observed:

> Ronald Reagan was the first modern president to arise from what might be loosely termed a popular political movement. Dwight Eisenhower had already clearly emerged as a national figure before taking over leadership of the Republican party. John Kennedy pushed himself into the Democratic nomination in a few brief years through media exposure and primary victories while never challenging the ultimate authority of party organizations. Johnson, Nixon, and Ford were in a sense all creatures of the established Washington community. Like Jimmy Carter, Ronald Reagan enjoyed a strong regional political base as a former governor and compiled a string of successes in presidential primaries. But unlike Carter's, Reagan's candidacy represented the culmination of almost fifteen years of grass-roots political agitation and organization across the nation.[4]

Thus, Reagan developed a base and developed at least a loose organization outside the party. In this way he encouraged a following that is ideological and "antipolitical", in Suzanne Berger's terms. As much concerned with "dismantling the state" as with controlling it,[5] Reagan's grassroots minions are not temperamentally attuned to the Washington world of political exchanges. They are not inclined to involve themselves in the practices of Congressional infighting or, for that matter, the actual details and drafting of legislation. More messianic than strictly political, this extra-parliamentary constituency helps Reagan distance himself from normal business-cycle politics and from the "let's go along to get along" style of Capitol Hill. Able to play the ideologues off against the professionals, Reagan can artfully manage political and political-economic outcomes from above.

Thus, to an unprecedented degree Reaganism is movement politics. Reagan's candidacy and presidency reflect the considerable power of right wing anti-statist constellations of socially conservative, self-consciously patriotic, and anti-modernist impulses. Heclo and Penner note:

> The fact that the Reagan presidency grew out of such a political agglomeration, and not simply from the virtuoso performance of a political entrepreneur (as with Kennedy and Carter) or from a long Washington apprenticeship (as with Johnson, Nixon, and Ford), had important implications for the incoming administrations economic approach. Economic policy positions were more than policy positions; they tended to become articles of faith during the long march to the White House.

They argue that Reagan, accordingly, possesses two "unique predispositions" when compared to all other postwar candidates: first an "explicit set of deeply held beliefs about the American economic order," and second, "a willingness to be less than normally deferential to elite opinion, particularly that of the established economics profession."[6]

Reagan's ideological zeal and populist base make him also unusually reluctant to accept the pressures of political and business elites who do not share his economic and social beliefs. This reluctance can be operationalized because Reagan's New Right organizational base in fundamentalism, television preachers and direct-mail advocates frees him to use traditional party and congressional leaders or discard them with little cost. Stalwarts such as Baker or Dole are expendable, particularly in the second term. They may even come to represent the objects of anti-Reagan organization, as in the case of Dole's elevation to majority leader of the Senate. The danger to Reagan of a Congressional rebellion by Taft traditionalists is strangely ambiguous, however, given the unusual character of Reagan's support and the odd public relations motif which dominates the evaluations of his presidency. A failure to achieve legislative passage of significant elements in Reagan's lame-duck program (for example, tax reform) may well mean less to him and to his followers than would normally be the case. For such rejection of a Reaganite program by professional politicians succumbing to the power of special interests — as the Reagan scriptwriters would certainly put it — might help galvanize the "moral majority" for post-Reagan mobilization.

Thus a whole range of typical constraints on the making of policy (and especially economic policy) are neutralized: the pragmatic horse-trading of administrations with congressional partisans, the need to mobilize support from rival party factions, the pressure of elite opinion from professional economists, the inchoate pressure of "business confidence" as a check on radical economic policy overtures. In these ways a second crucial condition for the emergence of a highly *dirigiste* regime is met. Reagan's apparently uncanny freedom to maneuver is secured by the fact of an independent and antipolitical political base. Likewise, Reagan's willingness to take unusual and highly controversial policy steps is enhanced by a political biography which has rewarded him well for ideological assertiveness. Every element in his situation invites the radical politicization of economic policy-making which has been a signal feature of his government.

THE POLITICS OF THE DEFICIT

The third condition for the maintenance of a presidency which is secure from many of the routine pressures of economic and political elites is perhaps the most revealing, for it shows the institutional distortions in American economic policy formation which the Reagan administration has exploited to secure unusual independence. This is a complicated tale: the emergence of a *dirigiste* state which politicizes economic policy to an unusual degree and which, at the same time, avoids the constraints which are typically imposed through the interplay of Keynesian coalitions. So it is, perhaps, best to start from the most clear and pressing manifestations of Reaganomics — the deficit.

There seems little doubt that the "politics of the deficit" is emerging as a major test of Reagan's ability to politically neutralize economic failures. As the 99th Congress convened in January, 1985 at the start of Reagan's second term in office, the administration admitted that the deficit would be higher than its previous projections had indicated. The budget was projected to exceed $200 billion in 1985, and David Stockman, chief architect of Reagan's program for economic recovery and Director of the Office of Management and Budget, revealed to Senate Republicans that the Reagan plan to reduce the budget would fall short — by $40 billion in fiscal 1988 — due to slowed economic growth and the President's refusal to reduce the military budget.

The *New York Times* reported the opening of Congress, which is usually a day for optimistic assurances by the majority, pro-forma broadsides by the opposition and the swearing in of new members, under an unusually downcast headline: "99th Congress opens somberly in deficit shadow." Senate Majority leader Dole, from the President's own party, and Democratic Speaker of the House, Tip O'Neill of Massachusetts, were scarcely distinguishable in their call for Congressional leadership to secure deficit reduction, whatever Reagan's position. Nearly a year later when the flush of Reagan's victory had passed, there was widespread agreement in the Congress that the deficit was still "the No. 1 problem facing the country," and worse — that House and Senate efforts to legislate a balanced budget by 1991 were "a political fraud."[7] Nor did the passage of the Gramm—Rudman measure in December, 1985 which sets a $144 billion target for fiscal 1987 relieve Congressional anxieties. At the same time business elites, as will become clear, have been strangely unified in their concern about the growing deficit, and extremely critical of the administration fiscal and monetary policies which they consider to be largely responsible for the current dangerous situation.

So deficit politics represents a crucial measure of the administration's capacity to steer a course which is boldly at odds with congressional voices and with capitalist interests: both with the expressed interests of capitalist elites and, quite probably, with the objective circumstances required for a healthy economy and steady, widespread capital accumulation. Here, then, in the President's stumbling reversal of the candidate's high-profile assurances of a balanced budget (as in his later return to the credo) we see this administration's peculiar independence in clearest focus.

To date two points are clear about Reagan's deficit politics. First, the selling of the budget and the subsequent intrigues which surround monetary policy and the machinations of the Federal Reserve Board (Fed) represent Reagan's *dirigisme* at its most impressive. Secondly, the politics of the deficit marks the furthest extent of the Reagan administration's distance from the stated interests — and very likely from the "real" interests — of a wide variety of capitalist elites.

Business elites are, to be sure, justifiably delighted about a set of policies and non-policies promulgated by this fervently pro-capitalist government. Indeed, administration favors are handed around to a wide set of capitalist interests. The evisceration of the Occupational Safety and Health Administration (OSHA) and the Environmental Protection Agency (EPA) helps the ailing smoke-stack industries, while the "drill we must" attitude of the Energy Department and the transformation of the Department of the Interior into a reserve of anti-environmentalist crusaders frees the energy industry and developers from irritating intrusions.[8]

Likewise, the substantial deregulation of banks helps the most powerful financial institutions rationalize accumulation strategies at the expense of their weaker thrift-industry competitors and makes it easier for them to recoup some of the considerable losses suffered as a consequence of bad third world debt. Finally, the high unemployment fostered by administration policies; the politicization of a National Labor Relations Board which permits union-busting efforts as never before and systematically delays the hearing of complaints (often past the point of relevance); the cruel PATCO example and harsh administration warnings that postal workers who threatened job actions would be dismissed; the pejorative labeling of trade unions as "special interests" — all this contributes materially to the capacity of management to intimidate their employees and to sustain profit ratios at the expense of labor.

There can be no doubt that the Reagan administration has in many ways turned the energies of the federal government to the advantages of the private sector. Nevertheless, capitalist elites are not sanguine about Reagan's economic policy. In fact there are unmistakable signs of alarm in unexpected places. Richard Corrigan summarizes well the curious phenomenon of an archly pro-business government generating substantial disfavor, not by its policies directed towards the business community, but by more fundamental directions in macroeconomic policy.

> [E]ven though the government is no longer such a nettlesome presence to the business community because of what it is doing in this or that location, the business community today seems united as never before by its concerns over how much harm the federal government is causing as a result of the ever-larger deficits it is running.
>
> In other words, business representatives seem much less worried about what the government is doing to them directly, with its regulations, as they are by what the government is doing to them indirectly, by borrowing so much money. In economic jargon, their worries have been transformed from the micro to the macro level.[9]

This last point is crucial, for it is easy to notice the policy plums provided particular capitalist interests and then ignore the global insensitivity of the Reagan administration to the general interests of capital which require a healthy economy with a good growth prospectus, sound money, and moderately pitched and fairly steady interest rates. The deficit reveals the possible nihilistic edge to macroeconomics transformed into macropolitics.

Capitalists and their elite representatives have been quicker than most observers to recognize the dangers. By the mid-point in Reagan's first term in office an impressive array of business leaders and corporatist representatives of capital were raising what, considering the sources, must be considered a shrill cry of warning. The "Peterson Group" led the attack on administration policy through a series of two-page advertising spreads issued by The Bipartisan Budget Appeal which appeared suddenly in a set of prominent newspapers. In these ads, five former Treasury Secretaries and a few dozen senior corporate executives — including powerful figures in banking such as the chief executive officers of Chase Manhattan, Bank of America, Manufacturer's Hanover, Continental Illinois, and Chemical Bank — joined Peter G. Peterson, a former Commerce Secretary, in sending a warning to Reagan and to the Congress.

They argued that decisive action was needed to mitigate the severe consequences of growing deficits.

Tomorrow's big deficits, and the high long-term real interest rates that will accompany them, are already doing serious damage now and will wreak even more havoc in the coming decade and beyond. Without savings available to fuel productive investments, the economy will face nearly perpetual stagnation.[10]

Once the Peterson group began the top-level criticism, it soon became clear that anti-deficit sentiment was widespread among corporate and banking elites. Most significant, it brought together capitalist fractions whose particular interests — from small domestic-oriented manufacturing to the internationalist wing of finance capital — characteristically place them at odds. After all, one hardly thinks of Chase Manhattan as being "interest-sensitive" in quite the same way as the housing industry which relies on low mortgage rates for survival. Nevertheless, the opposition to Reagan's fiscal policy extends from the Peterson Group, which is dominated by internationalist political and capitalist/financial elites, to the more humble and, in a sense, more representative business and manufacturing interests.

In January, 1983, the National Federation of Independent Business, the American Business Conference, and the National Association of Manufacturers took the very unusual step of convening a joint press conference to insist that Reagan do something to reduce deficits in fiscal 1984.[11] Typical of non-multinational manufacturing, which relies heavily on ready credit and the ability to sell products overseas, the textile industry has strongly registered its dismay at rising deficits which it holds responsible for both high interest rates and an overvalued dollar. J. Randolph Penner, publisher of the trade journal, American Textiles, notes:

> While a strong currency is desired, the abnormally powerful dollar is the major cause of our inability to sell products abroad. Why? — high interest rates. However, the huge deficit is the real culprit, since government has to borrow so heavily to service debt, leaving it considerably less money to lend to the private sector. That creates a lender's market, and high interest rates.[12]

Not to be outdone by Peterson, former Democratic Treasury Secretary Henry H. Fowler and former Republican chair of the

Council of Economic Advisors, Herbert Stein, formed an organization called the Committee to Fight Inflation. They also demanded that the administration take definite steps to reduce the deficit.[13]

A common concern unites these diverse representatives of the business and financial communities as they leave behind partisan political disputes and the routine imperatives of competition and intra-class rivalries. It is the same concern which dominates conversation at business meetings, such as those convened by the Center for the Study of American Business and the Conference Board. As the Peterson group put it, "The 1980s should be a decade of investment, not a decade of red ink."[14]

Despite the anti-deficit unity expressed by business leaders, it is not easy to prove that deficits cause high interest rates or the other economic difficulties for which they are routinely blamed. Donald Regan, Reagan's Secretary of the Treasury for the first term and the start of the second, for example, denies that there is any linkage between high deficits and high interest rates, blaming high interest rates instead on a fear of inflation.[15]

More to the point, however, diverse business elites seem to accept uniformly a gloom-and-doom litany that unchecked deficits cause interest rates to rise, and that this development has a multiplier effect of serious consequences. As writers in the American Banking Association (ABA) trade journal note, applying the conventional wisdom,

> Because of the lack of progress in reducing deficits implied by the President's budget, the Treasury will continue its heavy borrowing in the credit markets, and the government will probably crowd out private borrowers.[16]

As interest rates rise, "crowding out" causes investment to fall. Stagnation and decline in international competitiveness at a national scale are then sure to follow — or so the argument goes.

Whatever the truth to this theory, it seems clear enough that no capitalist elites want any part of this deficit. Domestic-based manufacturers find loans too costly and overseas sales increasingly difficult; multinationals are hurt by slow growth and sluggish credit markets for private and corporate consumers both at home and abroad; bankers are forced into high-profit, high-risk ventures, the continued legacy of the demand on first world financial institutions to recycle the post-1973 windfall of petrodollars.[17]

THE ADVANTAGES OF DEFICIT BUILDING

The phenomenon of business rejection of Reagan fiscal engineering is notable in itself, and highly suggestive of the strange proclivity of this government to set economic policy by its own inner lights and to permit unusual macroeconomic gambling with very high stakes. With Reagan more capitalist than the capitalists, the only surprise is that business is unified at Reagan's expense. One curious question remains about the burgeoning federal deficit. If the policy (and non-policy) of deficit growth antagonizes business and threatens the economy — what's in it for Reagan?

The answer lies in the multiple political uses to which this particular economic problem can be put by the administration, an understanding revealed by an unusual source. Just before Martin S. Feldstein left Harvard to chair Reagan's Council of Economic Advisors, he inadvertently revealed the political gains hidden behind the economic losses. On October 5, 1981, in an address to the American Paper Institute on Kiawah Island, South Carolina, Feldstein discussed the deficit in terms of the classic crowding-out argument, but added a distinctive statist twist to the story. As Feldstein noted:

> Since the government deficit means that the government must borrow more, the natural consequence of a deficit is a rise in the real interest rates on all debts. During the '60s and the '70s, the [Federal Reserve Board] repeatedly tried to prevent this rise by increasing the money supply. Of course, the rapid increase in the money supply meant that on balance, there was an excess demand in the economy, and this in turn led to higher and higher rates of inflation.[18]

Feldstein drew the obvious conclusion that when the government competes for funds with private borrowers, the government pushes interest rates up and "crowds out private investment." Feldstein observed somberly, but not surprisingly, that the loss in private capital formation which resulted is the main cost of high deficits. To this point Feldstein's Kiawah analysis simply reinforces the argument of the Peterson Group and others. But despite the measured words which very nearly dampen the insights, Feldstein went on to reveal a crucial political truth about Reagan's spending excesses which makes the whole exercise of balanced budget crusader turned profligate spender a good deal more explicable. Noting the reasonable concern that deficits would reduce the rate of capital formation, Feldstein examined the *advantages* for Reagan.

> [T]he causal link between deficits and inflation is really very weak. There's certainly no basis for the panicked fear of inflationary deficits now being expressed by some financial investors and Members of Congress.
>
> Why then are both the Administration and Congress screaming so much about inflationary deficits? The Administration's goal is to reduce the growth of government spending. They understand that failure to do so means a reduction of capital formation, a new set of tax increases or both.
>
> But that's very hard to explain to the general public. The goal of reducing the government's share of GNP from 22 percent to 20 percent is just not a cause around which the public will rally, for which the public will support cuts in food stamps or school lunches or medical benefits. In contrast, the goal of preventing inflation by balancing the budget is such a cause. So the Administration is trying to rouse public support for its spending cuts with shrill warnings that a failure to do so will lead to ever-increasing inflation.

Thus, the fact of apparently uncheckable federal deficits and the way that the deficit is sold in Washington (and in Peoria) shows the hard edge of Reagan's statist politics. In fact, economic malfeasance constitutes the basis of a highly polished political campaign. Deficit politics becomes the rational basis for the two strongest elements of the Reagan political miracle: imperial defence and social de-integration. In mortal combat with an "evil empire" the US must be always vigilant: the deficit is caused by wasteful social programs. Our military responsibilities are burdensome, to be sure, but we must pay the price of freedom even if unavoidable economic sacrifices are the consequence. Domestic spending is another matter.

Whether or not deficits actually drive up inflation, Reagan uses the fear of inflation — the way Thatcher used immigration — to drive a wedge between *us* and *them*. We are the solid citizens, Americans who are concerned about inflation and the threat it represents to *our* nation's international competitiveness. *They* are profligate spenders, the Democrats in the House who defend unnecessary high-cost programs pressed by special interests and led by the drunken sailor mentality of Mondale and Ferraro (as one 1984 Republican convention speaker noted). *They*, too, are the welfare cheats and the not "truly needy" who should no longer be coddled. Remarkably, economic policy failure fuels political success, as Reagan's own deficit building provides him with the practical logic with which to champion his de-integrative appeals.

ECONOMIC POLICIES AS DISPLACEMENT STRATEGIES

This is the truest expression of these unusually ideological and determined statist governments. Whatever their ostensible purpose and design the economic policies of Reagan, like those of Thatcher, are best understood politically as displacement strategies. There is one critical difference, however, which divides the British from the American case. Thatcher must deflect failure inward, while greater economic and geopoltical influence still permits the United States to enjoy the considerable privilege of socializing the costs of its economic decline globally and pushing the consequences of economic mismanagement outward.

Thus, in the UK, the government induces a colliery closure program which stampedes miners into a divisive and persevering strike. The miners are, at a stroke, rendered the "enemies within" — Thatcher actually used the term — and as such lumped in with the "fascist generals" who ruled Argentina during the Falklands war.[19] They are held responsible not only for police violence, but for the pervasive atmosphere of class antipathy and even for the UK's industrial decline. This is a calculated campaign of intimidation and innuendo which exposes the raw edge of Thatcher's de-integrative strategy. She must gamble with high stakes on political divisions within the working class: between militant leaders like Arthur Scargill, President of the National

Union of Mineworkers (NUM) and rank-and-file workers; between the unions in the declining manufacturing sectors and the white-collar unions which are gaining in numbers and in influence; between the suburbanized core of the new Tory majority and the working-class basis of Labour's hope for renewal.

In the United States, policy failure can still be side-stepped more majestically and with considerably less risk. The remaining hegemonic powers still provide the US with sufficient capacity to configure the world order at least partly to its needs. If self-interested aims can no longer be achieved through the front door of multilateral agreements and Bretton Woods, then they can be pursued through the back door of unilateral budgetary excess and benign fiscal neglect. An historic budget deficit pushes interest rates up, sucks capital into US markets, fuels the nicely timed 1984 pre-election "economic recovery" — and displaces a considerable fraction of the costs of imperial decline onto all those nations, European and third world, which have lost potential investment capital to American markets.

In this way Reagan can still call the tune but others, abroad and at home, are asked to pay the piper. A Reagan re-election campaign poised for certain victory could absorb the irritability of business elites at very low cost: where else could they go? Meanwhile, the real costs of decline are assumed elsewhere. American automobile workers (at General Motors plants) and miners represented by the United Mine Workers accepted in September, 1984, contracts which granted them only between 2.5 and 3 percent annual pay increases for a 3-year period and 40 months, respectively. Reflecting wider sentiments in the business and financial communities, the *New York Times* described the agreements as "a blow to inflation" and hailed the General Motors agreement as an "historic deal" which would improve American international competitiveness.[20]

With a record trade deficit of $24.4 billion for the second quarter of 1984; early reports on the quarter ending September 30 indicating a substantial slump in growth; with GNP increases estimated at 3.6 percent at an annual rate or barely one-half the increase of the second quarter; and, a half-point rise in consumer prices for August, more than twice the average for the previous 3 months — government sources and business analysts were looking to find the increasingly ephemeral indications that the recovery was real. Reasonably enough, they played the UMW and GM deals for all they were worth.

Whatever the true contours of the 1984 political business cycle, these agreements (like the effects of American deficit spending on foreign investment strategies) are very significant. They indicate the displacement power of Reagan's economic strategies. A whole host of governmental outputs — the neutralization of OSHA and the EPA, the weakening of the NLRB as an instrument for the redress of workers' grievances in disputes about union recognition, the campaign to delegitimize trade unions and dismiss them as special-interest PACs — contributes to a climate of intimidation. Altogether, for labor unions in the US, it is a time for strategic entrenchment at best. Union rights are jeopardized and the proportion of all employed workers belonging to trade unions has fallen to 23 percent.[21] The unions are declining in prestige, and management has defeated unions in recognition elections in a majority of recent cases (55.2 percent).[22] Under these circumstances the best unions can hope for are successful defensive battles to maintain jobs and to secure modest wage goals, and they can hope to duck some of the blame for low growth and declining international competitiveness.

Economic mismanagement does not derail the Reagan and Thatcher governments because their insularity from traditional pressures renders economic problems more amenable to political manipulations than is usually the case. No policy can lose, so long as they can make the victims pay for the government's mistakes. How else can we understand these remarkable Teflon administrations where errors of judgement, wild reversals of policy, and economic failures never seem to stick?

THE INDEPENDENCE OF THE EXECUTIVE

The politics of the deficit illustrates the statism of Reagan's administration not just because it marks his independence from capitalist elite pressures, nor even because of its success as a political displacement strategy. Deficit politics demonstrates also the curious *inner* dynamics of this government: not only the state's renewed capacity to evade class pressures, but the executive's remarkable independence within the state. Where the politics of fiscal policy is involved, monetary policy cannot be far behind and with it the Federal Reserve Board — as "independent agency" and lightning rod for criticism about the management of economic policy — comes to the fore.

The politicization of the Fed is, of course, not new to its role in the Reagan era nor an innovation fostered by the current chair, Paul Volcker. Few deny that the Fed is enmeshed routinely in political business cycle machinations. The Fed "not only follows the election returns when it makes monetary policy," notes Alfred J. Watkins, "but it also tries to influence them, usually by boosting the money supply and forcing down interest rates in time to make an incumbent President's record more palatable."[23] Similarly, Robert J. Shapiro challenges the "hallowed belief in the Federal Reserve's independence," noting in 1982 the clear influence of elections on growth rates in the money supply.

> With one exception, the money supply has expanded faster during the two years preceding every presidential election since 1960 than during the two years following. Or consider Arthur Burns's fate [as chair of the Federal Reserve Board] when he criticized the direction of Nixon administration policy in the spring of 1971: he quickly found himself excluded from the policy discussions concerning the imposition of wage-price controls and the end of the Bretton Woods world money system, decisions vitally affecting Reserve policy and operations.[24]

It is not that Volcker departs from this tradition, just that he may engage in Fed politicking in a rather unconventional way. It was during the Carter administration, of course, that the normal connection between growth in monetary supply and an incumbent's preparation for re-election was broken. As one observer noted,

> From 1977 to the middle of 1979, the economy experienced one of the longest peacetime expansions in its history. Real GNP grew at an annual average rate of 4 percent, and unemployment fell from 7.7 to 5.8 percent. But then the decline set in. In 1980, the growth rate of real income dropped to zero, workers' real weekly earnings fell by almost 3 percent, and unemployment skyrocketed back to

7.5 percent. Inflation, whose containment had been a major announced administrative objective, was still almost double digit on election day. Not since Herbert Hoover had a president presided over an election-year economy that behaved so diametrically opposite to what social science and common sense would suggest to be the outcome of a reasonable re-election strategy.[25]

There is, in fact, a piece of gallows humor attributed to Volcker, which suggests something of his political acumen and says a good deal about what the independence of the Fed means to him as a political and ideological resource:

> As Jerry Ford left the White House he handed Jimmy Carter three envelopes, instructing him to open them one at a time as problems became overwhelming. After a year, Carter opened the first envelope. It said, "attack Jerry Ford." He did. A year later, Carter opened the second envelope. It said, "attack the Federal Reserve." He did. Three years into his term, and even more overwhelmed by the economy, Iran, Afghanistan and so forth, Carter opened the third envelope. It said: "prepare three envelopes."[26]

As Gerald Epstein remarks, "Jimmy Carter appointed Paul Volcker to be chairman of the Federal Reserve; when the dust settled it was Volcker who remained to tell jokes on the Carter presidency."[27] In a similar vein, Watkins concludes, "As a fiscal conservative who is more at home with Reagonomics than with any alternative the Democrats might devise, why shouldn't [Volcker] use his considerable power to help his friends and punish his enemies?"[28]

Whether or not the Federal Reserve Board should be used as an instrument for dispensing political justice, it certainly has been used this way by Volcker. Through an extraordinary breach of security, a decision by the Fed's Open Market Committee to switch its attention from M1 (to M2 and M3)[29] was leaked just as the Bureau of Labor Statistics was revealing in October, 1982 that the unemployment rate had topped 10 percent for the first time in years.

Money growth suddenly accelerated and, for the first time in 8 months, the stock market soared, the prime fell 1½ points, mortgage rates dropped by a similar margin, and auto loans tumbled by 3 percent. As if from above, the administration got the sign it needed that Reagonomics was working, and the Republicans maintained control of the Senate — by 43,000 votes spread across five states — in the mid-term election in 1982.[30]

It is possible to question the propriety of his political interventions, but one can only marvel at the tactical canniness and political skill with which Volcker employs the considerable resources of his office. Eager to aid ideological compatriots and to ease into early retirement even benefactors who are no longer in favor, Volcker is clearly well suited to the subtle job of turning the Fed's much vaunted, much exaggerated independence to good use for the administration. As one economic analyst noted:

> Created by congress, [the Federal Reserve Board] enjoys nominal "independence" to insulate it from political pressures. But . . . this is something of a charade: the arrangement makes the Fed. a convenient agent — and scapegoat — for actions seen as necessary but unpopular by Congress or the White House. It institutionalizes institutional irresponsibility by elected officials.[31]

This general structure property conditions the relationship between the Fed and any administration and helps create an important sphere of independence for the American executive. Likewise, the independent capacity of Congress to modify the annual budget submitted by the administration — or offer its own, as with the "Dole budget" which figured prominently in debate over fiscal year 1986 — helps secure the President from attack for economic mismanagement.

The Volcker role *vis-à-vis* the Reagan executive does not represent a new structural or organizational configuration of economic management powers, but it does indicate greater artfulness, and perhaps more ruthlessness, in the performance of conventional duties by the Board's chair. It certainly represents one dimension of Reagan's atypical capacity to remove himself from the regular interplay of interests, and it adds another. Volcker has enhanced Reagan's capacity to turn economic defeat into political victory and has helped secure the executive's unusual independence within the state in two crucial but not obvious ways: by abandoning the Fed's control over interest rates and by warring with the Treasury over the deficit. The first, an apparently technical change in Fed policy — the switch from targeting interest rates to pegging monetary aggregates — has created an impressive freedom for political maneuver by the Reagan administration and, perhaps not quite coincidentally, for the Fed itself.

Traditionally, "the board maintains its considerable freedom to operate by hiding behind a confusing welter of obscure terms and statistics."[32] Watkins explains the source of this apparent irrationality.

> In 1975, Congress passed House Concurrent Resolution 133 instructing the Fed to "maintain long run growth of the money and credit aggregates commensurate with the economy's long run potential to increase production." According to the terms of that edict, the Fed would set noninflationary targets for money supply growth, report those targets to Congress, and most importantly, do its best to achieve them. . . .
>
> The Federal Reserve Board considered those instructions to be unwarranted limitations on its independence, so it complied with the letter of the law while doing everything in its power to violate the spirit. Congress demanded money supply targets, so the Fed presented a bewildering array of targets and constantly shifted the base period from which its performance was to be judged. By adopting these confusing procedures, the Fed could always point to the fact that it had indeed hit one of its targets as measured from one of its arbitrarily chosen, and constantly changing, starting points. Congressional oversight, meanwhile, degenerated into endlessly trivial debates over the relative merits of any particular target, the starting date from which to measure the Fed's performance, and whether the Fed should aim for the top, middle, or bottom of any particular target.[33]

FROM REAGANOMICS TO "VOLCKERISM"

This strategic mystification of policy by the Fed ended abruptly in October, 1979, just in advance of Reagan's election as President. At a meeting of international bankers in Belgrade, OPEC finance ministers and representatives from a variety of Western European central banks threatened to "dump their dollars on the international markets and precipitate a disastrous dollar devaluation unless the United States adopted stringent anti-inflation policies."[34]

Curiously, this was just the opening Volcker needed, both to turn congressional instructions to his own use and to create a political space for the administration. The Reagan forces badly needed a means to displace the criticism that would certainly be leveled at the government which had quite knowingly brought on a recession to cure inflation. Watkins explains the strategic cleverness of the Volcker move.

> Using the Fed's traditional interest rate targetting procedures, Volcker could have made the politically suicidal announcement that the Fed was going to peg interest rates at approximately 20 percent. But the anti-Fed forces in Congress had in fact given him a more expedient way to say the same thing. Volcker simply announced that the Fed would redouble its efforts to hit the congressionally mandated money targets, and that to guarantee success, the Fed would pay much less attention to interest rates.[35]

Thus, in October, 1979, the Fed embraced monetarism, a policy package which quite knowingly reduces inflation by inducing recession (and raising unemployment). Volcker's was an astute maneuver, given the phobic anti-inflationary fervor of the late 1970s and the strong monetarist consensus in economic policy circles. That he could snatch a two-way political victory out of the verbal assaults at Belgrade makes the move even more impressive.

First, Volcker could quiet congressional critics, in the short run by appearing to succumb to their pressures for strict control of growth in the money supply. In so doing he may have reduced their taste for strictly monetarist instruments altogether, and diminished their proclivities for their sometimes irritating, but seldom influential, oversight. "Bluntly stated, Volcker has proven beyond all doubt that monetarism can reduce inflation," noted one observer, "but he has proven it so decisively and so ruthlessly that Congress may soon forbid the Fed to use it ever again."[36]

Not only was the independence of the Fed enhanced this way but, second and more important here, Volcker could do the President a crucial favor. By making the Fed the monetarist and pragmatic counterbalance to the supply-side zealotry of the administration's tax-cutting strategy which oriented its first wave of economic policies, Volcker could help Reagan locate himself above the fray. Equally significant, he could displace criticism for the negative consequences of recession from the administration to the Board, thus fulfilling handily the Fed's scapegoat function.

Thus, the switch from a failing effort to control interest rates to an ostensibly successful policy of controling monetary aggregates paid considerable political dividends. As Clark explains,

> Although never admitted by government officials, the prescription for curing inflation was low growth and high unemployment, and the Fed was the blunt instrument of that policy. Fed officials themselves did not acknowledge the pain their actions would entail. . . .
>
> To induce slower growth and declining inflation, interest rates had to rise. And the adoption of the monetarist techniques had unlocked the political shackles that had kept the Fed from doing that. It could and did peer narrowly at M1 and the other monetary aggregates while barely casting a glance sideways as interest rates began their upward march.[37]

Volcker's willingness to take the lead in fostering this therapeutic recession was only the first indication of the political uses to which the Federal Reserve Board could be put. As Reagan's Economic Recovery Program foundered, the Fed under Volcker spearheaded a campaign to secure for Reagan an unusual dimension of autonomy within the state — and to create that very special Teflon protection from the economic policy failures of his own administration.

Believing initially that economic expansion was compatible with a program to reduce inflation, and that extensive spending cuts would shortly follow, the new President proposed both a sharp increase in military expenditure and a large tax cut.[38] Economic recovery would be fueled by a four-point recovery program consisting of the cuts in federal spending, reductions in both corporate and personal income tax, deregulation, and monetary restraint. Affecting the anti-statist pose typical of his outsiders' politics, Reagan blamed government for the economic troubles he inherited, stating in an early address to Congress:

> The federal government, through tax, spending, regulatory and monetary policies, has sacrificed longterm growth and price stability for ephemeral short-term goals. In particular, excessive government spending and overly accommodative monetary policies have combined to give us a climate of continuing inflation. . . .[39]

Unfortunately for Reagan, however, his new initiatives were insufficient to resolve the intractable problems faced by the American economy which made sustained growth unlikely — and lower inflation and growth quite impossible. Sawhill and Stone note the uncertain results of Reagan's recovery program:

> Interest rates began to rise, and the economy headed into a recession as the ink was still drying on the 1981 spending and tax legislation because slower money growth was already working to depress economic activity. By the end of 1982 real gross national product ... was lower than it had been three years earlier and the unemployment rate had risen to nearly 11 percent, its highest rate since the Great depression.[40]

This result was, of course, just what Volcker and his colleagues knew it would be. The Fed anti-inflation plan choked the Reagan recovery plan, but inflation did come down: consumer prices which rose 12 percent in 1980 increased by less than 4 percent in 1982.[41] Also by fiscal year 1982 the federal budget deficit exceeded $100 billion for the first time (it was, in fact, $110.7 billion), and the debt service paid by the government, announced as $100.8 billion also broke the unfortunate $100 billion barrier for the first time.[42]

THE INTRA-STATE DIVISIONS

Thus the situation was ripe not only for an energetic display of hand-wringing by Reagan stalwarts, but for an aggressive display of finger-pointing, too. Was the tightening of the money supply stifling growth — and causing the deficits (in which case monetarism had failed)? Or was fiscal and tax policy forcing the deficit to dangerous heights — and causing interest rates to rise to a point where they stifled investment (in which case Reagonomics, and the supply-side tax cuts which were its centerpiece, had failed)? It is no surprise, but nevertheless very significant, that the Treasury and the Federal Reserve Board diagnosed the problem differently.

One year into Reagan's first term of office a pitched battle erupted between Volcker at the Fed and Donald T. Regan, Reagan's loyal Treasury Secretary (later White House chief of staff). The issues in the dispute were precisely as one would expect. In January, 1982, Regan challenged the Fed's approach to controlling monetary aggregates, insisting that the Fed's policy instruments needed to be "sharpened, redeployed, and made more precise." The *Wall Street Journal* reported that Regan argued strenuously to diverse and very public constituencies — administration appointees and big city financial officers — that the "'uneven pattern' of money supply growth has kept the financial markets nervous." This followed remarks by the President that a "recent surge in money supply [was] sending 'the wrong signal' to the money markets and [might have] hinder[ed] the administration's economic recovery program."[43]

Within a few weeks the internal dispute was even more out in the open and apparently growing in intensity. Noting that the administration was divided on how much pressure should be exerted on Volcker in an election year — and on what direction that pressure should take — the *Wall Street Journal* summarized the growing intra-state controversy in unusually caustic terms.

> Treasury officials have been growing angry in recent days, however, because of the financial markets' poor performance, which has been widely attributed to warnings about federal budget deficits. Much of the stock market's recent decline has been attributed to warnings by Mr. Volcker last week that budget deficits threaten to keep interest rates high and weaken the economy.
>
> Treasury officials, who include members of both the monetarist and supply-side schools, play down the role of deficits in determining interest-rate levels but attach great significance to monetary policy. At meetings in recent days, Secretary Regan and his aides have concluded that Fed policy ought to err on the side of ease. . . .[44]

Indeed, the dispute which heated up in advance of the mid-term elections of 1982 was still boiling as the time for Reagan's re-election neared, amidst charges (and the required official denials) that "the White House was 'setting up' the Fed as a scapegoat should the economy turn sour."[45] The *American Banker* reported that a House Banking Committee session in June, 1984, concerning the rise in interest rates, turned into a sharp exchange between very partisan witnesses. The ongoing dispute between the Fed and the Treasury was unresolved, as Linda W. McCormick noted:

In yet another round of finger-pointing testimony — this time before the House Banking subcommittee on domestic monetary policy, a Treasury official blamed the Fed for keeping interest rates high, and Fed officials continued to lay the blame on the budget deficits kept in place by the administration and Congress.

The assistant Treasury Secretary for economic policy claimed that market uncertainty over the Fed's handling of monetary policy had "boosted" interest rates by 2—4 percent; Cleveland Fed President, Karen N. Horn countered with the argument that high deficits explained the increase in interest rates.[46] After the election nothing seemed changed as Donald Regan continued to criticize the Fed handling of the money supply and threatened action to reduce its "independence."[47]

The split between the Fed and the Treasury is obvious, and the cause is, at least at one level, easy to see. The very success of the Federal Reserve Board's monetarist strategy launched in October, 1979 — to bring down inflation, but forsake any effort to stabilize interest rates — has helped make the problem of interest rates a new source of real concern.

Thus the Fed consciously opened itself for attack; and it is also obvious that the growing federal deficit takes equal pride of place as the major source of macroeconomic worries. "The Federal Reserve's experiment with monetary control is a failure," noted Allan H. Meltzer, a professor of political economy and public policy at Carnegie-Mellon University and co-chair of the Shadow Opoen Market Committee. "Since the experiment began in October 1979 the volatility of money growth, short-term interest rates, long-term interest rates and exchange rates have been raised beyond previous levels and more than necessary." In an effort at equal-handedness, which probably reflected a common "plague on both your houses" attitude among business and academic observers, Meltzer agreed that the public and congressional blame on the budget deficit, as well as Fed policy for growing interest rates, was at least partly valid. "The deficit contributes to higher interest rates but can't explain why interest rates fell in May [1982], rose in June and fell in July." In the end "[u]ncertainty and skepticism" about Fed policy in conjunction with less ephemeral pressures associated with the rising deficit cause the problem. As Meltzer concludes: "The markets see the extraordinary deficits that must be financed in the next six months, and they wonder how well the Fed's faulty control system will respond."[48]

So the feuding, at the least, represents predictable bureaucratic infighting to deflect blame for a serious and complex circumstance, where no single agency — as Meltzer and innumerable others suggest — deserves to assume the entire burden. The Fed/Treasury controversy reveals much, however, about Reagan's capacity to use intra-state divisions to foster an unusual sphere of personal and institutional independence for the White House.

The handling of these controversies about economic management suggests the considerable advantages which accrue to a President as a consequence of the fragmentation and irresolution of the American political system of economic management. This represents a crucial difference in the Anglo-American comparison, for British traditions of firm Cabinet/governmental responsibility at the political level, combined with the greater concentration and coordination of economic management functions, make the nation's chief executive officer bear strict responsibility for policy.

On the contrary, the combination of the carefully architected "independence" of the United States' central bank and a strategically resourceful, inscrutable and determined leader of the Federal Reserve create an interesting opening for the displacement of policy away from the President. Add a genuine dispute about causality in a complex multivariate world with unparsimonious realities and ideologues (supply-siders versus monetarists) who seek single-factor partisan explanations. The result is a location for the President suitably above the fray, where he can operate apart from competing interests.

We also know that the Treasury Secretary was a fiercely loyal Reaganite, whose commitment to the President takes precedence over narrow ministerial loyalties or ideological preferences. The fact that Reagan shifted him early in the second term to White House Chief of Staff is highly suggestive of these qualities in itself, but the *New York Times* report of the exchange of jobs between Regan and James A. Baker, Regan's predecessor as chief of staff and successor at Treasury, eliminates any doubt on the point:

Donald T. Regan, the loyal Treasury Secretary whom President Reagan made his chief of staff today, has been an enigma through the first four years of the Administration. It has never been clear, as his views on issues have shifted and changed over that period, where he really leans.

The simple answer is that Donald Regan shifts and leans where the President leans. Rarely since he was first appointed to the Treasury has Mr. Regan stood apart from the President on the nation's major economic questions — the budget deficit, growth, taxes, budget cuts — that often produced open splits within the Administration and sometimes even within the White House staff.[49]

So Reagan has not one scapegoat, but two, so he can disdain the feuding and appear to foster unity within the administration. This is, of course, a role the President performs with some aplomb. For example, on February 18, 1982, at the height of Treasury anger at the Fed for the poor market performance and Fed counterattacks about the danger of a growing budget — and amidst press reports that Regan was pressuring Volcker[50] — President Reagan issued the following formal statement to the press before one of his carefully orchestrated news conferences.

One of my major concerns today is high interest rates. They hurt everyone — people who must borrow, families who want to buy a new home, businesses struggling to get ahead. High interest rates represent the greatest single threat today to a healthy, lasting recovery. The high level of current interest rates reflects two concerns in the financial community — some fear that the Federal Reserve Board will revert to the inflationary monetary policies of the past; others worry that this administration will tolerate ever-widening budget deficits. Well, I want to make it clear today that neither this administration nor the Federal Reserve will allow a return to the fiscal and monetary policies of the past that have created current conditions.

I have met with Chairman Volcker several times during the past year. We have met again earlier this week. I have confidence in the announced policies of the Federal Reserve Board. The administration and the Federal Reserve can help bring inflation and interest rates down faster by working together than at cross-purposes.[51]

The point is that the administration and the Fed work together *precisely because they do work at cross-purposes.* The monetarism at the Fed provides the administration with the political advantages of reduced inflation, and at the same time displaces to itself any criticism for high interest rates. This is a rationality crisis with considerable advantages to the President, and it is encouraged by a significant shift in the norm of Fed—Treasury relations.

A CHANGE IN INSTITUTIONAL NORMS

Traditionally, the Federal Reserve has steered monetary policy with relatively little interference or direction from the administration, since "federal reserve sympathizers" filled the key Treasury position — the undersecretary for monetary affairs — for the 35-year period which preceded the Reagan—Volcker era. Accordingly, throughout the postwar period "there was no development . . . of an alternative to the Federal Reserve's broad policy lines." Under Johnson the Council of Economic Advisors offered an institutionally weak alternative to the slackening of monetary constraints, and under Nixon the House and Senate Banking committees routinely but ineffectually criticized the Fed policy administered by the Nixon loyalist, Arthur Burns.[52]

Only under Reagan, with the 1981 appointment of Beryl Sprinkel, a member of the Shadow Open Market Committee, as undersecretary for monetary affairs has the Treasury itself launched "a line of policy thinking totally at variance with the traditions of the Federal Reserve." As Newton observed, "These changes in the Treasury were volcanic in their possibilities for the Federal Reserve because they indicated the establishment of a powerful countervoice to that of the Fed in administration policymaking."[53]

Unable to control the broad range of fiscal powers within the government — and indeed within cabinet discussions and White House briefings — the Federal Reserve Board really was "independent" (or at least cut off) for the first time in modern American politics. Enmeshed in a battle for the triangulation of policy (with the Treasury and Congress), the Fed acquired a carefully circumscribed space in which it could derive autonomous policy gestures. It could, as a consequence, become the more perfect scapegoat and agent of presidential misdirection. The

Reagan Recovery was responsible for bringing down inflation. But as interest rates rose, the Federal Reserve and Volcker were blamed. Monetarism became "the Fed's Failed Experiment" as the *Wall Street Journal*'s stentorian headline — for an article written by one of Sprinkel's colleagues on the Shadow Open Market Committee — affirmed in July, 1982.[54]

In this way the nexus of budgetary and monetary policy has become a crucial source of *Reagan*'s independence. The very fragmentation of the institutional bases for economic policy formation and the carefully constructed ideological and program-matic divisions among the Fed, the Treasury, and the Congress help secure the autonomous sphere for maneuver of the presidency — and help Reagan relocate economic defeats elsewhere.

THE WITHDRAWAL FROM LEGISLATIVE POLITICS

Thus the Fed/Treasury relationship is perhaps the most signifi-cant, but certainly not the only, institutional basis for Reagan's unusual withdrawal from the administrative, class, and party pressures which routinely constrain executive initiatives. As previously mentioned, Reagan's extraparliamentary and anti-political bases have permitted him to eschew efforts to secure party approval and support in Congress, and to bypass the traditional exchange relations which govern a President's approach to doing politics — and building future victories — in the House and the Senate.

This point is well made by Lester M. Salamon and Alan J. Abramson, who are concerned about a Reaganite cult of the personality that makes the building of durable legislative coalitions unnecessary.

> The building blocks for such a coalition were available in the senior Republican leadership in the Senate and House, as well as in some of the centrist Democratic leadership in the House, such as Budget Committee chairman Jim Jones and Ways and Means Committee chairman Dan Rostenkowski. While working with these leaders on occasion, the Reagan administration also frequently left them "twisting in the wind." During the first year, for example, the administration tended to bypass the Republican leadership in the

House, dealing directly with the Boll Weevils and other Democratic moderates or conservatives on the crucial budget and tax bills. Similarly, in the initial budget battles of 1981 the administration persisted in advancing economic projections deemed indefensible by most of the Republicans on the Senate Budget Committee. As the credibility of these projections began to dissolve in the latter part of 1981 and into 1982, so too did the president's support among congressional moderates and conservatives, the groups most likely to have formed a stable working majority for him. Rather than meeting this moderate block midway, Reagan's style of governance, particularly after the first year, has been marked by ideological intransigence, last minute compromises, and opportunistic maneuvers that frequently alienated potential allies.[55]

It is both true and commonly noted that institutional fragmentation in the United States reduces the coherence and, very likely, the effectiveness of economic policy. "[T]he structures of government [in Britain, Sweden, and Western Europe more generally] generally seem to concentrate authority over the whole budgetary process," notes Andrew Martin.[56] Reagan's genius is to turn this fragmentation to advantage, so the very lack of coordination between monetary and fiscal policy becomes a source of presidential resilience and empowerment.

REAGAN'S USE OF THE OMB

There is one final element to the strategy: the relationship of the White House to the bureaucracy of the Office of Management and Budget. The OMB with David Stockman as director assumed unusual prominence, particularly in the heady early days of Reagonomics when the agency was told by the President-elect to find $40 billion to cut — and soon, in time for the first budget message. Stockman was the cutting edge in the budget reductions, heading a budget working group which systematically isolated each Cabinet member in turn. The Secretaries then found it nearly impossible to withstand pressure to reduce expenditures. "Each meeting will involve only the relevant Cabinet member and his aides with four or five strong keepers of the central agenda," explained Stockman to William Greider, a journalist confidant.

"So on Monday, when we go into the decision on synfuels programs, it will be [Energy Secretary James B.] Edwards defending them against six guys saying, by God, we've got to cut these back or we're not going to have a savings program that will add up."[57]

One result of the pressure for quick results was a mad passion for work by Stockman and senior appointed staff aides, and a resulting simplification of procedures and substantive deliberations. "I just wish that there were more hours in the day or that we didn't have to do this so fast," remarked Stockman. "I have these stacks of briefing books and I've got to make decisions about specific options. . . . I don't have time, trying to put this whole package together in three weeks, so you just start making snap judgments." This acceleration of the review process resulted in the introduction of a new term into the budget process: "zero out." Old war-on-poverty programs like the job-training schemes funded under the Comprehensive Employment and Training Act (CETA) and the Community Services administration were zeroed out, the budget eliminated in a single fiscal year.[58]

These extreme examples of top-down budgeting were very effective, for once again they avoided the routine checks on presidential initiative which normally slow down the process and enhance OMB influence. "Stockman's agency did in a few weeks what normally consumes months," remarked Greider. "[T]he process was made easier because the normal opposition forces had no time to marshal either their arguments or their constituents and because the President was fully in tune with Stockman."[59] The procedure was astonishingly simple. Stockman would draw up a proposal and would introduce it to the budget working group, quickly if possible "before the new Cabinet officers were fully familiar with their departments and prepared to defend their bureaucracies."[60] When the relevant Cabinet member was sandbagged and a decision was reached by the working group, a memo would be sent to Reagan and the President could indicate approval by checking the appropriate box. "Once he checks it," noted Stockman, "I put that in my safe and I go ahead and I don't let it come back up again."[61]

Effective and speedy, the Reagan method of rapid budgeting occasioned a severe reduction in the function of the OMB professional staff, even as it helped encourage growing executive and increasingly politicized control of the formulation of fiscal policy. Salamon and Abramson note the institutional changes which these procedures effected.

> Serving as it did as the centerpiece of the administration's entire program, the budget became an important vehicle of expanding presidential control over policy. In the process it also became politicized as never before, and consequently lost considerable credibility. The loss was costly not only for the president's relations with Congress . . . but also for the institutional health of the Office of Management and Budget [OMB], the presidential staff agency ultimately responsible for developing the president's budget each year. Despite the undisputed competence of Stockman, the budget director, and despite the prominence of the agency as a whole under Reagan, the permanent OMB staff has lost certain of its functions thanks to the practice of "top-down budgeting," which, in a context of heightened political sensitivity, threatens professional norms and institutional capacities.[62]

This politicization of the budgetary process in the early days of the Reagan administration, like the White House withdrawal from the normal exchange relations which dominate executive/legislative interaction, secured for Reagan an unusual sphere of autonomy — an institutional basis for enormous political leverage — in the formulation of economic policy. The institutional and ideological consolidation of the budgetary process, combined with the fragmentation of economic policy between the Treasury and the Federal Reserve Board, has given Reagan the best of all arrangements. He can control and rapidly implement policy, all the while encouraging intra-state divisions.

Thus, Reagan secures the high ground of economic principle and reserves for himself the successes — reduced inflation and the recovery before the 1984 election. The failures are Volcker's and even the deficit, which has united business as never before against this most sympathetic of all presidents, becomes a crucial ideological tool for sustaining the de-integrative policies since the reduction in transfer payments is ostensibly required as a matter of fiscal rectitude. The administration's need to meet the deficit-reduction requirements of Gramm—Rudman only intensifies these pressures.

The Reagan administration has initiated significant institutional changes, with uncertain repercussions. At the same time the indications concerning the economic success record are by no means clear. In this regard neither the deficit gloom which engulfed official Washington at the beginning of Reagan's second term nor the studied optimism which pervaded British financial circles through much of 1985 represent the best points of reference from which to assess these governments.[63] As I hope to demonstrate, the success of the Reagan and Thatcher administrations should be measured also by reference to the social and political implications of the de-integrative strategies they pursue and the pattern of ideological misdirection they foster, issues which will help frame the discussion in the final chapter.

8
Politics in the Age of Reagan and Thatcher

The deepening international recession following the oil shock of 1973 strained the institutional arrangements of the postwar settlement, shattered the uneasy alliance between domestic Keynesianism and international liberalism in the United States, and ended *Pax Americana*. The decline of American hegemony does not make international economic cooperation impossible, but it does erode the existing institutional principles and reduce the costs of non-compliance.[1] This uncertainty in the "international regime" contributes, also, to the openness of domestic politics.

Accordingly, we are now observing a period of disequilibrium in international affairs and uncertain experiments in domestic political arrangements. Decline and stagnation have unleashed a formidable array of new political forces of the left and right — and some which stretch the interpretive logic of traditional left—right distinctions.[2] These movements which are often anti-state (anti-big government, anti-bureaucratic) have challenged the tradition of alternation of government between similarly constituted mainstream parties which are willing to acquire the ready-made institutions of state power. Their ranks include everything from the German Greens to neo-fascist National Front groups in the UK and France, but also: women activists, anti-nuclear movements, taxpayer revolts, gay rights organizations, and political agitation by immigrant and guest workers and by discontented youth.

These new political movements are unsettling. Unlike traditional extraparliamentary parties which, even by their radical oppositions, confirmed the centrality of state power and the precedence of traditional state forms, these new political movements foster belief in a "crisis of democracy" or a "legitimation crisis" even when they play more or less strictly by accepted parliamentary rules. In Germany the Free Democrats have been dislodged as the fulcrum which has kept the political system at a homeostatic center. The March 6, 1983 Bundestag election which brought The Greens to national prominence was viewed by many conservatives as a *Schicksalswahl* ("election of destiny") which represented a choice "not only between freedom and socialism but, more forebodingly, between order and chaos."[3] Even where they are neither numerically nor strategically significant, new political movements may place in doubt accepted institutional arrangements and political verities. Like the mobilizations during Italy's "hot autumn" 15 years before, the nuclear freeze campaign in the UK, led by the women at Greenham Common, has had significant consequences for the inner cohesion and outer "governability" of traditional left parties.

None of this is intended to suggest that these movements are the basic source of instability in European domestic politics, simply that they can be part of a comprehensive pattern of government uncertainty. More generally the decline of economic competitiveness makes statecraft an increasingly difficult art, as much for the left governments in France and in Sweden as for the right governments in the UK and the US. In France an ambiguous economic record by a Socialist government has led to an inordinate collapse of its political support with no modernizing coalition anywhere on the political map ready to provide new stability.[4] In Sweden, despite the enthusiasm elsewhere for its innovative approach to social democratic transformation through the socialization of an increasing share of investment funds (the "Meidner Plan"), the policy has been implemented only in a politically weakened form. Economic decline has reduced the incentive for support by the more advantaged trade union sectors and, more generally, strained the traditions of solidaristic wage bargaining.[5]

Thus, any evaluation of the success of the Reagan and Thatcher governments must be placed in the context of a near-universal incapacity of governments to secure either a significant complement of the aims their adherents sought or a representative sample of the positive outcomes which were long assumed to be the routine outcome of policy during the era of the Keynesian welfare state. Whether discussed in terms of the social rights of citizenship, the growth of the integrative capacities of the systems of political representation or the state-guaranteed prosperity and political moderation of "modern capitalism" — many influential observers saw in the postwar settlement a promise of economic growth, political stability, and social cohesion.[6]

Today the transitory character of the postwar settlement and KWS, the historically contingent and fragile quality of the institutional arrangements, and the ethos of compromise, seem much clearer. It was far easier before the political implications of the global recession of the 1970s were as obvious as they are today, and before Reagan and Thatcher, to be lulled by the seeming permanence of the 30-year reign of Keynesianism. It was, in fact, common to grant an undeserved status of capitalist universality to the atypical arrangements of the long postwar period of relative prosperity and at least moderate labor peace and social harmony.

This book is an effort to see past these politically dangerous and intellectually limiting illusions. I have tried to explain why the universalist ethos of welfarism associated with the KWS lost validity, and to chart the emergence and consolidation of the Thatcher and Reagan governments. I have discussed why these governments are highly unusual in a set of structurally determined features. They are atypical of postwar Conservative or Republican governments, ideologically motivated to an unprecedented degree for modern British and American administrations, and highly statist. Through the application of powerful de-integrative appeals which fragment opposition, by the withdrawal from corporatist arrangements (in the UK) and the artful manipulation of intra-state institutional divisions (in the US), and by the adventitious exercise of *machtpolitik* these governments secure unusual discretionary powers, both within the state and above the normal interplay of class and elite interests.

Their success to date involves the manipulation of fears to divide populations and the assimilation of hopes in unlikely guises. In the 1980 campaign for the Republican nomination, now Vice President George Bush referred to Reagonomics as "voodoo economics" — but there is nothing magical or mysterious about the consolidation of state power by the forces of the new and old right in these two countries. Politics in the age of Reagan and

Thatcher is deeply rooted in the decline of international standing, and in economic competitiveness, and in the erosion of the Keynesian/welfarist/growth consensus. Indeed, the evolution of these unexpected governments is only part of a much broader pattern of political disquiet and uncertainty which enmeshes the capitalist democracies today.

The uncertainty of Western economies and the decline of American hegemony have produced a transition in European politics, but unlike the period of the postwar settlement and the emergence of the Keynesian welfare state, this transition involves divergence rather than consensus, the repolarization of East—West relations, and the reinvigoration of radical and highly ideological alternatives to mainstream welfarist politics. The decline of the KWS represents more than the eclipse of an economic theory or a reduction in welfare provision: it represents the erosion of support for an historic vision of society.[7] It also represents a change in the way the progress and success of government initiatives are evaluated.

As Adam Przeworski and Michael Wallerstein explain, the system of class compromise and political canalization of dispute during the height of the KWS was not without its advantages, and its passing introduces considerable difficulties.

> [B]y most criteria of economic progress, the Keynesian era was a success. Whether or not this was due to the efficacy of Keynesian economic policies or was merely fortuitous is a matter of debate. Nevertheless, output grew, unemployment was low, social services were extended and social peace reigned. Until the late 1960s, Keynesianism was the established ideology of class compromise, under which different groups could conflict within the confines of a capitalist and democratic system.[8]

It is equally true and significant, moreover, that during this era policies and governments were evaluated in accordance with KWS principles. What mattered was their capacity to fulfill the full employment and enhanced equality pledge which was the architectonic basis for the postwar settlement. Growth was not their achievement, but followed from the "unexpectedly dazzling"[9] and thereafter apparently natural performance of capitalism in the postwar period. Therefore governments were not judged quite so much by their ability to promote successful economic performance, since productivity increases, a reduced incidence of strikes and "full" employment, high rates and increased levels of domestic investment and an upward growth curve were all routine and nearly universal occurrences among the capitalist democracies. Accordingly, it seemed reasonable to evaluate governments by reference to social rights and democratic norms, not simply performance.

Not just the material effects of economic policy mattered, but also the effects of policy on the *moral economy*.[10] These were different standards of success than those typically applied to the governments of Reagan and Thatcher — or for that matter, of Mitterrand and Papandreou — today, when the issues of the economy are so pressing.

EVALUATING REAGAN AND THATCHER

There are, of course, solid historical reasons for this change in evaluative motif. Before the economic problems of the 1970s the taken-for-granted fact of continued economic growth left to the state a fairly circumscribed role, as Berger explains:

[W]hether [what] the good the state was to provide was a plan or anti-inflationary measures or investment subsidies for highways, the expectation was that state intervention would be most effective when it served to reinforce and accelerate "natural" economic tendencies, and would be least effective when it aimed to change society and economy in accordance with political priorities. If political considerations led governments to decide to protect traditional producers against competition, or to build Concordes, or to introduce workers self-management, then policy would bump into the inevitable constraints of running an industrial economy and would succeed at distorting its course only at costs so high as to make likely an ultimate reversal in course.[11]

With "natural" economic tendencies nowadays presumed to be far less reliable, and with many governments politically re-invigorated and more ideologically directive, the possibility of successful governmental management of the political economy is considerably reduced, and the meaning of that success transformed. Most crucially, today governments are evaluated in terms of their ability to do what they were encouraged *not* to do in the easier postwar world of growth and compromise — by their ability to "change society and economy in accordance with political priorities."

This is a reasonable approach and yet it is one full of risks. Capitalist economies are cyclical and government economic policies these days — as with the Volcker anti-inflation plan launched in October, 1979 — involve explicit bottom-line trades of one foreordained negative consequence for another. The "American economy has demonstrated impressive resiliency and America's economic performance has improved substantially,"[12] observed Martin Feldstein in the summer of 1985. Inflation has dropped from 13 percent to a manageable 4 percent annual rate, and GNP has increased more than 12 percent during the 2 years of generalized recovery. William Benedetto, head of corporate finance for Dean Witter, Reynolds, called Reagan's re-election "an investment banker's dream world"[13] — but an annual budget deficit in excess of $200 billion and the overvalued dollar were no dream for export sectors which depend on strong foreign sales. The US merchandise trade deficit quadrupled between 1981 and 1984 and was expected to rise in 1985 to about $140 billion (or 3½ percent of the GNP)[14] Thus the general industrial recovery has not included crucial sectors: agriculture, timber, steel, chemicals, parts of high-technology industries. Accordingly the recovery is unbalanced and may, as one observer noted, "reduce the overall strength of the economy."[15]

Likewise, the British economy presents a set of highly contradictory characteristics: real industrial investment 13 percent higher in the third quarter of 1984 than in the third quarter of 1983; industrial and commercial profits (excluding those derived from North Sea oil) in the first half of 1984 increased by 17 percent in real terms from the comparable period a year before; output per worker increased at an annual rate of 3.1 percent (from 1981 to 1984), and total output improved by 2.7 percent per annum for the same period. Private industrial investment rose by about 13 percent in 1985 and exports rose by 7 percent. The retail price inflation held at 5 percent for the fourth quarter of 1985 and was expected to fall by 4 percent or below in 1986. There are, however, a set of less hearting economic indicators also available: import penetration rose from 24.8 percent in 1978 to 30.8 percent in 1983, and manufacturing employment fell from 7.193 to 5.970 million; the number of bankruptcies rose from 3902 to 1978 to 5700 in 1982, and company liquidations during this same period from 5086 to 12,067; between 1979 and 1983, the number unemployed rose by 1.8 million to reach some 15 percent of the workforce in real terms[17] — or at an average annual rate between 1981 and 1984 of 0.04 percent.[18]

On balance, therefore, the record of the Thatcher government is both mixed and broadly consistent with ideological and programmatic preferences. In 1985 the economy continued to expand: fixed investments and exports have grown because of high liquidity and the fall in sterling early in the year, while consumer demand slumped and some significant destocking developed. Both the government's most impressive success (inflation) and its most serious economic failure (unemployment) hold generally true to form.

As these radically inconsistent data indicate, economic performance criteria, which may appear to be the most scientific and practical, are in fact ephemeral and highly political from the start. There can be reasonable disagreement about whether a government should be applauded or criticized for lowering inflation at the expense of higher unemployment, or bringing down interest rates by slowing growth. There are claims to be made that a nation's economy suffers structural problems — the American budgetary or trade deficits, the British import penetration and unemployment — that are intractable and for which governments should not be blamed excessively. It is, I think, undeniable that governments select constituencies to advantage and disadvantage by the choices of economic policy they pursue, and that these choices are ideological and highly political.

Hence the meaning and distribution of economic success and failure immediately politicizes the ostensibly neutral categories of economic performance. It does not follow from this that economic performance criteria are meaningless, rather that the meanings themselves must be carefully scrutinized and evaluated. In the end these economic criteria are no more "neutral" or "scientific," but only a good deal less honest than the clearly enunciated standards of Marshall and Kirchheimer and Shonfield: the most extensive citizenship rights to commodious living consistent with capitalism; the continued political integration of outgroups; an effective macroeconomic policy to harmonize the interests of diverse producers groups while retaining as high a quotient of governmental accountability as possible. How shall these governments — and their re-election successes — be evaluated?

AFTER THE VICTORIES

There is a great tendency in American journalism to treat politics like sports. Thus the set of three presidential debates (each, by the way, referred to as a "round") in 1984 between Reagan and Mondale were analyzed not for their programmatic implications, but almost exclusively by reference to who "won" or "lost" — and "could Mondale deliver a knockout punch?" It seems that Mondale could not, so it was Reagan who got to toss the coin to determine who kicked off in the subsequent football championship game (the Super Bowl) and Reagan who took the oath of office to begin his second term on "Super Sunday." Nor is the *New York Times* unwilling to extend its sports journalism to foreign contests, treating readers interested in the debate over the abolition of the Greater London Council (GLC) to the catchy headline: "Thatcher vs. Red Ken: Winner to Take London."[19]

In this context it is hard not to consider the Thatcher and Reagan re-elections as "walkovers" or to deny their considerable victories. While some claim that Labour lost the 1983 election, rather than the Conservatives winning it,[20] there is evidence to suggest that decline in Labour support was linked to both an erosion of sentiment for the social democratic project and the continued influence of the suburbanization of the Tory party. As Ivor Crewe observes:

> Defection from Labour was widespread across the entire social spectrum of the Labour vote. But it was especially heavy on the periphery of its social constituency — 38 percent of 1979 non-manual Labour voters switched in 1983, 36 percent of its white collar union vote switched, and so did 33 percent of its non-union

vote. The largest-scale switching occurred among homeowners (44 percent switched from Labour), working class owners as much as middle-class owners. The Labour vote held up best — although still not very well — among council tenants (21 percent switched), blacks (21 percent), and those over 65 (25 percent). But there is scant comfort for Labour here. Council tenants are a slowly diminishing group; blacks are a tiny minority; and those over 65 will rapidly depart from the electorate.[21]

The news for anti-Reagan forces was hardly more encouraging, for Reagan won in an equally impressive manner. According to polls conducted by CBS news and the *New York Times*, Reagan was preferred to Mondale by a majority of women, men, whites, blue-collar workers, and voters under 25, while Mondale carried 90 percent of the black vote, and a slight majority of Jewish voters and voters in union households.[22] Journalists looking for relief from writing yet another landslide story, discovered that the gender gap had closed somewhat (from an 8 to a 4½ percentage difference between male and female support for Reagan, with a majority of women now supporting Reagan) — but that a big "marriage gap" had opened. Polling data indicated that married people supported Reagan (63 percent to 37 percent), but single people supported the President by a reduced margin (52 percent to 47 percent).[23]

There is no denying the extent of the victory. Nor (as with Thatcher) would it be appropriate to neglect the signs that an electoral mandate may also portend a worrisome change in the moral economy. Nevertheless, it was something of a surprise to find both these points made with equal force in the *New York Times* semi-official valedictory on the Reagan re-election:

Whatever history's judgment on President Reagan, no one can accuse him of having entered the White House through the back door. On Tuesday, he won a second electoral landslide, and this time piled up a mighty popular vote to go along with 525 electoral votes, the largest total in the history of presidential politics. These voters were not driven his way by war or economic collapse. Mr. Reagan's opponent, former Vice President Walter F. Mondale, was a solid political figure, so he clearly did not win by being perceived the lesser of two evils. Rather, six out of ten voters said clearly and unambiguously that they wanted him to be President. In that sense, the election was a triumphant affirmation of Mr. Reagan's popularity.

Yet there was a darker side to the 1984 contest. Mr. Mondale, in a sad, dignified final speech to supporters in his home state of Minnesota, affirmed his commitment to the underprivileged, intimating, as he has all year, that there was a troubling appeal to self-interest at the heart of the Republicans' message. And the potential for racial division that has been a part of Mr. Reagan's politics since his opposition to the Civil Rights Act in 1964 seemed heightened: more than 90 percent of the black voters refused to endorse the Reagan mandate.[24]

As the *New York Times* article implies, it may be appropriate to look beyond the figures — both the exit polling data and the economic performance records — when evaluating these governments. It is undeniable that so far Reagan and Thatcher have satisfied a sufficient number of voting citizens that their politics represents the best approach to governance in a post-welfarist, post-hegemonic order. But is the cost of this new brand of politics too high when assessed in terms of reduced democratic participation, divided political communities, and more attenuated control of the executive?

The close of the *New York Times* commentary above suggests an appropriate point of departure for an effort to see deeper meanings in these election returns, for it brings into focus the de-integrative strategies of the current US and UK governments. I think it is clear that both the Thatcher and Reagan governments — through active policies and by indifference — have increased racial polarization in their societies. When Thatcher expresses sympathy for those who feel swamped by the small inflow of New Commonwealth and Pakistani passport-holders (some 30,000 in 1981), endorses a new British Nationality Act which restricts citizenship with full rights of settlement exclusively to patrials and to those already legally resident in the UK, and then rejects her own minister's plan for treating the problems of urban decay and youth unemployment which helped promote Britain's riots in 1981 (and again in 1985)[25] — the indications of a *them* vs. *us* divide on racial lines seems very clear.

Likewise, regarding the US, Robert Lekachmen notes simply that "The Reagan Administration is the most racist in recent history," and concludes, "[t]he president and his co-conspirators have been conducting undeclared war against blacks and Hispanics, welfare clients, women, children, and blue-collar workers."[26] While this is a difficult assessment to enforce, it is probably safe to say that the Reagan administration has reversed a pattern of political integration of racial minorities in the United States.

During the Reagan years the ability of victims of discrimination to sue the state has been reduced by the Supreme Court's use of doctrines of sovereign, judical and prosecutorial immunity and by a set of more restrictive criteria for determining standing. Decisions concerning the right to bring cases involving both educational and employment policy have indicated that the court is generally unwilling to provide group remedies for group wrongs. Of course, the behavior of the Supreme Court cannot be linked in any transparent way to administration policy; but it is reasonable to try to gauge the implications of a Justice Department which refuses to pursue discrimination cases, resists affirmative action in hiring policy, has argued to the Court that previously established protections be revoked, and a President who invokes the racist code words "states rights" (used in efforts to defeat federally legislated integration of public facilities twenty years ago). Haywood Burns explains:

> Added to [the Supreme Court's] conservative predilection on racial issues are the urgings of an Administration and Justice Department that unashamedly seek to turn back the civil rights clock. Until now the Burger Court has demonstrated a measure of independence. Its resolve may be weakening, and will be in even greater jeopardy if the political climate grows more reactionary after the November election and if President Reagan gets the opportunity to put his stamp on the Court.[27]

Climatological changes are difficult to predict, although Burns' fears are, I think, fully justified. It is clear, moreover, that an evaluation of the Reagan and Thatcher governments in terms of the precepts of the KWS does not depend mainly on speculations about what comes next. Have marginal or politically disenfranchised groups become increasingly integrated into the affairs of state? Have citizenship rights proceeded along their expanding evolutionary path? Has economic policy been set to harmonize diverse interests in society?

Where economic policy and de-integrative strategies come together, the answers to these questions are unmistakable. In the United States it is easy to detect the process of the feminization and "racialization" of poverty: between 60 and 80 percent of the recipients of federal welfare programs cut by the Reagan administration have been low-income women and their children.[28] Nationwide, 80 percent of the caseload for families that receive AFDC involves female-headed households and, in New York City the figure is 91 percent.[29] In 1981, 45 percent of all black children lived in poverty (compared to 14.7 percent of white children) — and for children in black female-headed households the poverty rate was 68 percent.[30] It is perhaps less widely known that for white women "the social welfare economy" (both government and private sector contract work) accounted for 39 percent of all new jobs between 1969 and 1980; for black women it accounted for fully 58 percent of the jobs gained during this period.[32]

Accordingly, women, blacks, and especially black women have been disproportionately affected by the reductions in force (RIFs) mandated by federal budget cuts. The Office of Management and Budget estimated that budget cuts for Fiscal Years (FYs) 1981—1984 would reduce the federal government's non-defense employment by 8 percent (150,000) by 1987. The Federal Government Service Task Force estimated that of the employees to be laid off by the end of FY 1982, fully three-fifths were in the social welfare agencies. Finally, the Task Force noted that among the first 12,000 RIFs, women in the upper managerial—professional levels (GS12 or higher) were RIFed at a rate 150 percent higher than their male counterparts — and black administrators were laid off at a rate 200 percent higher than white administrators.[32]

Thus women in general, and black women in particular, have been doubly hurt and marginalized by the reduction of transfer payments: once as a disproportionate number of the recipients and once as late entrants to the labor market. Accordingly, the "Reagan revolution" has economically disadvantaged and marginalized two central constituencies which had been partly integrated into the affairs of state by the KWS programs and the New Deal/Kennedy coalition politics of the War on Poverty. At a stroke, the best hopes of a generation of postwar thinkers for political integration and the expansion of the social rights of citizenship have been denied. The consequences cut deep into the political life in the UK as in the USA, and affect the very meaning of capitalist democracy.

It seems clear that the vision of a cohesive and variegated political community — in which the coalitional politics of the KWS involved diverse constituencies in the creation of a political agenda — has been shelved. Thus the terms of the reconciliation between capitalism and democracy have been recast. The prerogatives of private capitalist elites are expanded. The safeguards offered the politically weaker groups — ethnic and racial minorities, women — are substantially reduced. Democratic participation has shrunk in some ways to nineteenth-century proportions as the dimensions of capitalist power expand commensurately. This is what it takes to restore confidence in the US and break the power of British trade unions; but the social costs measured in terms of reduced participation and democratic control of government have not yet been fully assessed.

BEYOND THE WELFARE STATE

It is a sign of the times, and an indication of the power of the Reagan and Thatcher governments to construct a divided and amoral political community, that political discourse is often so shallow today and anti-capitalist perspectives so quiet. With the human price of reduced welfare provision so high and the division in society growing — leftists often forgo more exacting standards by which to judge contemporary governments in order to participate in a defensive struggle to bolster the no longer fashionable principles of the KWS. In so far as the availability and the level of transfer payments represent for many the difference between meager existence and outright privation, the battle for welfare *provision* is necessary but the *welfare state* is past saving. In fact, it never really was.

The expression "welfare state" never described the structural attributes of given nation-states or governments. Rather, as Ian Gough asserts, "the very term the welfare state reveals the ideological nature of most writing about it."[33] Clusters of social-welfare policy and institutionally reinforced cultural expectations about expanding entitlements may have summarized a stage of development of the contemporary state. Likewise, welfare provision of a particular variety and level of fiscal generosity represented "a constituent feature of modern *Capitalist* societies."[34] But the "welfare state" is not the ultimate resting place of capitalism: perhaps it is the highest stage, but certainly not the final stage of capitalism.

It is now all too clear that the KWS represented a transitory motif of class compromise, a fairly long but nonetheless limited *durée* which was determined by the contingent interplay of political forces within a context set by exceptional economic performance. There is no welfare state, only a set of welfare provisions. Designed to offset the brute force of capitalism — and, equally, the physical frailities of the species (old age, invalidity, etc.) — these policies are often accompanied by a set of corporatist arrangements to ease their implementation. The social policies and the institutional provisions of the KWS alike were typical of an unusual period, perhaps never to be repeated.

The demise of the institutional arrangements, legitimating strategies, and social policy packages of the KWS defines not only a new age of politics — but also a new set of possibilities for the re-invigoration of progressive politics. Indeed, it is possible that highly ideological governments of the right, like that of Reagan and Thatcher, which reject the premises of the class compromise and the harmonization of interests, and which assert a more radical executive autonomy, may at the same time also encourage new forms of resistance. A short reprise of how Reagan and Thatcher each acquired power may help provide clues to what might happen next.

At an elementary but crucial political level the vicissitudes of electoral and party politics provided the ideological opening for Reagan and Thatcher. Edward Heath's U-turn towards an incomes policy and his celebrated defeat after a challenge to the miners in 1974 diminished the appeal of conventional Toryism, and thereby allowed Thatcher to secure the Conservative Party leadership. The collapse of the "Social Contract" leading to the "winter of discontent" in 1978 belied the Labour government's corporatist vision and eroded its traditional base of support. Otherwise, the resounding victory of Thatcherite Toryism in May, 1979 would have been unthinkable.

Similarly, Reagan's election would have been impossible but for the débacle of Nixon's Watergate and the drawn-out failures of the Carter administration in economic and foreign policy. Nie, Verba and Petrocik argued just a year before his election that Reagan, like Goldwater, was ideologically too extreme to win the election.[35] But time and again during the campaign Carter was unsuccessful in his attempts to paint Reagan as an extremist. Despite Carter's fiscal conservatism and his repudiation of the traditional Democratic commitment to full employment, which brought the "Misery Index" (inflation plus unemployment) to new highs, the Democrats were blamed for the failures of the Carter years. The voters responded by electing a new and different conservative to office. Ironically, the failure of one kind of conservative economic policy generated an ideological opening for another. Reaching up his sleeve, Reagan produced supply-side economics, a program with uncertain economic merit, but considerable political success — not least because it enabled Reagan to distinguish himself from Carter. Thus, in both the United Kingdom and the United States, the capture of the party by an unconventional ideological faction followed a critical failure by more traditional conservative leadership. National victory at the polls in each case took the form of a response to the lingering ineptitude of the center—left alternative.

The preconditions for the emergence of Thatcher and Reagan are also political in a second, more profound, way. As the stable formula of domestic Keynesianism and international liberalism broke down, free trade orthodoxies were eclipsed and the celebration of the KWS cut short as the egalitarian social values of welfarism lost hold. Tarnished by the failures they managed during the KWS, there was declining support for traditional parties as the standard bearers of belief. This accompanied a growth in "antipolitical" parties and movements — representing "peripheral" nationalism, taxpayers' revolts, ecologists. There was growth in antinuclear activism, "new right" movements, women's movements, etc. As Berger observed, "[i]n the seventies, the dominant political response to the new transparence of the state [was] to try to dismantle it. . . . Never before has this conception of politics shaped new political ideas on both the Left and the Right."[36]

At the same time the decisive decline in economic growth — which can scarcely be exaggerated as a grounds for the emergence of the Reagan (and Thatcher) governments — caused the tensions immanent in society, where ideology had not really disappeared and interests beneath the national political consensus had never been resolved, to emerge with new force. The class compromises which marked the Keynesian political order receded throughout Western polities and nowhere more rapidly than in the US and UK. In the US and UK left forces — as labor movement and/or party — were not able to fill the ideological opening in national politics, nor could they forge antipolitical elements into a durable force or apply the outpouring of radical political sentiment to clear political purpose. Meanwhile, Thatcher and Reagan galvanized right wing antipolitical and antistatist sentiments and, exonerating even the most self-interested anti welfarist beliefs, they united diverse constituencies. Relying on very good timing for very dubious theories[37] they offered ready "solutions" to the unsolvable problems of contemporary capitalism.

In short, the Reagan and Thatcher governments emerged when an electoral opening coincided with a deep erosion of the principles, a failure of the practices, and a destabilization of the institutions of the KWS. Thus there was an assault on society's equilibrating mechanisms with many dimensions: a decline in geopolitical standing, a crisis in economic spheres, a breakdown of compromises and institutions for mediating and containing claims among the most powerful groups in society, a collapse in central belief structures which provided an element of coherence and some basis for commonality among otherwise divided interests. Reagan and Thatcher were able to offer an alternative vision of society with which to mobilize an electoral majority, posit new-sounding economic doctrines, and discredit the mediating institutions of the KWS. How long can this new politics of Reagan and Thatcher hold together? Have the tensions immanent within the politics of Reagan and Thatcher begun to undermine their mission?

THE TENSIONS WITHIN

From the very beginning of Reagan's 1980 campaign his strategists recognized that his success as a candidate, and potentially as President, required that sharp programmatic and ideological distinctions be drawn between issues of civil rights/human rights and economic policy. They understood that traditional liberal ethics — fairness in government action which concerned diverse interests, income levels, ethnic groups, races; commitments to equal opportunity and reduced racial discrimination; provision of welfare for the "truly needy" — remained grounded in solid majoritarian values. Reagan's job was to distinguish this set of political constants from the ideologically vulnerable social democratic objectives of the labor movement and highly identified Democratic liberals: redistributive welfarist measures; expanded provision beyond "true need" and outside traditional governmental responsibility as defined in the US (for example, health care and housing); affirmative action to reduce racial and gender-based patterns of discrimination. Reagan accepted instinctively what pollsters repeatedly confirmed, that any widespread perception that he lacked compassion or unfairly advantaged the wealthy or opposed equal opportunity would damage his candidacy — and his presidency — among at least two crucial groups of potential supporters. Moderate Republicans and independents who supported mild KWS principles and improved civil rights would be put off. Equally important, "populist" or "new politics" Democrats and independents with a greenish tinge — who opposed big business and "special interests" (including trade unions) — might be lost in considerable numbers.[38]

Although the President held these supporters together in electoral terms remarkably well through two campaigns, there is reason to suspect that a real tension exists between the economic policy and the civil rights/human rights stand of the administration. Economic policy has jeopardized Reagan on the crucial fairness issue. This process began as early as 1981, with the passage of the Economic Recovery Tax Act. ERTA was so generous to business investors, notably in high-technology computer-based firms, for example, that the value of allowable deductions and credits often exceeded the tax liability on increased income. Thus, for equipment investments "the depreciation system . . . turned from a tax to a net subsidy, and equipment purchase provided excess deductions and credits that could be used to shelter from tax, income from other sources."[39] ERTA even permitted investing firms with income too low to accommodate all permissible tax benefits to transfer or sell these benefits to other companies.

Neither the reversal of tax policy reflected in the Tax Equity and Fiscal Responsibility Act of 1982 (TEFRA) nor the administration support for a simplified tax plan in Reagan's second term have quieted fears that the self-interests of those in the Reagan coterie have dictated the terms of his tax policy. One Washington journalist noted:

> President Reagan's Tax Proposals for Fairness, Growth and Simplicity are a radical assault on the progressive income tax, a knee in the groin for workers and a windfall for those whose income derives from speculation in stocks and bonds. It is eminently fair to the very rich, provides genuine relief for the very poor and is so complex that the Commissioner of internal revenue has said he will need more help to administer it.[40]

Such responses to Reagan's most carefully planned exercise in economic policy fairness suggest that Reagan's critical need to maintain a public perception of equity on economic matters is difficult to sustain and may be seriously eroded.

Even more crucial than tax policy misadventures, Reagan's turnabout on the deficit and the administration's inability to significantly stem record government overspending, have considerably strained his political support. According to a highly respected Washington source, the word "panic" was used to describe reaction to Reagan budget deficits by Republican members of Congress, and by the Main Street merchants who are the core of the GOP. Nor did the remarkable reversal in one of Reagan's central governing doctrines go without notice. It was reported that Reagan's acceptance of record deficits was seen as comparable to a call by Edward Kennedy for increased unemployment to fight inflation.[41]

By summer 1985, a sluggish economy, concerns about tax reform, and the deficit made Reagan's second presidency appear to be drifting without clear direction. The President was politically mishandling the budget, which increased internecine division among the Republicans, amidst aggressive charges from House Speaker Tip O'Neill that the administration "has no plan whatever for dramatically cutting the budget" — a partisan claim nevertheless confirmed both by ranking Republicans and government reports.[42] Most nettlesome for Reagan — given his characteristically confident air — were the findings of a *Time* magazine poll conducted in late July: three out of four registered voters had "only a little confidence" or "none at all" that Reagan could successfully revise the tax law, reduce the deficit, or reach an arms reduction agreement with the Soviet Union.[43] The *New York Times* warned ominously in a graphic headline: "For the President, the Tough Part Could Be Just Beginning."[44]

Nor was the Thatcher government free from political damage which flowed from problems in its economic policy. The Thatcher government has staked a lot on the argument that inflation is a monetary phenomenon which can be remedied by free market processes: negatively by the elimination of prices and incomes policies and the restriction of trade unionist abilities to "artificially" increase the cost of labor; positively by operating the PSBR to ensure a decline in monetary growth.[45] Unfortunately for the government, Thatcher's second term offers some indication of growing difficulties in the political management of serious economic problems. Both the Treasury and the Confederation of British Industry predicted strong growth and moderating inflation,[46] but available data painted a rather different picture: at 7 percent for the 12 months to May, 1985, inflation was double what it had been 2 years before, and industrial production, while rising 5 percent over the 12 months to April, 1985, remained 2 percent below its peak in the second quarter of 1979 when Margaret Thatcher became Prime Minister.[47]

Not surprisingly unemployment continued to rise, standing officially at 13.1 percent in June 1985, up 0.6 percent from a year before.[48] As economic analyst Gavyn Davies observed:

> As Mrs. Thatcher's second term has progressed with relatively little sign of a down-turn in unemployment, the political salience of the issues seems to have increased. No longer is it possible for the government to argue convincingly that more time is needed to

make their policies work. Simultaneously, a more politically-credible alternative is beginning to emerge from the opposition parties. The Conservatives know that the race is on to do something about the unemployment figures.[49]

Indeed, recent polls conducted by Market and Opinion Research International (MORI) suggest

a consistent deterioration in the government's standing that may well endure: apart from a brief "remission" around the bomb attack at the Conservative Party Conference in Brighton in October, 1984, there is the clear indication of a steady loss of satisfaction in the way Thatcher is doing her job as Prime Minister (from 48 percent approval in January, 1984 to 35 percent approval in May, 1985) — and in the way the government is running the country (from 40 percent approval in January, 1984 to 26 percent approval in May, 1985). With unemployment viewed by 73 percent of respondents as the most important issue facing Britain and a growing pessimism about the economy — only 18 percent of those polled in May, 1985 thought the economic condition of the country was likely to improve — the loss of support for the Thatcher government is easy to understand.[50]

POLITICAL RENEWAL IN THE AGE OF REAGAN AND THATCHER

It is of course much harder to forecast what will happen next, and what the future will hold for the Thatcher government, as for the Reaganite forces as the President's last term draws toward a conclusion. But the history of their ascent should provide valuable guidance in considering potential political counterswings. I have argued that the emergence of the Reagan and Thatcher governments required their positive reconstruction of the negative facts of declining economic competitiveness and geopolitical influence. This process involved the confluence of at least three elements: an erosion of institutions and beliefs associated with the KWS which made dubious economic theories and de-integrative political strategies successful; the discrediting of mainstream conservative and center-left political tendencies which gave Thatcher's and Reagan's new brand of politics party-electoral openings; and the ability of Reagan and Thatcher to assimilate to their campaigns a disproportionate share of extraparliamentary and anti-state movement energies.

Reagan and Thatcher came to office and have consolidated power because they offered confident alternatives to the tired politics of Carter and Callaghan, rejected the politically unacceptable facts of geopolitical decline, and artfully forged firm arithmetic pluralities — conglomerate constituencies but not unified coalitions — from a set of disparate and particularistic interests.

None of the three conditions for support show unmistakable signs of collapse, nor are the British and American cases symmetrical; but some grounds for reasoned reflection do exist. It seems that some Americans are concerned about Reagan's fairness, and fully 75 percent have lost confidence in his ability to handle the deficit or introduce his long-heralded tax reform. Likewise, Britons display little confidence in Thatcher's performance, are increasingly worried about unemployment, and think that the economy under her direction is likely to get worse. Those patterns do not suggest a resurgence of KWS support, but they do indicate a significant disavowal of supply-side and monetarist nostrums, and perhaps some serious reaction against the social implications of Thatcher's and Reagan's policies. Thus the first condition — belief structures and legitimating strategies — can no longer be assumed for the Thatcher and Reagan projects.

By contrast, the second condition, the party-electoral opening, seems probably the most secure for Reaganite forces, and it is ambiguous but quite positive for Thatcher, also. In the former case there may be some difficulty in the forging of a post-Reagan reconciliation between New Right and other more traditional conservative currents, but the Republican party seems firmly located within a conservative orbit, and the Democrats seem quite unlikely to reconcile the different needs of the "rainbow coalition," the New Politics of a Gary Hart, and the traditional urban, middle-aged, unionized, ethnic constituencies of the New Deal Coalition.

Purporting to speak for a new generation of professional middle-class voters, during the 1984 campaign for the Democratic presidential nominations Hart stressed budgetary efficiency in social services as in defense, an industrial policy which paid little attention to the concerns of blue-collar workers who would bear the cost of high-technology conversions, and the need to improve the economic status of women through the application of comparable worth rather than traditional market mechanisms in the setting of wages. As observers noted, however, "[c]onspicuously absent from Hart's new ideas were any having to do with the working class or blacks."[51]

Thus, at campaign's end the three core areas of a potential Democratic majority — the blue-collar—ethnic—union base of Mondale, the young urban professionals and New Politics base of Hart, and the "Rainbow Coalition" of Jackson — remained divided. As yet there is no emerging basis for a new post-KWS Democratic Party coalition. Even though, as Theodore Lowi has argued, Reagan's conglomerate constituency is not comparable to the Roosevelt coalition — because the Republican victories in 1980 and 1984 did not penetrate local and state electoral patterns and because national policies divide the constituencies on ideological grounds[52] — the Democrats are likely to face in the near future similar electoral problems to those which defeated them in 1984.

In the British case, with the continued divisions within the Labour Party, and between the Party and the more assertive elements of the trade union movement, the Social Democratic Party—Liberal Party Alliance has been the prime beneficiary of the government's loss of standing. But for a temporary rise in support at the end of the miners' strike and following debate about an unpopular budget, Labour's support has gradually declined — from 38 to 40 percent in summer, 1984 to 34 to 36 percent from fall, 1984 to summer, 1985 and down just below 30 percent in fall 1985. Labour jumped six points after a spirited attack by the leader, Neil Kinnock, on Arthur Scargill at the annual conference, but the most dramatic polling story remained the rise of the Alliance. After its successes in local government elections the Alliance rose six points in early summer 1985 to a new postelection high of 30 percent — and by fall, at 32 percent, it was (at least momentarily) four points above Labour, which was in turn one thin point ahead of the Conservatives.[53]

As with the Democrats in the US, party opposition to the government remains potentially divided in the UK. It is difficult to envision Kinnock's Labour Party healing the wounds of the miners strike, reassembling a pre-Social Contract mainstream of active party—trade union unity, and recapturing the disaffected skilled workers and the other "new middle-class" elements which have strayed to the Alliance or to Thatcher's Conservatives. Almost certainly it will not be able to build on to the UK's potential New Politics alliances (discussed below) which have emerged from the disparate battles of the NUM, the GLC (Greater London Council), and the CND (Campaign for Nuclear Disarmament) movements. Thus the government may fear a hung parliament with a prospective BLP—Alliance entente but, with all the governing party's advantages in the timing of the general election and the setting of its agenda, that is not such a bad place for Thatcher to be mid-way through her second term.

STATE PRACTICE AND POLITICAL RESPONSES

This leaves the third, and perhaps most interesting, issue: each government's relationship to emerging extraparliamentary movements. Here not only the discrete policies of Reagan and Thatcher, but the altered operations of the state which they have effected, will influence the political outcomes.

I suggested initially — and the narrative has developed the theme — that politics in the age of Reagan and Thatcher involves a withdrawal of the state from the entanglement of corporatist arrangements, the centralization of state power, and the insulation of the executive from a variety of external interest and representational pressures. We are seeing now a President removed from the regular interplay of legislative interests and the constraints imposed by the politics of his own party. Reagan has manipulated economic policy to secure an unusual degree of insulation from diverse economic forces and interests.

We are likewise watching a Prime Minister who has used a military adventure to take her government above political business cycle pressures which were eroding her support, and has appropriated inordinate power to the central government for highly partisan and ideological reasons. Once Thatcher sent the taskforce sailing toward the Falklands/Malvinas in 1982, the use of British force against an inferior Argentine garrison seemed both foreordained and strategically necessary for Thatcher's domestic use. How better to foster traditional national unity than to spill blood against a "fascist junta" and in defense of the sovereign rights of British citizens (a dubious point in reference to the residents of these islands in the South Atlantic with only very attentuated citizenship rights)?

On the domestic front the unusual political use of state power, and the process of its increased centralization, are most clear in Thatcher's celebrated assaults on local government which have culminated in the outright abolition of the GLC and a set of big-city provincial counterparts. In a system with no federal tier — like American states or the German Laender — such developments have significant constitutional implications, for they represent an unparalleled reduction in "checks" on the central powers of the executive.

Efforts like these to consolidate power and remove the executive from countervailing political pressures are doubly significant. They raise important questions about the capacity for democratic control of powerful *dirigiste* states and may, at the same time, galvanize new oppositional forces. Have the changed modus operandi of the British and American executives — and the reversal of KWS legitimating strategies — provoked new possibilities for active resistance? There are noteworthy, if as yet inconclusive, signs of political renewal.

In the United States, despite efforts to consolidate a trade unionist—rainbow politics in the aftermath of the 1984 campaign, and to shift the balance of power in the Democratic Party accordingly, the fissures outside the party have tended to match the divisions within. Thus, apart from defensive struggles to keep the US from even more aggressive action in Central America, perhaps the most successful campaigns have emerged in response to Reagan's anti-welfarist posture and pro-family politics. The patriarchal messianism of the New Right, an increasing awareness of the "feminization of poverty" as a consequence of cuts in welfare state programs, the growing battle for comparable worth, the de-funding of nutrition programs for pregnant women (the WIC program), a broad-based attack on reproductive rights culminating in thirty or more bombings of abortion clinics amidst presidential support for anti-abortion activists — all this has galvanized political campaigns with substantial results. Some WIC programs have received local or state funding, the "marital rape" exemption has been abolished in more than half the states, and reproductive rights organizations have effectively organized to reduce sterilization abuse and prevent any further restriction on the availability of abortions through a "right to life" constitutional amendment.[54] Thus, in the United States, oppositional politics has remained, by and large, diffuse and reactive, organized through a range of largely autonomous and local political organizations.

In the United Kingdom, by contrast, it may be that the vigor of government assaults and the centrality of the victims — the GLC, the NUM — have created a movement of potential cohesion among previously unrelated oppositional elements. Have the attacks on unions culminating in the miners strike, the erosion of democratic norms symbolized by the abolition of local councils, and the callousness of economic policy and the raw violence of the state reflected in police behavior, baseless accusations, and government indifference surrounding the riots in Handsworth, Brixton, and Tottenham in fall, 1985 — fundamentally altered political forces in the UK?

On this point NUM president Arthur Scargill is probably right in saying at the end of the miners strike, "The greatest lesson of the last twelve months is the struggle itself."[55] In fact it was a lesson learned by many, and sometimes in surprising quarters. Peter Jenkins, noting that the miners' strike was no simple North—South issue as it had often been portrayed, observed that "support for the miners was nowhere stronger than at the GLC and Lambeth borough council."[56] Indeed, unexpected lessons were learned: by miners that women could take powerful leadership roles in political confrontations and that what black youth and Irish republicans had long said about state initiated violence might be true; by George Moores, who chaired South Yorkshire's police committee, that "[the] government has declared a class war [and] wants to drive the working class into submission. . . ."[57]

These lessons provide the possibility of new solidarities which could sustain wide resistance movements, but the signs are ambiguous. NUM President Arthur Scargill, who never before showed the least interest in the empowerment of women, campaigned passionately — although unsuccessfully — for a rules change in the NUM which would have granted women who were active in support groups associate membership in the mineworkers' union.[58] However, there is little evidence either that women in the mining communities generally invited this new function or that strike time solidarities — among miners, support groups, GLC activities, and antinuclear/peace groups — have been sustained in the post-strike status quo ante of mounting dole queues, urban riots, and the breakaway from the NUM initiated by the Nottingham miners.

For every small gesture of growing unity, like the activities of Save Easington Area Miners (SEAM) which combines trade unions, women's groups, and church associations in an effort to save the community,[59] there are larger illustrations of classic rifts and organizational incapacity. The Kinnock—Scargill confrontation at Labour's 1985 conference is a perfect example. The miners' pleas that the party would reimburse the union for sequestered funds and that a future Labour government would reinstate the dismissed miners was passed when the Transport and General Workers backed the NUM, but the resolution failed to achieve the two-thirds majority needed to commit the party executive to include the policy in the next general election manifesto. The result: a victory for Kinnock as measured in the polls, but a guarantee of resentments, divisions, and vituperative exchanges later, when the Labour Party will need most to unify its industrial base (including the NUM) with its parliamentary moderates and, if it is to be successful, run with and not against the solidarities which were forged during the miners strike and the struggles in defense of local councils.

Like the sense of empowerment that comes out of struggles in the United States to challenge the patriarchal dimensions of Reaganism, these new solidarities in the United Kingdom represent the possibility of more active and broader-based opposition. There are, however, considerable difficulties to overcome. The politics of Reagan and Thatcher have created the opening for new political alliances — in the US between professional women and poor women trapped by the decline of the social welfare economy, and in the UK between community activists and trade unionists fighting to reclaim lost democratic rights. But the de-integrative strategies have also exacerbated old racial, class, and gender divisions, and spawned new intra-class competition.

Catapulted to power on bromide assurances of renewed national greatness, improved economic performance, and firm political direction, Reagan and Thatcher have in fact recast uncertainty in new and far more dangerous terms. They have marginalized constituencies which were politically integrated during the era of the welfare state and have reduced in significant ways the social rights of citizenship. Reagan prospers amidst assertions of economic recovery and renewed international leadership, while Thatcherism is characterized as "government by lethargy and conflict."[60] Despite these ostensible differences, the two governments have much in common. The means Reagan and Thatcher have used to consolidate power — de-integrative strategies which divide a nation's people, innovative use of the executive to secure unusual independence — raise serious questions about their exercise of power. In the end, politics in the age of Reagan and Thatcher leaves much in doubt about the contemporary compatibility between capitalism and democracy.

Notes

INTRODUCTION

1. For a very revealing account of this period of the Carter presidency, see: Joseph A. Califano, Jr, *Governing America: An Insider's Report from the White House and the Cabinet* (New York: Touchstone/ Simon and Schuster, 1981), pp. 418–429. Unless otherwise noted, background references are from Califano.
2. *New York Times*, July 13, 1979, pp. A1, A10.
3. Quoted in Califano, p. 427.
4. *New York Times*, July 15, 1979, p. 20E.
5. *New York Times*, July 16, 1979, p. A10.
6. Califano, p. 428.
7. TUC–Labour Liaison Committee, *Economic Policy and the Cost of Living* [The "Social Contract"] (February, 1973). See: Stephen Bornstein, "States and Unions: From Postwar Settlements to Contemporary Stalemate," in S. Bornstein *et al.* (eds), *The State in Capitalist Europe* (London: Allen and Unwin, 1984), p. 88.
8. David Coates, *Labour in Power? A Study of the Labour Government, 1974–1979* (London and New York: Longman, 1980), pp. 11–27, 67–80.
9. Joel Krieger, "Britain: Phased out by Phase Three?" *Working Papers for a New Society* (March–April, 1978), pp. 17–19.
10. *New York Times*, July 22, 1979, p. 1E.
11. For a good discussion of the political ramifications of incomes policies see: David Butler and Dennis Kavanagh, *The British General Election of 1979* (London: Macmillan, 1980), pp. 23–27.
12. Strategy Group, The President's Commission on Industrial Preparedness, *Making America More Competitive: A Framework*, [1985], pp. 8–20.
13. *Making America More Competitive*, p. 5.

14.   Richard E. Caves and Lawrence B. Krause, "Introduction and Summary," in R. Caves and L. Krause (eds), *Britain's Economic Performance* (Washington, DC: The Brookings Institution, 1980), pp. 1—19.

CHAPTER 1

1.   See: Arthur Schlessinger, Jr., *A Thousand Days*, (Boston: Houghton Mifflin, 1965), p. 644.
2.   Claus Offe, "Advanced Capitalism and the Welfare State," *Politics and Society* (Summer 1972), pp. 484—485.
3.   See, for example: Andrew Shonfield, *Modern Capitalism: The Changing Balance of Public and Private Power*, (Oxford and New York: Oxford University Press, 1978), pp. xiii—xv, 3—67. I have paraphrased in part remarks from pp. 3—6.
4.   Samuel Bowles, David M. Gordon, and Thomas E. Weisskopf, *Beyond the Wasteland: A Democratic Alternative to Economic Decline* (Garden City, New York: Anchor Press/Doubleday, 1983), p. 68.
5.   Robert O. Keohane, *After Hegemony: Cooperation and Discord in the World Political Economy* (Princeton, New Jersey: Princeton University Press, 1984), p. 37. This argument relies heavily on Keohane, pp. 31—37.
6.   C. Fred Bergsten, "The United States and the World Economy," in J. Michael Finger and Thomas D. Willet (eds), *The Internationalization of the American Economy* (Sage/*The Annals of the American Academy of Political and Social Science*), vol. 460 (March, 1982), pp. 12—13.
7.   US Department of Commerce, International Trade Administration, *An Assessment of U.S. Competitiveness in High Technology Industries* [1983].
8.   Bergsten in Finger and Willet, pp. 13—14.
9.   *New York Times*, July 16, 1979, p. A10.
10.   See, for surprisingly similar discussions from rather different perspectives: David P. Calleo, *The Imperious Economy* (Cambridge, Mass.: Harvard University Press, 1982) and Alan Wolfe, *America's Impasse: The Rise and Fall of the Politics of Growth* (New York: Pantheon, 1981).
11.   Ajit Singh, "U.K. Industry and the World Economy: A Case of De-Industrialization?" in Charles Feinstein (ed.) *The Managed Economy: Essays in British Economic Policy and Performance since 1929*, p. 249.

12. Organization for Economic Co-Operation and Development, *Paris: OECD Economic Surveys: United Kingdom* (February, 1983), p. 51.
13. Commission of the European Communities, *The Competiveness of the Community Industry* (Luxembourg: Office for Official Publications of the European Communities, 1982), pp. 17—19.
14. Adam Przeworski and Michael Wallerstein, "Democratic Capitalism at the Crossroads," *Democracy*, vol. 2, no. 3 (July, 1982), pp. 52—68.
15. John D. Stephens, "Impasse and Breakthrough — In Sweden: After the Contradictions of Social Democratic Policy," *Dissent* (Summer, 1981), p. 316.
16. Jonas Pontusson, "Behind and Beyond Social Democracy in Sweden," *New Left Review*, no. 134 (January—February, 1984), p. 92.
17. See: Pontusson, p. 86.
18. See: George Ross and Jane Jenson, "Pluralism and the Decline of Left Hegemony: The French Left in Power" (unpublished paper presented at the American Political Science Association annual meetings, August, 1984).
19. Hans-Ulrich Wehler, "Bismarck's Imperialism 1862—1890," *Past and Present* (August, 1970), p. 140.
20. Paul Smith, *Disraelian Conservatism and Social Reform* (London: Routledge and Kegan Paul; Toronto: University of Toronto Press, 1967), pp. 160—161.
21. Smith, p. 161.
22. David P. Calleo, *The Imperious Economy* (Cambridge, Mass. and London, 1982), pp. 10—11.
23. Otto Kirchheimer, "The Transformation of the Western European Party Systems," in Joseph LaPalombara and Myron Weiner (eds), *Political Parties and Development* (Princeton: Princeton University Press, 1966).
24. T. H. Marshall, "Citizenship and Social Class," in David Held *et al.* (eds), *States and Societies* (Oxford: Martin Robertson, 1983), pp. 257—258.
25. Colin Leys, "Thatcherism and British Manufacturing: A Problem of Hegemony," paper presented to the annual meetings of The American Political Science Association, August, 1984, p. 11. For a somewhat different interpretation, see: Michael Useem, *The Inner Circle: Large Corporations and the Rise of Business Political Activity in the U.S. and the U.K.* (New York and Oxford: Oxford University Press, 1984), pp. 71—74, 169.
26. Leo Panitch, "Trade Unions and the Capitalist State," *New Left Review*, no. 125 (January—February, 1981), p. 40.

CHAPTER 2

1. E. J. Hobsbawm, *Industry and Empire* (Harmondsworth: Penguin/ Pelican, 1983), pp. 29—31.
2. This discussion closely follows that of Stuart Hall, "The Rise of the Representative/Interventionist State, 1880's—1920's," in Gregor McLennan *et al.* (eds), *State and Society in Contemporary Britain* (Cambridge: Polity Press, 1984).
3. G. Dangerfield, *The Strange Death of Liberal England* (New York: Capricorn, 1961), p. viii.
4. See: Hall, pp. 11—21.
5. Hobsbawm, p. 240.
6. Keith Middlemas, *Politics in Industrial Society: The Experience of the British System Since 1911* (London: André Deutsch, 1979), p. 154.
7. Stephen Bornstein, "States and Unions: From Postwar Settlement to Contemporary Stalemate," in S. Bornstein *et al.* (eds), *The State in Capitalist Europe* (London: Allen and Unwin, 1984), p. 75.
8. Grahame Thompson, "Economic Intervention in the Post-War Economy," in Gregor McLennan *et al.* (eds), *State and Society in Contemporary Britain* (Cambridge: Polity Press, 1984), pp. 91—93.
9. Ian Gough, *The Political Economy of the Welfare State* (London: Macmillan, 1979), pp. 76—78.
10. OECD, *Social Expenditure 1960—1990: Problems of Growth and Control* (Paris: OECD, 1985), pp. 23—29.
11. John Saville, "Labourism and the Labour Government," in *Socialist Register 1967* (London: Merlin Press, 1967), p. 53. See also: Tom Forester, *The British Labour Party and the Working Class* (New York: Holmes and Meier, 1976), pp. 52—67.
12. David Coates, *Labour in Power? A Study of the Labour Government 1974—1979* (London and New York: Longman, 1980), p. 10.
13. Peter Gay, *The Dilemma of Democratic Socialism: Eduard Bernstein's Challenge to Marx* (New York: Columbia University Press, 1952), p. ix, quoted in H. M. Drucker, *Doctrine and Ethos in the Labour Party* (London: George Allen and Unwin, 1979), p. 89.
14. Coates, pp. 4—5.
15. Samuel H. Beer, *Britain Against Itself: The Political Contradictions of Collectivism* (New York and London: Norton, 1982), p. 89.
16. Coates, p. 17.
17. See: David Butler and Dennis Kavanagh, *The British General Election of 1979* (London: Macmillan, 1980), pp. 23—27.

18. See: Butler and Kavanagh, pp. 27—30; Coates, pp. 11—27, 67—80. Unless otherwise noted the figures which follow are derived from these sources.
19. Coates, pp. 79—80.
20. Beer, p. 6.
21. Michael Rustin, "Different Conceptions of Party: Labour's Constitutional Debates," *New Left Review*, no. 126 (March—April, 1981), p. 20.
22. C. A. R. Crosland, "The Transition from Capitalism," in R. H. S. Crossman (ed.), *New Fabian Essays* (New York: Praeger, 1952), pp. 38—45.
23. Tony Benn, "An Interview with Eric Hobsbawm," in Martin Jacques and Francis Mulhern (eds), *The Forward March of Labour Halted?* (London: Verso, 1981), p. 87.
24. See: Coates, pp. 39—44. See, also: "The U.K. and the IMF: 1976," Harvard Business School Case 1—379—168, unpublished.
25. David Coates, "Labourism and the Transition to Socialism," *New Left Review*, no. 129 (September—October, 1981), p. 14.
26. Ken Coates, "The Choices Before Labour," *New Left Review*, no. 131 (January—February, 1982), p. 38.

CHAPTER 3

1. Samuel H. Beer, *Britain Against Itself: The Political Contradictions of Collectivism* (New York and London: Norton, 1982), p. 175.
2. Martin Jacques, "Thatcherism — The Impasse Broken?" *Marxism Today* (October, 1979), pp. 7—8.
3. Andrew Gamble, "The Decline of the Conservative Party," *Marxism Today* (November, 1979), p. 7.
4. Krishnan Kumar, "Thoughts on the Present Discontents in Britain: A Review and a Proposal," 1979, unpublished, pp. 2—4.
5. Kumar, p. 3.
6. Samuel H. Beer, *British Politics in the Collectivist Age* (New York: Vintage/Random House, 1965), p. 390. Beer notes the transformation himself in his *Britain Against Itself*, p. xiii.
7. Beer, *Britain Against Itself*, p. xiv.
8. Herbert Marcuse, *One Dimensional Man* (Boston: Beacon Press, 1964), p. 9.
9. Anthony Sampson, *The Changing Anatomy of Britain* (New York: Random House, 1982), p. 35.

10. See: Sigmund Freud, *Civilization and Its Discontents,* Joan Riviere (trans.); James Strachey (ed.) (New York: Norton, 1962), p. 61.

11. Jacques, p. 7.

12. Sir Geoffrey Butler, *The Tory Tradition* (London: J. Murray, 1914), republished by the Conservative Political Centre (1957) pp. 67—81, quoted in Beer, *Britain Against Itself*, p. 175.

13. Peter Kellner, "Variations on a Theme by Norman Tebbit," *New Statesman*, vol. 105, no. 2719 (April 29, 1983), p. 7.

14. Kellner, p. 7.

15. Gamble, p. 7.

16. Sampson, p. 37.

17. Beer, *Britain Against Itself*, pp. 84—85.

18. Sampson, p. 37.

19. Andrew Glyn and John Harrison, *The British Economic Disaster* (London: Pluto Press, 1980), pp. 72—74.

20. Glyn and Harrison, pp. 57—90.

21. Gamble, p. 9.

22. David Butler and Dennis Kavanagh, *The British General Election of 1979* (London: Macmillan, 1980), p. 154.

23. Butler and Kavanagh, p. 187.

24. Butler and Kavanagh, pp. 189—190.

25. *The Right Approach: A Statement of Conservative Aims* (London: Conservative Central Office, 1976), p. 50.

26. Butler and Kavanagh, p. 190.

27. *The Right Approach*, pp. 53—54.

28. Butler and Kavanagh, p. 191.

29. Butler and Kavanagh, p. 185.

30. *The Right Approach*, pp. 47—48.

31. Barry Troyna, "Reporting the National Front: British Values Observed," in Charles Husband (ed.), *Race in Britain: Continuity and Change* (London: Hutchinson, 1982), pp. 265—267.

32. Butler and Kavanagh, p. 185.

33. Butler and Kavanagh, p. 185.

34. Anthony Mark Messina, "When Parties Fail: Race and the Emergence of Extra-Party Movements in Britain," September, 1981, unpublished, p. 34.

35. Butler and Kavanagh, p. 195.

CHAPTER 4

1. John Curtice and Michael Steed, "Appendix 2: An Analysis of the

Voting," in David Butler and Dennis Kavanaugh (eds), *The British General Election of 1979* (London: Macmillan, 1980), pp. 390—393.

2. Butler and Kavanagh, p. 336.

3. James R. Lewis, "Regional Policy and Planning: Convergence and Contradiction," in Stephen Bornstein *et al.* (eds), *The State in Capitalist Europe* (London: George Allen and Unwin), p. 145.

4. I refer to two-party swing, the average in the change in the Conservative share of the total votes cast for Conservatives and Labour only. Unless otherwise noted, all references to swing refer to two-party swing.

5. Curtice and Steed, pp. 394—396.

6. Butler and Kavanagh, p. 384.

7. *The Economist*, June 2, 1979.

8. Anthony Mark Messina, "When Parties Fail: Race and the Emergence of Extra-Party Movements in Britain," September, 1981, unpublished, p. 35.

9. Cf. Messina, pp. 16—17. Unless otherwise noted electoral data is derived from Butler and Kavanagh, "Appendix 1: The Statistics," pp. 353—389.

10. Butler and Kavanagh, p. 399.

11. Michael Jones, "The Tories: Bringing the House Down," *Marxism Today*, (May, 1980), p. 10.

12. Samuel H. Beer, *Britain Against Itself: The Political Contradictions of Collectivism* (New York and London, 1982), p. 82.

13. Butler and Kavanagh, p. 340.

14. Ernest Barker (ed.), *Social Contract: Essays by Locke, Hume, Rousseau* (New York: Oxford University Press, 1962), p. 194n.

15. David Lipsey, "The Reforms People Want," *New Society* (October 4, 1979), p. 13.

16. Peter Taylor-Gooby, "Public Belt and Private Braces," *New Society* April 14, 1983.

17. Stephen Jay Gould, *Hen's Teeth and Horse's Toes* (New York and London: Norton, 1980), p. 24.

18. Amy Gutman, *Liberal Equality* (Cambridge, England: Cambridge University Press, 1980), p. 156.

19. Otto Kirchheimer, "The Transformation of the European Party Systems," in Joseph LaPalombara and Myron Weiner (eds), *Political Parties and Political Development* (Princeton: Princeton University Press, 1966), p. 178.

20. *Los Angeles Times*, December, 1978, cited in Lipsey, p. 13.

21. *New York Times*, August 26, 1983.

22. David Hall, *The Cuts Machine: The Politics of Public Expenditure* (London: Pluto Press, 1983), p. 7.
23. Hall, p. 3.
24. The government subsidy (the Rate Support Grant) but not the council spending financed directly by local rates (i.e., property/occupancy taxes), was governed by the cash limits regulations.
25. Hall, p. 51.
26. Hall, p. 107; Michael O'Higgins, "Inequality, Redistribution and Recession," paper presented to a conference on "The Thatcher Government and British Political Economy," Center for European Studies, Harvard University, April 19–20, 1985.
27. See: Hall, p. 68.
28. *The Campaign Guide: Supplement 1978* (London: Conservative Research Department, 1978), p. 120.
29. *The Campaign Guide*, p. 120.
30. Steve Iliffe, "Dismantling the Health Service," *Marxism Today* (July 1980), p. 14.
31. Hall, p. 22.
32. Iliffe, p. 14.
33. Michael O'Higgins, "Privatization and Social Welfare: Concepts, Analysis and the British Experience," paper presented to the Columbia University Seminar on Privatization.
34. Iliffe, p. 16.
35. *The Economist*, June 4, 1983, p. 42.
36. *The Economist*, p. 43.
37. John Solomos *et al.* "The Organic Crisis of British Capitalism and Race: The Experience of the Seventies," in Centre for Contemporary Cultural Studies, *The Empire Strikes Back* (London: Hutchinson, 1982), p. 14.
38. Tom Rees, "Immigration Policies in the United Kingdom," in Charles Husband (ed.), *Race in Britain* (London: Hutchinson, 1982), pp. 86–87.
39. Rees, p. 88.
40. Michael Dummett and Ann Dummett, "The Role of Government in Britain's Racial Crisis," in Husband (ed.), p. 126.
41. Dummett and Dummett, pp. 101–102.
42. Solomos *et al.*, p. 27.
43. Solomos *et al.*, p. 23.
44. Solomos *et al.*, p. 26.
45. Solomos *et al.*, p. 15.
46. *Manchester Guardian Weekly*, October 13, 1985, p. 1.

47. Huw Benyon and Peter McMylor, "Decisive Power: The New Tory State against the Miners," in H. Benyon (ed.) *Digging Deeper* (London: Verso, 1984), p. 33.
48. See: "Appomatox or Civil War?" *The Economist*, 27 May, 1978; Benyon and McMylor, pp. 35—36.

CHAPTER 5

1. Michael Roskin, "From Pearl Harbour to Vietnam: Shifting Generational Paradigms and Foreign Policy," *Political Science Quarterly*, vol. 89, no. 3 (Fall, 1974), pp. 563—576.
2. David P. Calleo, *The Imperious Economy* (Cambridge Mass.: Harvard University Press, 1982), p. 159.
3. Fred L. Block, *The Origins of International Economic Disorder: A Study of United States International Monetary Policy from World War II to the Present* (Berkeley: University of California Press, 1977), p. 33.
4. Alan Wolfe, *America's Impasse: The Rise and Fall of the Politics of Growth* (New York: Pantheon, 1981), p. 145.
5. Wolfe, p. 146.
6. For an excellent summary of the erosion of British-American financial collaboration, see: Richard N. Gardner, *Sterling Dollar Diplomacy: The Origins and the Prospects of our International Economic Order* (New York: McGraw-Hill, 1969), pp. 71—100.
7. Wolfe, p. 147.
8. Block, pp. 50—51.
9. *Manchester Guardian*, March 23, 1946, quoted in Gardner, p. 267.
10. Gardner, p. 268.
11. Gardner, p. 126.
12. Roy F. Harrod, *The Life of John Maynard Keynes* (London: Macmillan, 1951), p. 635, quoted in Gardner, p. 268.
13. Sylvia Porter, "U.S. to Exploit World Bank," *New York Post*, May 9, 1946, quoted in Gardner, p. 266.
14. Calleo, p. 24.
15. See: Calleo, pp. 15—17.
16. Calleo, p. 17.
17. Joshua Cohen and Joel Rogers, *On Democracy: Towards a Transformation of American Society* (New York: Penguin, 1984), p. 102.
18. Cohen and Rogers, p. 100.
19. Samuel Bowles, David M. Gordon, and Thomas E. Weisskopf,

Beyond the Wasteland: A Democratic Alternative to Economic Decline (Garden City, New York: Anchor/Doubleday, 1983), p. 68.

20. Cohen and Rogers, p. 100.
21. Block, p. 164.
22. Labour Party, *Report of the Annual Conference 1976,* p. 188, quoted in Jim Tomlinson, "Keynesian Revolution in Economic Policy?" *Economy and Society,* vol. 10, no. 1 (February, 1981), p. 72.
23. See: Wolfe, p. 51.
24. Herbert Stein, *The Fiscal Revolution in America* (Chicago and London: The University of Chicago Press, 1969), p. 240.
25. Bowles *et al.,* p. 68.
26. Wolfe, p. 116.
27. See: Cohen and Rogers, pp. 93—95.
28. Block, p. 168.
29. Wolfe, p. 120.
30. Seymour E. Harris, *The Economics of the Kennedy Years* (New York: Harper and Row, 1964), p. 28.
31. Wolfe, p. 123.
32. Stein, p. 294.
33. Calleo, p. 5.
34. Stein, p. 4.
35. Harris, p. 5.
36. Ronald Frederick King, "Presidential Economics and the New Frontier," Midwest Political Science Association, April, 1980, p. 11.
37. Calleo, p. 12.
38. Stein, p. 401.
39. Stein, p. 401.
40. Calleo, p. 14.
41. Calleo, p. 11.
42. King, p. 4.
43. King, p. 46.
44. King, pp. 46—47.
45. Calleo, p. 18.
46. Calleo, p. 21.
47. Harris, p. 150.
48. Harris, p. 150.
49. Calleo, p. 24.
50. Cohen and Rogers, pp. 108—109.
51. Calleo, p. 61.
52. Alan Wolfe, "Capitalism Shows its Face: Giving up on Democracy," in Holly Sklar (ed.), *Trilateralism: Trilateral Commission and Elite Planning for World Management,* (Boston: South End Press, 1980), p. 298.

53. William Tabb, "The Trilateral Imprint on Domestic Economics," in Sklar (ed.), p. 213.

CHAPTER 6

1. James Schlesinger, "The Eagle and the Bear," *Foreign Affairs*, vol. 63, no. 5 (summer, 1985), p. 961.
2. Commission of the European Communities, *The Competitiveness of the Community Industry* (Luxembourg: Office for Official Publications of the European Communities, 1982), p. 38. See also: C. Fred Bergsten, "The United States and the World Economy," in J. Michael Finger and Thomas D. Willet (eds), *The Internationalization of the American Economy*, Sage/*The Annals of the American Academy of Political and Social Science*, vol. 460 (March, 1982), pp. 12–13.
3. Richard E. Foglesong, "Making Sense of the Industrial Policy Debate: The U.S. Case," paper prepared for the Annual Meeting of the American Political Science Association, Hilton Hotel, New Orleans, August 28–September 1, 1985, p. 8.
4. See: Foglesong, pp. 5–11.
5. Walter Dean Burnham, "The 1980 Earthquake: Realignment, Reaction, or What?" in Thomas Ferguson and Joel Rogers (eds), *The Hidden Election* (New York: Pantheon, 1981), p. 98.
6. Fred I. Greenstein, "The Need for an Early Appraisal of the Reagan Presidency," in Fred I. Greenstein (ed.), *The Reagan Presidency: An Early Assessment* (Baltimore and London: The Johns Hopkins Press, 1983), p. 12.
7. Burnham, p. 100.
8. Burnham, p. 122.
9. Alan Wolfe, "Capitalism Shows its Face: Giving Up on Democracy," in Holly Sklar (ed.), *Trilateralism: The Trilateral Commission and Elite Planning for World Management* (Boston: South End Press, 1980), pp. 297–298.
10. Thomas McCarthy, "Translator's Introduction," in Jurgen Habermas, *Legitimation Crisis* (Boston: Beacon, 1975), p. vii.
11. Samuel H. Beer, *Britain Against Itself: The Political Contradictions of Collectivism* (New York and London: Norton, 1982), pp. 107–148.
12. Mike Davis, "The Political Economy of Late Imperial America," *New Left Review*, no. 143 (January–February, 1984), p. 30.
13. Hugh Heclo and Rudolph G. Penner, "Fiscal and Political Strategy in the Reagan Administration," in Greenstein (ed.), p. 25.
14. Ferguson and Rogers, p. 27.

15. Bergsten, p. 13.
16. Bergsten.
17. See: Ferguson and Rogers, pp. 40—52.
18. Burnham, p. 127.
19. Burnham.
20. *National Journal*, November 8, 1980, p. 1876.
21. *New York Times*, November 9, 1980, p. 28.
22. Burnham, p. 109.
23. Rosalind Pollack Petchesky, "Antiabortion, Antifeminism, and the Rise of the New Right," *Feminist Studies*, vol. 7, no. 2 (summer, 1981), p. 207.
24. Petchesky, pp. 207—211.
25. Ferguson and Rogers, p. 4.
26. Zillah R. Eisenstein, *Feminism and Sexuality: Crisis in Liberal America* (New York: Monthly Review Press, 1984), p. 29.
27. *New York Times*, November 9, 1980, p. 28. It should be noted that women in favor of the ERA represented 22 percent of the sample and that women opposed to the ERA represented 17 percent of the sample. My analysis of the exit poll data follows closely that of Burnham. Unless otherwise noted, all opinion data on the election follows from the *New York Times*/CBS News Poll.
28. *National Journal*, November 8, 1980, pp. 1876—1877.
29. Burnham, p. 106.
30. *National Journal*, November 8, 1980, p. 1877.
31. Burnham, p. 107.
32. Burnham, p. 102.
33. See: Greenstein, p. 5; Heclo and Penner, pp. 26—27.
34. Heclo and Penner, p. 27.
35. Davis, pp. 12—13.
36. Davis.
37. See: Burnham, p. 114.
38. Burnham, p. 111.
39. Davis, p. 12.
40. Alan Crawford, *Thunder on the Right: The "New Right" and the Politics of Resentment* (New York: Pantheon, 1980), p. 176.
41. Crawford, p. 176.
42. Crawford, p. 176.
43. Petchesky, pp. 221—222.
44. New Right attitudes concerning liberal freedoms are also inconsistent in so far as they also advocate state withdrawal from the family with reference to spousal and child abuse. The pattern suggests a predominance of patriarchal over Lockean concerns. I am indebted

to Kristin Booth Glen for a recognition of the significance of this point.

45. Petchesky, p. 222.

46. Peter Steinfels, *The Neo-Conservatives* (New York: Touchstone/ Simon and Schuster, 1979), p. 15.

47. Crawford, p. 211.

48. A. James Reichly, "The Reagan Coalition," *The Brookings Review*, vol. 1, no. 2 (winter, 1982), p. 8.

49. Reichly, p. 8.

50. Wolin, quoted in Steinfels, pp. 17—18.

51. Alan Wolfe, "Sociology, Liberalism and the Radical Right," *New Left Review*, no. 128 (July/August 1981), p. 5.

52. Benjamin Ginsberg and Martin Shefter, "A Critical Realignment? The New Politics, the Reconstituted Right, and the Election of 1984," in Michael Nelson (ed.), *The Elections of 1984* (Washington, DC: CQ Press, 1985), pp. 10—19.

53. Ginsberg and Shefter, pp. 20—21.

54. See: Matthew Hooberman and Roger Wilkins, "Jesse Jackson in Person," *New Socialist*, no. 24 (February, 1985), pp. 34—38.

55. See: Reichly, p. 7.

56. Schlesinger, p. 958.

57. Wolfe, p. 5.

CHAPTER 7

1. Ralph Miliband, *Marxism and Politics* (Oxford: Oxford University Press, 1977), p. 74.

2. The position represented here is that of Nicos Poulantzas. The quotation appears in: Robin M. Blackburn, (ed.), *Ideology in Social Science: Readings in Critical Social Theory* (London: Fontana, 1972), p. 245.

3. For the clearest expression of this perspective in the work of Claus Offe, see: Claus Offe and Volker Ronge, "Theses on the Theory of the State," in Anthony Giddens and David Held (eds), *Classes, Power, and Conflict: Classical and Contemporary Debates*, (Berkeley: University of California Press, 1982), pp. 249—256.

4. Hugh Heclo and Rudolph G. Penner, "Fiscal and Political strategy in the Reagan Administration," in Fred I. Greenstein, (ed.), *The Reagan Presidency: An Early Assessment* (Baltimore: Johns Hopkins Press, 1983), pp. 24—25.

5. See: Suzanne Berger, "Politics and Antipolitics in Western Europe in the Seventies," *Daedalus*, vol. 108, no. 1 (winter, 1979), pp. 27–50.

6. Heclo and Penner, in Greenstein, p. 25.

7. *New York Times*, January 4, 1985, pp. A1, A17; October 20, 1985, p. 4/1.

8. Richard Corrigan, "Unified by Deficits," *National Journal*, vol. 15, no. 5, (29 January, 1983), p. 232.

9. Corrigan, p. 232.

10. Corrigan, p. 232.

11. Corrigan, p. 232.

12. J. Taylor, *America's Textiles*, vol. 13, no. 3 (March, 1984), p. 6.

13. Corrigan, p. 232.

14. Corrigan, p. 232.

15. Stanley Siegalman, "Editor's Report: What's Current in D.C.? — Politico's Update Editors," *American Druggist*, vol. 189, no. 6, p. 3.

16. Peter S. Nagan and Kenneth A. Kaufman, "Threat of Growing Fed Deficit is Crucial to Credit Markets," *ABA Banking Journal*, vol. lxxiv, no. 5 (May, 1982), p. 10.

17. See: Phil Battery, "What the IMF Means to Main Street, U.S.A.," *ABA Banking Journal*, vol. lxxv, no. 4 (April, 1983), p. 8.

18. Timothy B. Clark, "Will Economic Growth End the Deficits Or Will thw Deficits Stifle Growth?," *National Journal*, vol. 15, no. 2 (January 8, 1983), p. 65. All references to Feldstein's Kiawah Island address are based on the Clark article.

19. *The Miner: Journal of the National Union of Mineworkers*, Special Issue, August 17, 1984, p. 7.

20. *New York Times*, September 23, 1984, pp. I/26, IV/2.

21. Andrew Hacker (ed.), *U/S: A Statistical Portrait of the American People* (New York: Viking Press, 1983), p. 137. The figure is for 1980.

22. Hacker, p. 137. The figure is for the year ending September 30, 1980.

23. Alfred J. Watkins, "Paul Volcker and the Politics of the Federal Reserve Board," *Working Papers for a New Society*, vol. 10 (March–April, 1983), p. 27.

24. Robert J. Shapiro, "Politics and the Federal Reserve, *The Public Interest*, no. 66 (winter, 1982), p. 126.

25. Gerald Epstein, "Domestic Stagflation and Monetary Policy: The Federal Reserve and the Hidden Election," in Thomas Ferguson and Joel Rogers (eds), *The Hidden Election* (New York: Pantheon, 1981), pp. 141–142.

26. Epstein in Ferguson and Rogers, p. 141.

27. Epstein in Ferguson and Rogers, p. 142.
28. Watkins, p. 28.
29. M1 is a measure of cash in circulation, deposits in checking accounts, and travelers checks. M2 is a broader gauge of the money supply which (in addition to everything included in M1) includes deposits in money market funds and savings accounts. M3 includes, in addition, certificates of deposit and Treasury securities. See, for example, "Review of the Month: Money Out of Control," *Monthly Review*, vol. 36, no. 7 (December, 1984), p. 10.
30. See: Maxwell Newton, *The Fed: Inside the Federal Reserve — The Secret Power Center that Controls the American Economy* (New York: Times Books, 1983), ch. 1; see also Watkins, p. 26)
31. Robert J. Samuelson, *National Journal*, vol. 15, no. 1 (January 1, 1983), p. 27.
32. Timothy B. Clark, "The Politics of Money Could Determine Volcker's Fate as Chairman of the Fed," *National Journal*, vol. 15, no. 24 (June 6, 1983), p. 1214.
33. Watkins, p. 29.
34. Watkins, p. 29.
35. Watkins, p. 29.
36. Watkins, p. 28.
37. Clark, p. 1214.
38. See: Isabel V. Sawhill and Charles F. Stone, "The Economy: The Key to Success," in John L. Palmer and Isabel V. Sawhill (eds), *The Reagan Record* (Ballinger, 1984), pp. 69—71.
39. *New York Times*, February 19, 1981; also see: Teresa Amott and Joel Krieger, "Thatcher and Reagan: State Theory and the 'Hyper-Capitalist' Regime," *New Political Science*, no. 8 (spring, 1982), pp. 18—19.
40. Sawhill and Stone, pp. 70—71.
41. Sawhill and Stone, p. 71.
42. Clark, p. 63.
43. *The Wall Street Journal*, January 21, 1982, p. 6.
44. *Wall Street Journal*, February 15, 1984, p. 14.
45. *Wall Street Journal*, March 1, 1984, p. 4.
46. Linda W. McCormick, "Fed, Treasury Again Exchange Blame for Rising Interest Rates at Hearing," *American Banker*, vol. 149 (June 11, 1984), p. 12.
47. *Hartford Courant*, December 1, 1984, p. C3.
48. Allan H. Meltzer, "The Results of the Fed's Failed Experiment," *Wall Street Journal*, July 29, 1982, p. 18.
49. *New York Times*, January 9, 1985, p. A1.

50. *Wall Street Journal*, February 15, 1984, p. 2, 14.

51. Newton, pp. 232—233.

52. Newton, pp. 121—122.

53. Newton, p. 123.

54. *Wall Street Journal*, July 29, 1982, p. 18.

55. Lester M. Salamon and Alan J. Abramson, "Governance: The Politics of Retrenchment," in Palmer and Sawhill, p. 59.

56. Andrew Martin, *The Politics of Economic Policy in the United States: A Tentative View from a Comparative Perspective* (Beverly Hills, Calif. and London: Sage, 1973), p. 21.

57. William Greider, *The Education of David Stockman and Other Americans* (Dutton, 1982), p. 20.

58. Greider, pp. 20—21.

59. Greider, p. 20.

60. Greider, p. 19.

61. Greider, p. 20.

62. Salamon and Abramson, p. 63.

63. See: *Financial Times*, June 24, 1985, p. 1.

CHAPTER 8

1. See: Robert O. Keohane, *After Hegemony: Cooperation and Discord in the World Political Economy* (Princeton: Princeton University Press, 1984.)

2. See: Suzanne Berger, "Politics and Antipolitics in Western Europe in the Seventies," *Daedalus*, vol. 108, no. 1 (winter, 1979), pp. 47—50.

3. Andrei S. Markovits, "West Germany's Political Future: The 1983 Bundestag Elections," *Socialist Review*, vol. 13, no. 4 (July—August, 1983), pp. 67—68.

4. See: George Ross and Jane Jenson, "Pluralism and the Decline of Left Hegemony: The French Left in Power," paper presented to the national meetings of the APSA, August 1984.

5. See: Ulf Himmelstrand, "Action on the Stage," in U. Hillemstrand *et al.* (eds), *Beyond Welfare Capitalism: Issues, Actors and Forces in Societal Change* (London: Heinemann, 1981), pp. 255—315; Jonas Pontusson, "Sweden — Reformist Valhalla?" *New Left Review*, no. 143 (January—February, 1984), pp. 69—96.

6. See: T. H. Marshall, "Citizenship and Social Class," in David Held *et al.* (eds), *States and Societies* (Oxford: Martin Robertson, 1983), pp. 248—271: Otto Kirchheimer, "The Tranformation of European Party

Systems," in Joseph La Palombara and Myron Weiner (eds), *Political Parties and Development*; Andrew Shonfield, *Modern Capitalism: The Changing Balance of Public and Private Power* (Oxford: Oxford University Press, 1978). It should be noted that each theorist also had doubts — about the justice of economic inequalities, about the growing marginalization of political parties as agents of social and political integration, about the bureaucratization of decision-making which threatened representative democracy — which should not be ignored and which will be discussed in part below.

7. George Ross, "What is Progressive about Unions?: Reflections on Trade Unions and Economic Crisis," *Theory and Society*, vol. 10, no. 5 (1981), p. 57.

8. Adam Przeworski and Michael Wallerstein, "Democratic Capitalism at the Crossroads," *Democracy*, vol. 2, no. 3 (July 1982), pp. 57–58.

9. Shonfield, p. 3.

10. See: E. P. Thompson, *The Making of the English Working Class* (New York: Vintage, 1966), originally published in 1963; also "The Peculiarities of the English," in E. P. Thompson, *The Poverty of Theory and Other Essays* (New York: Monthly Review, 1978), pp. 245–302 and especially, p. 254, originally published in 1965. My usage of the term is not identical with that of Thompson but there is some kinship. In both cases the concept implies a prior set of social attitudes, expectations, and habitual practices which condition a broad set of relations and which involve the abrogation of the *old* (a moral economy of "provisions" in the early nineteenth century, a moral economy of "laissez-faire capitalism" with limited state interference augmented by a clearly defined set of individually located "rights of citizenship" in the twentieth century) by a *new* and dynamic ethos (in the first case, industrial capitalism and in the second, the welfare state).

11. Suzanne Berger, "Politics and Antipolitics in Western Europe in the Seventies," *Daedalus*, vol. 108, no. 1, (winter, 1979), p. 29.

12. Martin Feldstein, "American Economic Policy and the World Economy," *Foreign Affairs*, vol. 63, no. 5 (summer, 1985), p. 995.

13. *New York Times*, November 11, 1984, p. 2E.

14. Feldstein, p. 996; *New York Times*, January 1, 1986, p. 1.

15. Feldstein, p. 996.

16. *Financial Times*, January 2, 1985, p. 9; *Financial Times*, January 2, 1985, p. 13.

17. Colin Leys, "Thatcherism and British Manufacturing: A Problem of Hegemony," paper presented to the national meetings of the APSA, August, 1984.

18. See: Commission of the European Communities, *European Economy* [Annual Economic Review Report 1984—85], no. 22 (November, 1984), pp. 52—53.
19. *New York Times*, August 2, 1984.
20. Ivor Crewe, "Why Labour Lost/Conservatives Won the British Elections," *Public Opinion* (June/July, 1983), pp. 7—60.
21. Crewe, p. 57.
22. *New York Times*, November 11, 1984, p. 2E.
23. *New York Times*, December 16, 1984, p. 40.
24. *New York Times*, November 11, 1984, p. 1E.
25. See: "Britain's Urban Breakdown," *The Economist*, April 3—May 22, 1982, pp. 2—9.
26. Robert Lekachman, *Greed is not Enough: Reaganomics* (New York: Pantheon, 1982), pp. 8—9.
27. Haywood Burns, "Racial Equality: The Activism is not Affirmative," *The Nation*, vol. 239, no. 9 (September 29, 1984), pp. 264—268.
28. See: D. Lee Bawden and John L. Palmer, "Social Policy: Challenging the Welfare State," in John L. Palmer and Isabel W. Sawhill (eds), *The Reagan Record* (Cambridge, Mass.: Ballinger, 1984), pp. 177—216.
29. Karen J. Hatcher, "The Feminization of Poverty: An Analysis of Poor Women in New York City," June, 1984 (unpublished), The Council of the City of New York.
30. The Center for the Study of Social Policy, "A Dream Deferred: The Economic Status of Black Americans," (Washington, DC: 1984), pp. i—ii.
31. Steven P. Erie, Martin Rein, and Barbara Wiget, "Women and the Reagan Revolution: Thermidor for the Social Welfare Economy," in Irene Diamond (ed.), *Families, Politics and Public Policy* (New York and London: Longman, 1983), pp. 102—103.
32. Steven P. Erie, "The Conservative Attack upon Women and the Welfare State in the United States: Potential for a New Progressive Alliance?" paper presented to the Tocqueville Society Conference on Community Action and Public Policy, Institut d'Etudes Politiques, Paris, France, May 6—7, 1985.
33. Ian Gough, *The Political Economy of the Welfare State* (London: Macmillan, 1979), p. 3.
34. Gough, p. 3.
35. N. Nie, S. Verba, and J. Petrocik, *The Changing American Voter* (Cambridge, Mass.: Harvard University Press, 1979).
36. Berger, p. 33.
37. For an interesting discussion of how "baseless" economic theories

gain Administration support and popular currency, see: Mancur Olson, "The Politics of Industrial Policy: Supply-side Economics, Industrial Policy and Rational Ignorance," American Enterprise Institute (1984).

38. *The Baron Report*, no. 144, February 15, 1982.
39. Perry D. Quick, "Businesses: Reagan's Industrial Policy," in John L. Palmer and Isabel V. Sawhill (eds), *The Reagan Record* (Washington: The Urban Institute, 1984), p. 297.
40. Bernard D. Nossiter, "Reform for the Rich: Reagan's Tax Package Unwrapped," *The Nation*, August 3—10, 1985, p. 74.
41. *The Baron Report*, no. 144, February 15, 1982, emphases omitted.
42. *New York Times*, July 31, 1985, p. A1; August 4, 1985, p. E1; August 11, 1985, p. E1.
43. *New York Times*, August 11, 1985, p. E1.
44. *New York Times*, August 11, 1985, p. E1.
45. See: Gavyn Davies, "The Macroeconomic Record of the Conservatives," paper presented to a conference on "The Thatcher Government and British Political Economy," Center for European Studies, Harvard University, April 19—20, 1985.
46. *Financial Times*, June 24, 1985, p. 1.
47. *The Economist*, June 22—28, 1985, pp. 28, 97.
48. *The Economist*, June 22—28, 1985, p. 97.
49. Davies, p. 29.
50. *British Public Opinion*, vol. VII, no. 5 (May, 1985) pp. 1—3.
51. Benjamin Ginsberg and Martin Shefter, "A Critical Realignment? The New Politics, the Reconstituted Right, and the Election of 1984," in Michael Nelson (ed.), *The Elections of 1984* (Washington, DC: CQ Press, 1985), p. 16.
52. Theodore J. Lowi, "An Aligning Election, A Presidential Plebisite," in Nelson, pp. 277—301.
53. *British Public Opinion*, vol. VII, no. 5 (May, 1985), pp. 1—2. See also: *Manchester Guardian Weekly*, May 12, 1985, p. 3; October 6, 1985, p. 3; *New York Times*, September 22, 1985, p. 21.
54. See: Rosalind Pollack Petchesky, *Abortion and Woman's Choice: The State, Sexuality, and Reproductive Freedom* (New York and London: Longman, 1984); also, Petchesky "Bombing Feminism," *The Nation*, vol. 240, no. 4 (February 2, 1985), p. 101; Thomas M. Shapiro, *Population Control Politics: Women, Sterilization, and Reproductive Choice* (Philadelphia: Temple University Press, 1985).
55. Peter Jenkins, "The Rift Round the Miners' Hearth," *Manchester Guardian Weekly*, vol. 132, no. 11 (March 17, 1985), p. 5.
56. Jenkins.

57. *Labour Weekly*, June 22, 1984, p. 1.
58. See: *The Miner: Journal of the National Union of Mineworkers*, Special issue, May, 1985. My observations are also based on a set of interviews with miners and members of support committees conducted in Dunscroft, Doncaster, South Yorkshire, on June 22–June 24, 1985.
59. Peggy Kahn, "A New Politics for Coal," *New Socialist*, no. 30 (September, 1985), pp. 29–30.
60. *Manchester Guardian Weekly*, October 13, 1985, p. 1.

Index